AN UNLIKELY DIPLOMAT

A MEMOIR

WARD OF THE STATE
ROYAL AUSTRALIAN AIR FORCE
NUCLEAR TESTS VETERAN
COLD WAR DIPLOMAT
FAMILY REUNION AFTER FORTY YEARS
BUSINESS

GEORGE J. KNOX

Published in Australia by Sid Harta Books & Print Pty Ltd,
ABN: 34632585293
23 Stirling Crescent, Glen Waverley, Victoria 3150 Australia
Telephone: +61 3 9560 9920, Facsimile: +61 3 9545 1742
E-mail: author@sidharta.com.au

First published in Australia 2023
This edition published 2023
Copyright © George J. Knox 2023

Cover design, typesetting: WorkingType (www.workingtype.com.au)

The right of George J. Knox to be identified as the Author of the Work has been asserted in accordance with the Copyright, Designs and Patents Act 1988.

All rights reserved. No part of this publication may be reproduced, stored in a retrieval system, or transmitted, in any form or by any means without the prior written permission of the publisher, nor be otherwise circulated in any form of binding or cover other than that in which it is published and without a similar condition being imposed on the subsequent purchaser.

ISBN: 978-1-922958-21-1

To my family — Judith, Adrian, Samantha, and Adam with all my love. To my brother Bob — together since the beginning.

Contents

Dedication	iii
Preface	ix
Acknowledgements	xi

Chapter 1	Woman Horse-Whipped	1
Chapter 2	A Brief Taste of Family Life & Wards of the State	4
Chapter 3	Castledare Boys Home & Men in Black Dresses	20
Chapter 4	Clontarf Boys Town	35
Chapter 5	The Foster Family & Bess	70
Chapter 6	The Air Force & The British Nuclear Tests	77
Chapter 7	Canada via the USA	92
Chapter 8	The Office of the Air Attaché Washington, DC	104
Chapter 9	Return to Australia and Meeting the in-Laws	131
Chapter 10	The Department & a Baby	135
Chapter 11	Posted to the Australian Embassy Moscow, USSR	140
Chapter 12	The Australian Embassy, Moscow, USSR	151

Chapter 13	Moscow to Santiago de Chile	207
Chapter 14	The Australian Embassy, Santiago de Chile	211
Chapter 15	Return to Australia & the Department of Foreign Affairs	247
Chapter 16	The Consulate-General, Chicago USA	251
Chapter 17	Back in the USSR	274
Chapter 18	The People, the "Elite" & the Church in the USSR	300
Chapter 19	Persona non grata & Farewell to Moscow	318
Chapter 20	Return to the Department & Resignation	327
Chapter 21	The Sunshine Coast & Into Business	336
Chapter 22	The Family Reunion After Forty Years	341
Chapter 23	The Last of Business and Return to Public Service	351

Figures

Figure 1	Men in black dresses	20
Figure 2	Castledare orphanage dormitory, 1945	28
Figure 3	AOC inspection of 25 Squadron (City of Perth), 1957	85
Figure 4	Enjoying breakfast at Maralinga, South Australia, 1960	88
Figure 5	The engagement, Washington, DC, 1965	124
Figure 6	Leaving the church on our wedding day, 1965	128

Figure 7	Diplomatic passport, cancelled, 1967	146
Figure 8	Presentation of Ambassador's credentials, Moscow, 1968	151
Figure 9	Diplomatic ID cards, Moscow, 1967	156
Figure 10	Missile on way to Red Square for May Day parade, 1968	202
Figure 11	Author and son Adam, Santiago, 1971	232
Figure 12	Author and Judith at Embassy function, Santiago, 1970	239
Figure 13	Author at an official function, Playboy Club, Chicago, 1974	267
Figure 14	Author and Judith at Government House, Adelaide, 1980	331
Figure 15	The restaurant at Kings Beach, Sunshine Coast, Queensland, 1981-1986	338
Figure 16	The newspaper headline of the family reunion, 1985	341
Figure 17	Father and son — thank you	339

All images are the property of the author.

Preface

I have found that writing about one's own life experiences has been emotionally draining, so much so that I had to leave it at times for several years. I shall endeavour to provide at least some clarity and understanding of the impact on one family in Western Australia during the Great Depression and Second World War (WW2) and the day-to-day struggle within the orphanages where my brother Robert (Bob) were placed.

Despite the above, I set myself goals that I was fortunate enough to achieve in the years that followed, at Clontarf Boys Town, by serving in both the Royal Australian Air Force, in Australia's Foreign Service as a career overseas officer and finally by returning to Federal government service as a protocol officer with the departments of prime minister and cabinet and foreign affairs and trade.

Some may disapprove of my referring to Department of Foreign Affairs and Trade officers and staff from other departments serving at Australian overseas missions as Foreign Service officers. However, while writing this memoir, I have found that it has simplified and encapsulated the core name of the many Australian Government departments that often serve at our diplomatic missions overseas.

I should have devoted so much more detail in this book to the wives and children of Foreign Service officers and the single staff who commit themselves to leave their family and friends for years at a time to face the difficulties, disruptions, illnesses, and dangers that so often occur while working at overseas missions. However, that would have been a book in itself.

George J. Knox

Acknowledgements

To the loves of my life — Judith, Adrian, Samantha, and Adam. Your passion, energy, patience, support, and encouragement to complete this memoir are appreciated more than you could realise and certainly more than I could adequately express to you in words.

To Bob — thank you for always being there for me and for being the driving force that reunited us all after so many years.

To dear Aunt Glady, the family historian. I express my deepest gratitude for providing me with such a detailed background on the tragic life of our mother and her children with such honesty, compassion, and love. Your input has helped me better understand and appreciate the hardships and abuse experienced by countless women in similar circumstances to my mother during the Depression and the pre- and post-years of WW2.

I would also like to emphasise that my siblings, Bob, Muriel, Kerry, Andrew, William, and I have maintained a love of life and the fondest appreciation for all you wonderful people who have contributed so much support, friendship, love, energy, and shared life experiences. You know who you are.

George

1

...and the newspaper banner read: "Woman Horse-Whipped"

The most important thing a father can do for his children is to love their mother.
Theodore Hesburgh

The first woman in my life was Marguerite Mary Ellen McKinnon, referred to by family and friends as Peggy. Her paternal grandparents, Henry and Marguerite Spalding married in Dublin, Ireland, and arrived in Western Australia as free settlers with their three children and their maid, Annie Pringle, in 1872.

Henry Spalding was a successful and wealthy businessperson and philanthropist and was the Mayor of Geraldton, the second-largest city in Western Australia. He held this office for many years. A suburb, golf course and several streets bore his family name or the first names of his children. Henry lost the family fortune in the 1929 stock market crash. The impact on the family unit was devastating.

Additional pressure was applied to the family during this challenging period of the Great Depression. Peggy

McKinnon, one of Henry's grandchildren, was nineteen years of age, pregnant, and unmarried. Her strict Methodist family considered her condition a disgrace. There were no social security benefits, family bonuses or other government assistance given to women in her situation at that time. She was very much alone.

The McKinnon family had to set about finding a husband for Peggy. There was an immediate answer to an advertisement in the *West Australian* newspaper from a farmer with teenage children. A marriage was quickly arranged.

The family must have breathed a sigh of relief because their daughter with a young child was to be married to a prominent farmer on a large property some distance away from the capital. What could be better? The family had been saved from the shame and stigma that would surely have followed. Peggy quickly learned that her role within the new family unit was to be a live-in servant. She was constantly subjected to physical and emotional abuse by her husband. Fist and boot were regularly used for the slightest transgression, as he saw it.

The event that finally broke her spirit occurred when the older step-children physically abused her son, who was by then just three years of age. As a final act of their bastardry, they secured her child onto the back of a horse and set it off into the bush. The horse returned to the homestead several hours later without the child. A search party found the distressed boy early the next morning.

1   ...and the newspaper banner read: "Woman Horse-Whipped"

Distraught throughout this experience, Peggy dared to raise her voice to her husband in defence of her child. He turned on her with more violence than she had previously been subjected to. His rage was such that she was almost beaten to death with a horsewhip and was left bleeding and semiconscious in the front paddock.

That night, when Peggy regained full consciousness, she wrapped up her son, packed a small case with personal items, and set out on foot for a neighbouring farm. She staggered and crawled at times, making her way through the bush with her son by her side. The neighbours took them both in, applied whatever medical assistance they could, and called the police. Peggy was rushed to Perth and hospitalised for several days.

The *West Australian* newspaper headline read — *WOMAN HORSE-WHIPPED*. No action was taken by the police. The marriage was annulled soon after and her son was adopted. Peggy reverted to her maiden name of McKinnon.

Two years later Peggy met George Robert Knox. She was 24 years old and he was 21 when he was informed of her "condition". Once again, she was pressured by her family into marriage, as was he. This was not exactly an auspicious start for either of them. Marguerite Mary Ellen (Peggy) Knox (nee McKinnon) was to be my mother.

The nation's men and women were needed in the armed forces and the factories. My father signed up with the Army and following his basic training he was assigned to the Tank Corps Training Unit at Wagga Wagga in western New South Wales.

2

A Brief Taste of Family Life & Wards of the State

1937–1955

The economy of Australia during this period was desperately trying to recover from the Great Depression. This was also a time when those young men and women planning marriage and starting a family were faced with considerable difficulties. Employment was still in the doldrums. Many of the unskilled men had to take on a nomadic lifestyle in order to support their families. My father was away for months before my birth looking for work in country towns and did not arrive home until two months after I was born.

The commencement of a slow but certain turnaround in the economy of the country in 1938 augured well for the newly married couple. However, while I was taking my first steps, other more devastating events were unfolding in Europe. The rantings of Adolf Hitler were becoming an increasing concern to all, as was the unprecedented build-up of the Nazi military machine.

War was declared by England against Germany on 3

September 1939. There was no formal declaration of war on Australia's part. We were part of the Commonwealth, and our government of the day quickly offered to support the British Empire.

The introduction of ration cards ensured that providing food, fuel, clothing, and other necessities of life was a constant challenge. My mother and grandmother had to cope alone, as was the case with so many other families, with their husbands, sons, and daughters away at war.

There were no refrigerators, washing machines, or many white goods, electrical appliances, or digital products that enhance our standard of living today. There is an old saying, "When the going gets tough, the tough get going". This was indeed the case for most families during those years of Depression and war.

My father had been in the Army for almost four years at this stage and had often been absent without leave (AWOL) to assist at home. He was finally discharged on compassionate grounds in late 1943.

I have no idea where we lived in Western Australia prior to Dad's military service, but Bob and I had been left with Gran, Dad's mother, at Plain Street, East Perth when he signed up with the Army. The younger of our siblings remained with our mother. Her rented home in Perth could not house us all.

The war had placed insurmountable strains and stresses on the marriage that endured the parenting of five children in almost as many years, and with another on the way. I was the first of their children. Dad had great difficulty in accepting his financial and parental responsibilities for his family and had returned to his wife and children an angry and distant man.

The drunken attacks on our mother were to become more frequent and violent in the years ahead, but none could have been as horrific as those recounted to me by the family historian from those years, our mother's younger sister Aunt Glady. The first occurred on the evening of 20 January 1939, when my very pregnant mother almost died. Dad had arrived home inebriated and found an unacceptable dinner warming in the oven. Mum had been in labour and trying desperately to organise herself for the trip to the hospital. Aunt Glady had been staying with us to care for me. I was then thirteen months old. Dad pummelled my mother down the hallway with his fists, ignoring her screams and pleading.

Finally, beaten to the floor, she screamed that the baby was coming. Aunt Glady protected and assisted her battered sister as best she could during the vicious onslaught. Seeing that her sister was in a dangerously distressed state, she ran to nearby neighbours who had a telephone and asked them to call an ambulance. It was too late. Robert (Bob) was born prematurely in the passageway of our home where our mother had collapsed.

Muriel was the third child and she did not fare much better than Bob in entering this world. Again, Mum was attacked while an ambulance was on the way, this time with a sharp-edged metal sugar bowl that was thrown at her. Medical staff were stitching and treating our mother's head wound while Muriel was being born. Kerry and Andrew (Lucky) followed in quick succession approximately twelve to thirteen months apart.

Dad, now a civilian, arrived at Gran's house one day with our mother and our younger siblings Muriel, Kerry, and baby Andrew, and we moved into a home at Kwinana, south of Perth, and close to a joint Australian and American Naval Station at Garden Island. The house had a rusting roof, unpainted fibro walls, and a hand pump for bore water in the middle of the backyard. A corrugated iron outhouse sat alone at the rear of the backyard at the edge of dense scrub. A large nickel refinery covers this area today.

A grey, fine dirt road with intermittent stretches of bitumen wound past our house, and on through the bush to end at the school. When the road was followed in the opposite westerly direction, it ended at our playground, the sandhills, the beach, and the Indian Ocean. The sandhills provided a barrier between the sea and our house.

I cannot remember laughter in our home whenever Dad was present. The only expressions of love and laughter I can recall during this period were during the warmer months when we washed our mother's hair on a Saturday or Sunday morning under the hand pump that was strategically placed between the house and the outhouse. While we were enjoying these precious moments with our mother, Dad would be either at the Rockingham Hotel drinking with his mates or would have moved on to the Saturday two-up game. For those who have no idea what a two-up game is, it is a gambling game in which coins are spun in the air, and bets are laid by those participating on whether the coin faces show heads or tails when they land.

A strong work ethic was instilled early. Everyone had to contribute to the household chores. If you could walk and talk, you could also work. We helped our mother with the washing on Monday mornings during the school holidays.

Once the washing chore had been completed, Mum saved a few saucepans of the still-hot laundry water for use in the kitchen sink, and put some more in the bathtub for us all to take turns in. Bob and I always tried to get in first because we were sure that the younger ones were having a tinkle in it.

The outhouse had a flap opening at the back to facilitate the can's replacement by the dunny cart man who came once a week. The outhouse precinct was also a favourite haunt for many species of snakes, spiders, and other undesirables such as Bob and me.

Bob and I were relentless in the pursuit of frightening our little sister Muriel whenever Dad was not at home, and therefore not a witness to her screams. We hid in the bush behind the outhouse when we knew she would be paying a visit. Once she was inside, we blew into a paper bag, quietly raised the flap at the rear, and slammed the bag between our hands. The Tom Thumb firecracker was our favourite tool of torture for our little sister! I sincerely hope that Muriel has never suffered from nightmares or other neurological problems as a result of these and many other dastardly acts perpetrated upon her by her older brothers!

Our two major sources of income were from acting as "cockatoos" at the local two-up game in the nearby bush on irregular Saturday afternoons, and on Sunday mornings we searched the nearby beach sandhills that were often frequented by American and Australian sailors and their girlfriends.

The duties and responsibilities of the cockatoos were quite simple. We climbed a designated tall gum tree in the bush near the main dirt road that ran by our house. Instructions on how to raise the alarm, how high we should climb up the tree, and what to say to the police if we were caught, were given by the local publican. We were also assisted up onto the lowest bough of the selected tree. We then had to climb as high as we could with one of us holding a stick, and the other an empty kerosene tin to beat on. We had to have a line of sight of the road and the two-up game in progress.

When a raiding party of the police was spotted, we beat on the kerosene tin with the stick as loudly as possible. We were doing well for a while and had avoided being caught, although, on a couple of occasions raiding policemen had pointed at us perched in the high branches and let us know that they would catch up with us later, but never did. We always earned a good bonus whenever we were successful in our alerts to the players.

The publican was very happy with us, as was Dad who was

a regular player. All was going well until one of the players gave us a common whistle used in the military and by police. We did not hesitate to accept this new alarm system, because the tin had been quite cumbersome when climbing, and hanging onto it when astride the bough of a tree.

On the same day we were given the whistle we spotted a group of men moving slowly through the dense scrub. I blew it with considerable enthusiasm. This caused a lot of panic and confusion because the group heading towards the betting ring were in fact more punters, not the police! Those already in the game, including Dad, frantically tried to gather up their money while the incoming group ran through the betting ring, past the scrambling players, and disappeared into the scrub beyond. Chaos reigned!

The punters eventually returned to the betting ring and set about getting the game going again. The whistle was confiscated. We were exonerated by the publican after he discovered the very unpopular man who had provided us with the new early warning device and failed to advise anyone what he had done. My whistle-blowing had added to the general chaos because the players thought the police had blown the whistle!

Soon after the whistle-blowing incident, Bob inadvertently let the kerosene can go when I had attempted to pass him a sandwich. The can made a lot of noise as it bounced and clanged off the boughs of the tree before finally coming to rest in the scrub below. We sat very still, hanging on to the trunk of the tree, terrified, as the punters, Dad included, quickly dispersed through the heavy scrub. This was the final straw. We were sacked as cockatoos, and Dad gave us a thrashing later that evening. Dad's broad "wharfie" belt, or his leather shaving strap, was the normal means of administering punishment to us wayward children! The worst part of Dad's regular application of discipline was not the actual beating, but the waiting period to receive it.

His venture into the business world eventually failed and caused considerable hardship for all of us, especially Gran. She had loaned Dad all her savings and offered her house as a guarantee on the loan he acquired for his truck and fruit and vegetable delivery business. He lost everything he invested in his business, and Gran lost her home and her life's savings. Dad's drinking increased, as did his wrath. Gran was alone and destitute. She moved to New Zealand to work as a live-in housekeeper for a family in Hamilton on the North Island.

Funds for the purchase of sweets and cakes were usually easy to come by, and at times I think Bob and I were supporting the entire household. For instance, we urchins of the dunes usually diverted from the track on the way home from the beach and searched the area for signs of a recent presence of American or Australian sailors from the nearby naval base. Sunday mornings were most profitable. A site looked promising if we spotted discarded chocolate and chewing gum wrappers, empty beer bottles, or cigarette packets. When we had completed our preliminary search, we sifted through the sand with our fingers for coins. We rarely missed out on a return thanks to the fob-like pockets of a seaman's uniform.

An incoming group of American sailors and their companions caught us unawares one day, but instead of getting a thick ear, we were paid a pound note and told to disappear. In those days a pound note was about all an adult labourer could expect for a day's work. If we had been successful in finding money, we had a spend-up at the corner store on cakes, soft drinks, and sweets, some of which we consumed before returning home. Any surplus monies were spent on special items for Mum who was usually at home alone with the younger children. Our cash flow from the sandhills was far more lucrative than had been our Saturday employment as cockatoos, and not so arduous.

On one foray into the dunes, we inadvertently left Muriel behind, not for some malicious or vindictive reason, but simply because she was so quiet and so small that we forgot she had been with us. We must have become distracted by success in our search for booty, and the routine of the trip to the corner store on the way home.

It was not until we had arrived home, and Mum asked where Muriel was that we knew we were in a heap of trouble. Mum became very upset and was about to call the police when Dad arrived home. There was a lot of shouting, and Bob and I knew that we could expect the belt or the shaving strap to make an appearance before too long.

We were all on our way out the front door to mount a search when a neighbour, with a group of sailors, came down the road with Muriel laughing hysterically, and waving to us with a bar of chocolate. The sailors were made to feel at home, and Dad plied them with beer until it ran out. Dad and his new friends then went off to celebrate some more at the nearby Rockingham Hotel.

We thought we were home-free and would escape punishment, at least until the next day. But this was not to be. The front door slamming was the signal we were hoping would not come. We were both dragged from the bed we shared with our two younger siblings and beaten until Dad was distracted by Mum screaming at him. We had tried desperately to put distance between the flailing strap and ourselves by running around the kitchen table. This only worked for a lap or two. We were finally shepherded into a corner, cowering, and trying to blunt the blows by covering our heads with our arms. All the while Mum was trying to intervene and shield us from the onslaught. She was also beaten black and blue and could not go out of the house for days.

These episodes of violence that I have referred to were witnessed by my mother's visiting teenage sister, Glady, who often stayed with us to assist with the children. Glady wrote her own record of much of what she witnessed during those years and passed her notes on to me.

I commenced my schooling at six years of age, which was the law at that time. Bob was deemed too young for school as a five-year-old, but my mother asked for and received special permission from the Education Department for Bob to accompany me. Permission was granted on the grounds that there was no bus or family transport to take us to the local primary school. It was either a trek through the bush or an even longer hike down a partially laid bitumen road.

Our first day at school was memorable for one reason. Bob was not at his desk after lunch. The whole school was emptied to search for him. Groups were sent off into the surrounding bush with teachers and students screaming out his name. Several minutes of this feverish activity passed until I was instructed by my teacher to return home to inform our mother of his disappearance. Bob suddenly emerged from under the school veranda as I was about to leave. In between heaving sobs, he told of the assault on him by a group of girls who had cornered him at lunchtime and insisted on kissing him in turn. It must have all been a bit too much for Bob. How he changed, and so quickly!

I loved school, and the actual journey itself to and from school always seemed like such a great adventure. Shoes were not a high priority within the budgets of many households at that time, and the powdery grey sand track leading through the scrub to the schoolhouse was blistering hot in summer. The longer journey via the partially paved road with its sections of melting tar proved more difficult. We ran as fast as we could for as long as we could so that the hot sand or the melting sticky black tar would not present too much of a problem with our bare feet.

Another encouragement to run as fast as possible through the bush was provided by the magpies and butcher birds that swooped on us during nesting season. There were also other distractions on the way to school, such as chasing blue-tongued lizards, goannas, rabbits, or whatever else crossed our path. The snakes we left alone.

We looked forward to Tuesdays because that was pick-up day for our outhouse canister by the "dunny man". We had a standing invitation to travel with him to school. We thought it was a great treat to ride on the high seat of the dray behind his large draught horse.

The contents of the canisters partially emptied behind us on the back of the dray as it swayed from side to side in the sections of the soft sand of the makeshift road. We laughed all the way to school, despite what must appear to have been a most repulsive experience.

Dad became increasingly violent during this period. I do not know whether it was the war; the copious amounts of alcohol he consumed; the stress of his failed business; no immediate promise of steady employment, other than casual work on the Fremantle wharves; a wife and five children with another on the way to support at twenty-seven or twenty-eight years of age; a combination of all of these factors; or perhaps it was a by-product of the times?

I can now appreciate and understand that the local pub would have acted as a release valve for men to network within the community, and to unwind after a gruelling and at times stressful day at work. However, there were those who did not have the emotional fortitude and sense of responsibility to realise when they had stayed too long, consumed too much, and failed to accept that the family unit also required and at times desperately needed their attention and assistance. My father was such a man.

As far as I am aware, there were no specific laws during those years to protect women and children from abusive and violent husbands, and there was no social security to support those women who were forced to flee their homes. Mum bore the brunt of Dad's drunken physical attacks for years without recourse to anyone or any organisation.

Dad expected a hot meal to be ready and waiting for him every evening, no matter what time he staggered home. No excuses would be tolerated. Mum tried to have us washed, fed, and in bed before he burst through the front door. If for some reason, or perhaps for no reason at all, the evening meal was not to his liking, the shouting would start. Screams would inevitably be followed by thumps. Relative quiet would then prevail, except for the mumblings of an incoherent drunk, the whimpering of our mother wherever she had fallen, and we terrified children peeing ourselves with fear and holding each other while shaking uncontrollably in that sagging, smelly old bed. Bob and I slept at one end of the bed and Muriel and her younger sister, Kerry, or Andrew, were at the other end.

We could do little to help our mother during Dad's tirades.

During daylight hours we ran out of the house and hid in the bush at the rear of the yard as soon as we heard the screaming start. We did not return until all was quiet. At night we were confined to the house and within the bounds of any conflict initiated. Escape was impossible.

Dad's brutality reached a climax in late January 1945, when neighbours called the police to the house. Mum had been beaten terribly with a long piece of garden hose. The screaming and shouting continued until neighbours called the police who arrived and took Dad away. An ambulance came for Mum and the younger children. Bob and I were still in our favourite hiding place in the scrub behind the outhouse. We would not come out until police officers called out that Dad had gone and assured us that Mum was alright and being cared for.

Our meagre personal belongings were packed into a large leather portmanteau that had been our grandfather's. A policeman took us to the local police station and settled us into a couple of bunks near his desk. The police drove us to Perth the next day and delivered Bob and me to officers of the Department of Child Welfare.

We were no longer a family unit. Our parents' relationship had deteriorated to such a degree that the state's Child Welfare Department decided that they were incapable of caring for us responsibly and that there was considerable danger in leaving us with them.

Bob, Muriel, and I were declared wards of the state on 7

February 1945. I had just turned seven and Bob was six when we were delivered to the Christian Brothers at Castledare Boys Home. Muriel, Andrew, and Kerry were taken straight to the nuns at St Joseph's Foundling Home. The two sisters were separated soon after. Kerry was fostered out when she was eighteen months old and Andrew was adopted almost immediately.

The last of the brood of this pathetic parental mishap was William. Our mother was in the Family Court in the process of divorcing our father and holding the newborn baby, William, when she was approached by a woman who had listened to her case and asked if she could adopt William. Our mother was in no position to say no.

The handwritten note on the Child Welfare Department's final report in the section entitled Circumstances and Character read as follows:

- The conduct of the children is good.
- The Father drinks and squanders money.
- The Mother's behaviour is good.
- The Charge — Destitute.
- The Judgement — To be placed in the care of the Child Welfare Department.
- The Term — Until eighteen years of age in each case.
- Date of Committal — 7 February 1945
- Court — Perth, Western Australia.

What followed was a period during which Bob, Muriel,

and I were stripped of family and ensured a loss of personal identity. We were to endure childhoods that were bereft of parental love and subjected to physical and emotional abuse, loneliness, and a sense of abandonment that is quite impossible to describe to anyone who has not travelled a similar road.

Fear and the uncertainty of what the next day may bring were constant companions in many forms during those years ahead at Castledare Boys Home and later at Clontarf Boys Town. We had no idea what had happened to Muriel or the other siblings until many years later.

3

Castledare Boys Home & Men in Black Dresses

1945–1948

Figure 1. Men in black dresses

Castledare Boys Home was handed over to the Christian Brothers by the Western Australian Government in March 1933 to receive young state wards and it became a junior orphanage to Clontarf Boys

Town which was bursting at the seams at that time. Castledare provided the opportunity for state authorities to separate the young boys, aged between five and ten years, from the older boys who remained at Clontarf until the outbreak of WW2.

Many of the orphans at Castledare from 1939 to 1945 were there because of the dislocation and disruption of family life caused by the war. Most fathers were either away engaged in war activities or were casualties. Women were taking up civilian positions in the factories or contributing in other ways to the war effort. The end of the war also presented additional problems with industrial unrest, shortages of goods and services, and a housing crisis. Maintenance of buildings was impossible to afford and therefore was continually deferred. Epidemics of ringworm and diphtheria broke out at Castledare during 1946 and 1947.

British child migration recommenced in post-war 1947, and the new influx tended to be quite different to those who arrived prior to WW2 in 1938 and 1939. They arrived at Castledare and Clontarf in an already crowded situation and apparently had little formal education. They had suffered extreme deprivation during the war and had experienced desperate insecurities. They were generally ill-disciplined, and when banding together presented a formidable challenge to the Australian boys and to the staff.

The influx of children from Great Britain was for some time a major cause of overcrowded classrooms, and other problems with the dining room, and toilets. A lack of general maintenance of the laundry and the absence of hot water for long periods presented major problems. Bed coverings were well-worn old stocks of ex-Australian Army and American blankets which were in such a state that they were barely adequate for use by such young children. In childcare terms, a state of emergency was declared and paper volleys flew between the state government departments and the British High Commission.

I believe the Western Australian government at that time provided Castledare and Clontarf Boys Town with eight shillings per week per boy for food and clothing. Another shilling per boy per week was allocated for the education of the child, but it was never enough — hence street appeals, annual field day events, and assistance from the West Australian Lotteries Commission contributed greatly in later years towards meeting the basic needs of the institutions and their charges.

Bob and I were driven to Castledare by a state government child welfare officer (CWO), who told us that we were going on a new adventure. He added that we would have a great time living and playing with lots of boys our own age. We had no idea what an orphanage was or what was in store for us, but he made it sound exciting.

An image that will always remain with me is that of the large man standing midway down the steps of the administration building's reception area awaiting our arrival. He stood in the semi-darkness of early evening dressed in what appeared to be a long black dress with a white collar that enclosed his neck, and I thought it was on backwards. Black beads and a large cross hung from the broadcloth band tied about his ample waist. His arms were folded across his chest. His unsmiling face and deep-set dark eyes indicated no sign of welcome or pleasantness.

The CWO handed a file to the grim giant in black and replied for us with our names and ages, but religion was questioned. We had no idea what they were talking about. We were told that with a name like Knox, we must be Protestants. The remainder of the handover took place in the reception office with papers signed and exchanged. After a brief discussion, that did not include us, the CWO departed.

We were then marched off to the locker room carrying between us our solitary leather portmanteau that had been filled to overflowing with all our personal clothing and belongings. Gran told us that our grandfather had brought it home with him after WW1 in Europe. It had been his cherished possession. We were told to undress and were given clothing items that were much too big. When we pointed this out, we were told that we would grow into them. We were also told that our good clothes and shoes and socks were only to be worn on Sundays for church services, or on Visitor's Day, which was every third Sunday in the month.

I asked if we could keep the pullovers and shoes that we had been wearing on arrival. We were told to address the man as "Brother", and as the other boys did not have pullovers and shoes, why should we? I could not understand the reference to calling these men in black dresses, Brothers — they were not our brothers!

The clothing and other personal items we had arrived with were placed in our portmanteau, which was then stacked on top of an assortment of cases that almost reached the ceiling. We never saw grandfather's bag or its contents again. We were then led into a dormitory and left standing outside a door at the end of the rows of beds by an older boy who delivered us to another brother who was in charge of our dormitory.

The dormitory was a sea of half-naked boys flowing to and from the showers with no-one appearing interested in our arrival, that is until we saw the black-robed figure standing at the far end of the dormitory staring in our direction. He was very tall, thin, and slightly hunched over. His hair was as black as a moonless night. He was a most frightening sight. This was our introduction to Brother Lawrence Murphy.

We were told that we would be sleeping on opposite sides of the dormitory, because we now belonged to one big family, and all the boys were our brothers. What? We had big brothers in black dresses and all the boys were also our brothers. We were very confused. We had our own family.

The final evening routine was for all boys to kneel by their beds and pray in unison with the dormitory brother-in-charge

3 Castledare Boys Home & Men in Black Dresses

calling out the Hail Marys and the Lord's Prayer. I joined in this litany of prayer by mumbling anything that came to mind. I had no idea what they were all muttering with heads bowed, hands clasped together, and eyes closed. A statue, which we were told was of St Joseph, stood at the entrance to the dormitory, and each evening after the prayers we would recite a communal prayer for the safety of Australia, and our fighting men and women away at war. Lights out immediately followed and thereafter no talking was allowed.

We had been through an exhausting and confusing couple of days. We had been directly involved in the brutal event that led to the involvement of the police taking our father away; been separated from our parents and our siblings; been placed in a police car and taken to the Fremantle Goal to spend the night in the care of a policeman; been handed over to a CWO and delivered to an orphanage; and finally, subjected to indoctrination of sorts in routine and discipline, which was confusing and an unpleasant experience. Bob and I did not feel that any of these events augured well for an early family reunion.

We cried the first night. Bob tried unsuccessfully to find me. He called out to me and I answered. The full impact of what was in store for us quickly became obvious when the lights came on, and Brother Murphy called for us both to come to him. He stood outside his private room holding a leather strap out in front of him. We were told to bend over, and he struck us both on the back of the legs and buttocks several times. He then told us more of the same was to come if we did not go to sleep immediately.

We were instructed the next morning by an older boy as follows: "You better sleep on your right side, and never on your left side. Brother will give you a whack if he finds you sleeping on your left side." I questioned this advice and was told that brother said that to sleep on your right side was to please your guardian angel, especially if he came for you during the night! To sleep on your left side was to invite the devil to visit. We never asked what would happen if we slept on our backs. It's a wonder we ever fell asleep at all! Fear seemed to pervade everything, even sleep.

The older boys whose age was between nine and ten did not waste any time during our settling-in period in describing what would happen if we were told to go to the brother's room. If you were instructed to stand outside you were in for a strapping, and if you were taken into the brother's room you were called a "pet". I had no idea what this reference actually implied until three years later when we were moved to Clontarf Boys Town.

The brother-in-charge of the dormitory arose before us and wandered around the beds swinging a large bell to rouse us. It was in your best interest to get out of bed the moment the bell rang, get washed, dressed, and have your bed made for inspection before all in the dormitory were allowed to proceed to the dining hall.

3 Castledare Boys Home & Men in Black Dresses

The iron beds were covered with thin fibre-filled mattresses, most of which had been subjected to many a urinary experience. Those boys who were bedwetters were humiliated in front of the entire dormitory, and more often than not were beaten prior to being marched off to the laundry with their wet sheets.

Saturday mornings were devoted to scrubbing the floors of the dormitories, cleaning toilets, and any other tasks as directed by the supervising brother. If you were in luck, you got to operate the kerosene blowtorches that occasionally appeared. These were used exclusively on the iron bed joints that were home to the plagues of unfriendly bed bugs. The insatiable appetites of the invaders encouraged them to vacate their hiding places and relocate to the juicy pastures of our heads.

The more severely infested boys had their heads shaved and iodine was dabbed on the bloody sores left by the more voracious of the bed bugs that had feasted on scalps. If the infestation was more widespread, we were all marched down to the farm sheds and had our hair close-cropped with shearing shears.

We were then lined up in front of the sheep-drenching troughs and told to kneel and hold our heads at least to the hairline under the yellow, burning sheep dip, and to keep them there until we were instructed to stand up, and make way for the next group.

Figure 2. Castledare orphanage dormitory, 1945

If you got any sheep dip in your eyes when standing up again, you were led screaming to the nearby water-filled horse trough to dunk your head in and try to gain some relief by washing out your eyes.

The meals were not culinary delights, but they were memorable during this period of three years at Castledare. The norm for the evening meal was either cold jellied pig trotters, tripe cooked in sour milk, Irish stew, or "Irish glue" as we called it because you could turn your plate to the side and it would not fall off, and other servings of unidentified gelatinous substances. Boiled turnips, swedes, and foul-smelling boiled cabbage were not enjoyable additions to the evening plate. Desserts appeared on special Saint's days — bread and milk pudding or sago pudding which we referred to as "cat's eyes".

Breakfast was always the same — thick, lumpy porridge, a

piece of bread and jam, and a mug of warm tea. Lunch was either a sandwich or leftovers from the evening before. Eggs, steak, chops, fresh fruit, salads, or confectionary items were never available to us. However, I think this would also have been the case with most Australian families, because of food rationing during and immediately after the war years.

We always looked forward to "piece time", so named because it was a rest period and we received a piece of bread. Molasses was used as an alternative spread when there was no jam. The molasses was kept in the dairy in 44-gallon drums. It was an acquired taste, and not too bad once you got used to it. The cows certainly loved it.

As already mentioned, our diet must have contributed in no small part to the chronic state of our bodies over those years. Ear infections were also a common occurrence, particularly after swimming in the river. My lips always seemed to be covered with blisters. Most mornings I could not open both my eyes properly, because they were sealed shut with pus that had dried overnight. Lengthy periods of picking away the outer layers of the dry and solid mass to gain at least partial sight were followed by some careful bathing to slowly clear the rest away. I believe Sandy Blight, a severe eye infection that was highly contagious, was the name given to this infection. This contagion was caused by swarms of black flies that would seek out the moisture of the eyes and could lead to blindness. They were always present on the playing fields and in the classrooms.

The most painful of all infections of the feet were "stonies". These were infected bruises and cuts to the soles of the feet that formed blisters, which filled with pus and a clear liquid that swelled the entire foot. When this happened, we had to find a needle to lance the swelling ourselves to spill the souring pus, and hopefully dry the infection out. A walk in the river and the muddy bank helped relieve the pain and entice the ever-present leeches to lunch.

The use of leeches was a popular method of cleansing wounds and open sores. We sat for as long as possible in the shallows of the dark brackish river that ran past Castledare and when we emerged, we had black squirming leeches clinging to the infected areas. Any leeches, if not already on the infection, would be picked from minor sores and moved to the area requiring greater attention. I admit it does sound pretty gross but this was a far more effective treatment than any provided at the infirmary.

The arrival of winter and the very cold temperatures with insufficient warm clothing and no shoes invariably meant we would again be subjected to the dreaded chilblains. Many of the boys, including myself, suffered unbearable pain from the swelling of toes and fingers that looked like little red cocktail sausages that were going to split open. It was impossible to stop scratching them. The itchiness never went away, and always ended up bleeding.

One of the dairy duties required bringing the cows in for milking early in the morning. Those boys suffering from chilblains eagerly stood in any freshly dropped and steaming cow manure. It was an absolute delight. Unfortunately, this only offered temporary relief.

Boils and carbuncles were also commonplace and were usually ignored and left to heal by themselves. If a trip to the infirmary was required then a poultice was applied and kept in place by a torn piece from an old sheet. The smell became unbearable after a couple of days, but it seemed to do the trick, and the leeches were always on standby should additional assistance with the healing process be required.

On one such occasion, when I was in the infirmary with a poultice covering a serious foot infection, a large complement of boys at the orphanage decided enough was enough, and they took off in all directions. Bob absconded with a couple of his mates early one morning but returned alone after only travelling for an hour or so. He mentioned later that he felt guilty leaving me behind. His absence had not been discovered by the brothers.

Many of these five-to nine-year-old children were loose in the countryside! The younger ones wandered back over the next couple of days, hungry and despondent. There were many stories of great adventures as they were "recaptured" by police and brought back to the orphanage. It took several days to get them all back. Those who were returned last were held in the highest esteem! The hidings they got did not appear to diminish the continued excitement.

The river was our major play area during the summer

months. If you could not swim you were considered a "squib" or a "wuss", and therefore unable to join in the fun in the marshes and mud on the other side of the river. Those who could make it across would jeer at those who could not.

One of the lay brothers came up with a great idea that helped a lot of us who were unable to achieve temporary freedom. He tied a rope around an old car tyre and bound the other end to a long pole. The student swimmer slipped his body halfway through the submerged ring of the tyre, and the brother walked along the jetty that ended in the deep water with the boy inserted in the tyre using whatever swimming stroke he had settled on, usually the "dog paddle". Once the boy had assumed a level of confidence and competency, the brother gradually lowered the tyre in the water to provide the boy with an opportunity to take a few strokes on his own. The tyre would not be taken away until the boy was ready.

I felt considerable relief and a sense of achievement when I finally made it to the other side and could feel the thick dark mud grasping my feet. It was a rite of passage, one of life's graduations that I would never forget. There were no volunteers for escort duty on the return trip. The return all by yourself was the final test, and you could not fail!

In the early stages of our stay at Castledare in 1945, we had one visit from our mother and one from our father. The visits were best described as cursory and dispassionate. Dad turned up with a woman, and made us stand in front of him while he asked, 'Who do you love the best boys?' We replied,

'You, Dad.' Even at a young age, we were quickly developing the skills of diplomacy and survival. We were not mature enough to question or argue the point of our abandonment. We certainly did not miss his beatings. I am sure we would have been ready in an instant if he had told us he was taking us out of the place. Perhaps it was a matter of "better the devil you know than the ones you don't!"

Mum also visited just once. She was with her mother, a stern, unsmiling and humourless woman. There were no hugs, kisses, or words of encouragement from Grandmother McKinnon. Our mother was much more affectionate but had little to say and cried a lot. Neither parent brought anything for us to eat, anything to read, or instilled any hope or hint that we would eventually be going home with them. In our mother's defence, I should add that she and her mother were barely surviving themselves.

Both parents must have decided to get on with their own lives because we did not have another visit from either of them at Castledare Boys Home, or during the years ahead at Clontarf Boys Town. We represented the past. I never saw or heard from my mother again, and the only other time I saw my father was when he resurfaced briefly when I was fifteen years old, but that was not a good experience.

I had turned ten, and Bob was just turning nine when we were told to jump up on the back of the orphanage's old truck that was fuelled by wood and coal. We were soon joined by two other sets of brothers, the Dixons and the Clarks. Years later, Ray Dixon joined the Commonwealth Police, now the Australian Federal Police, and his brother Keith joined the Navy. The Clarks were Aboriginal boys and excellent boxers.

It was now time to graduate to another institution, Clontarf Boys Town, where the punishments, work, and general discipline were to be far harsher than at Castledare. The move from Castledare Boys Home to Clontarf Boys Town held many fears for us all because we had heard all sorts of stories emanating from that establishment which was referred to by the boys as "Clony". Most of the boys we were to join there were aged between ten and sixteen. We were leaving a place where we had become the "big boys", to one that would once again place us on the bottom rung in the pecking order.

4

Clontarf Boys Town

1948–1952

It is so difficult, if not impossible, to describe the absence of any parental presence and guidance at that age. However, after three years at Castledare Boys Home, the introduction to Boys Town, and the absence of any further visits from our parents, we knew we were not going home again. We had no idea where our other brothers and sisters were. You did not dare ask. Emotional and physical hardships were served up daily in varying dosages. Most of us dealt with it. Others could not. The imagery and sense of a child's own hell was a personal experience that impacted in different ways and was very much dependent on the level of maturity and sensitivity of the boy.

Fear was a tool generally employed by the Church and instilled early. For instance, we would be going to hell if we were not baptised as Catholics! Fear of the men in black dresses always took precedence over all else because they existed in the present, whereas hell could perhaps wait for us sometime in the future.

The Royal Australian Air Force (RAAF) occupied Clontarf

Boys Town from 1942 to 1945 and used it as a training facility. Just before the RAAF's arrival, all those boys accommodated there at the time were moved to temporary accommodation at other institutions run by the Christian Brothers.

The furniture and all educational material, including the entire library and sporting equipment, were removed by the RAAF. Negotiations were held with them after they left Clontarf and items such as beds, tables, chairs, and cooking utensils were made available for our use.

The Commonwealth Salvage Commission released large quantities of surplus military clothing, bed linen, and blankets after the war. Some of us were issued with army shorts and woollen sweaters. The clothing was so big on the smaller boys that the sweaters reached to their knees, and the shorts had to be tied a couple of times around the waist with string to keep them up. No-one complained.

The population at Boys Town almost doubled with the influx of British war orphans and displaced children between 1947 and 1948. The older Australian boys told us the new arrivals were to be referred to as "Poms". This considerable increase in our numbers impacted food supplies and they became less varied. Dormitories became cramped, clean clothing was less frequent, the allocated times for toilets and showers were cut back, and the lack of general maintenance continued.

A lot of the Irish lads refused to side with the "bloody English", as they referred to them. Between 1950 and 1951, our numbers received another boost to an already overstretched orphan community with the arrival of the first child migrants from Malta. These boys were readily accepted by the Australian youths and became close friends, with some experiencing friendships that have continued over the years.

The most memorable event of all during this transition of growth was the war games. They established the pecking order and standing within the orphanage between the two warring factions of the Australians and the Poms. A reference without the same level of savagery could be made to William Golding's novel *Lord of the Flies,* and its major theme that humans are essentially barbaric, if not downright evil.

We often staged our own smaller skirmishes that were quite different. Instead of having two opposing tribes charging at each other, we picked two sides. One would be the "defensive" team, dug in or hiding in the bush, and the other would be the "offensive" team who would make a charge to try and overrun those defending their territory.

I have been reminded of one war game several times over the years with a comment from Bob — 'Look at the bloody hole that you can still see in my head.' My team was indeed the victor on that day. My valiant companions and I charged the positions being held by Bob and his team. Sticks were used as rifles. Pine cones were normally used as hand grenades. However, there were no pine cones available on this occasion, so broken pieces of house bricks were chosen without any warning to the enemy. Wily Bob had been sitting in a tree waiting to ambush us. I had only intended to toss my "grenade" high into the air, and have it land near their position. Unfortunately, the brick hit him on the forehead and he fell to the ground. He landed awkwardly, and by the time I reached him he was half sitting and trying to make sense of what had happened. The oozing blood and his silence scared the hell out of me. I thought I may have seriously maimed him. My efforts at apologising to Bob were ignored, and my own life was threatened to be short-lived as soon as he had been treated by the nuns at the infirmary. Victory on this occasion was not sweet. We agreed that in future no heavy hardware such as bricks was to be used and that we should focus more on the major battles with our real "enemy", the Poms.

If no work had been rostered for after the evening meal, we returned to the classrooms to study from 7 pm to 8 pm, then bed. Lights out were at 9 pm. No speaking was allowed after lights out. The shower facilities were similar to those at Castledare. Harassment was a necessary tool for those supervisory staff members in attendance to ensure the system and time frame for the movement of so many boys through the showers was achieved. Orphanages at that time were still recovering from the legacy of WW2. With few resources and staff, and many children in care, close supervision and tight discipline were the norms. Almost two hundred young adolescents had to be showered at multiple open outlets between sport or manual work, and the evening meal. In such an environment a sensitive youth could feel harassed where no harassment may have been intended.

No qualified medical staff or transport was readily available in these institutions to meet medical emergencies. Therefore, it was necessary for the staff to become involved in basic health care, which occasionally included inspecting the boys' private parts. This action was of some concern and embarrassment initially to the new arrivals from Great Britain.

Saturday was a work day until midday and included work such as delousing beds, assisting in the laundry and cleaning out the dairy and piggery. In addition, there always seemed to be a major project that we had to contribute extra time to, such as building extensions to existing buildings, chipping and cleaning old bricks for reuse on new building projects, slaughtering of farm stock, and so on. The younger boys collected old bricks from piles that had been scrounged from building and demolition sites and mixed cement (we called it "pudding") for the older boys who became expert bricklayers and builders under the supervision of a lay brother. Then and only then would there be time allowed for sport or general mischief.

We were expected to work harder during this early post-war period in order to meet the most basic maintenance and improvements to our surroundings. There was no-one else available to do the work.

Sunday was a church parade that required the wearing of shoes and socks until after Mass. The afternoon on the third Sunday of the month could be occupied with visitors. Shoes and socks would be retained for this occasion if you had been advised of visitors to set a good impression for those visiting. If there were no visitors, then swimming, fighting, scheduled sport, or simply socialising was the routine until tea time. Another Sunday church ritual — benediction — was to be attended either before or after the evening meal.

Establishing the right seating position in the dining hall was extremely important. For our little group, this was at the table at the back and to the left after entering through the main entrance, and therefore as far as possible away from the brother-in-charge who sat at the other end of the hall attempting to keep a watchful eye over all of us.

One of our number remained at the table to position himself at the table and seat nearest to the window which opened out to a high hedge and path leading to the dairy. It was also this boy's duty to ensure that the window was open prior to the commencement of Grace and that no other boys tried to hijack the table before his colleagues returned with their meals. He could then proceed to the kitchen to receive his own offering.

You did not dare to leave anything on your plate by the end of mealtime. Our "tosser" had to wait for everyone to stand for the commencement of Grace by the brother-in-charge to be distracted before he commenced throwing any questionable food out the open window and into the hedge. The desired result was only achieved with the correct trajectory, which would be a low strong shot that would direct the items into, not onto, the hedge. A high shot would lob it over the hedge onto the dirt path and draw attention to the activity if not removed immediately after leaving the dining hall.

Bob was the "tosser" on this particular occasion and his aim was woefully off. A heaping handful sailed over the hedge and struck Brother Campbell, a lay brother, who unfortunately for us was returning from his dairy duties. The stinking mass of colourful debris adhered to the side of his neck and head. Not a good look for a man in a black dress!

The brother stormed into the dining hall with the vegetables continuing to cascade down his cassock. After a quick glance along the line of tables near the windows, he spotted the open window and calculated the position of the tosser. He came directly to our table. He was not at all happy. We must have looked extremely guilty. 'Who?' was all he muttered. Bob raised his hand. The command that followed was bordering on hysterical, 'Come here you little shit!' This language is a guesstimate only — it could have been a lot stronger coming from this lay brother.

The first open-handed swing directed at Bob's head missed as he instinctively ducked. Bob tried to escape from this screaming man of the cloth who followed him around the table, knocking us all over in the process. However, the second blow was more accurate and cannoned Bob into already upturned benches, boys, and chairs. The brother dragged Bob from the floor and roughly shook him while at the same time he was demanding to know why he was such an ungrateful little shit throwing good food out the window. Silence followed, and because there were no tears this further infuriated the increasingly hysterical brother. The dong appeared, and as each blow fell any remaining vegetable debris flew in all directions.

The entire dining hall was in an uproar. The brother-in-charge was on his feet ordering all the boys to remain seated and continued to call for silence, to no avail. This must have been a green light to the rest of the boys to rid themselves of any inedible items still on their plates because a food fight started at the other side of the hall where no brothers were present.

As soon as the two brothers moved from one side of the hall to the other to quell the disturbance, the other side would restart throwing their mixed parcels of cabbage, turnip, and swede. Some of these items struck the brothers as they tried to corner the ringleaders. It probably only took a couple of minutes for the brothers to regain control, but it seemed a lot longer at the time.

Our table of eight, all of whom were believed to have been responsible for initiating the disturbance, were called to the brothers' table and swift justice was dispensed. But that was not the end of it. We were then instructed to remain in the dining hall to clean every last morsel from walls, windows, floors, and furniture.

The cook, Mr Kadama, at Boys Town until 1949 or 1950, was an elderly, almost illiterate Japanese citizen with very little English language. He had worked as a cook on a pearl-diving boat before the war at Broome in the far north of Western Australia.

Mr Kadama was extremely paranoid about the authorities coming to arrest him and take him away to an internment camp. Boys Town was a sanctuary for him. He did not appear to understand that WW2 ended in 1945. Perhaps nobody bothered to tell him! He went missing one day. Our search parties gave up after a thorough search of the grounds and surrounding bush. We thought he had done a "runner".

The next morning, one of the older boys working in the kitchen became aware of barely audible sobbing. He said he could not locate the source until he found cigarette stubs on top of an old, unused wood stove. He described how he peered up into the brick chimney above the stove, and there he was, covered in soot with bulging red eyes that oozed thick wet tracks down his cheeks. It took a lot of persuasion to get Mr Kadama down and cleaned up before the brothers found him. We heard later that someone had cruelly told him the authorities were coming for him.

We briefly experienced an interesting and much-appreciated distraction to our normal dining routine when we were given WW2 C-Rations. There were two stories about where they came from. One was that they were supplied by a group of US naval officers who had visited the orphanage, and the other was that they were found by a lay brother at a nearby garbage dump. The biscuits were so hard we had to soak them for a while in the water. The small tins of Spam were highly prized and the rock-hard chocolate substitute would last for ages but left a sour and chalky taste.

Boans department store and the Mills and Ware biscuit factory were the two suppliers of the highly regarded biscuit pieces. Once a month a few of the boys were selected to board the truck and head off to Perth to visit both these suppliers. We filled large boxes with pieces of broken biscuits that had been aside for us. We also received supplies of fruit and vegetables from Boans that were not presentable for sale to the public. They were nowhere near as popular as the biscuits.

"Piece time" at Clontarf had eventually progressed past the piece of bread and jam that we received each day. A large wooden tea chest of the broken pieces of biscuits would be carried out into the yard by the senior boys, and the distribution of a handful to each boy was deposited into the shirt front, which was held out for collection.

I was in charge of the furnace in the boiler room for some time. The boiler room supplied the hot water for the showers and kitchen, and I found this to be very rewarding work requiring little effort on my part. It was certainly a step up from the toilet block duties.

I kept my piece time biscuit pieces with mould or weevils that had been cast aside to make "bickie soup". I always invited Bob and my closest friends to bring their own supply plus a jam tin or other suitable container. We simply added water to the crushed biscuit pieces stirred this into a thick, brown mush and placed the containers on the furnace grating. It always tasted great, especially when a little jam was added to sweeten the feast.

For a brief period, Bob scored the choice job of scraping and washing the plates after the brothers had finished their meals. The pigs missed out on any bones, even the ones that did not have any meat on them. We placed the bones on the gratin and waited for the marrow in the bones to start to bubble from the ends. It was then time to take them out. We sucked the warm marrow out and chewed on the burned and softened bones — wonderful! The boiler room was also a favourite venue for anyone who had other edible items for trade or consumption.

Although waiting on the brothers was a job to hang out for, it did have its moments. For example, one boy engaged as a waiter was punished for spilling soup while serving at the brothers' table. He returned to the kitchen with tears streaming down his face. The tears quickly gave way to a wicked cackle as he relieved himself of piss and vengeance into the brothers' soup urn before delivering the remaining plates to their table. The brothers complimented the cook on the soup. The boy became a legend.

Some of us ate grass seeds that we found on and around the playing fields. We called them "puddings". Each stalk had a tiny sack of sweet juice at the tip. We must have looked quite a sight as we grazed across the playing fields near the river, on our hands and knees picking at the grass like a herd of cows. This may have originally been referred to as "bush tucker".

Peanuts not presentable for sale to the public were occasionally donated to Boys Town for pig food. A good proportion of this delicacy never made it to the pigs. Certainly not to the four-legged variety. The peanuts were an unexpected luxury. Word spread very quickly when the truck pulled up at the piggery for unloading. Volunteers came from everywhere.

Another source of food was the Canning River. Mullet and garfish were the almost exclusive resident fish population. We inherited another little piece of survival knowledge from the Aboriginal boys. We were shown how to use what they called the "kylie" to catch fish.

The kylie was either a V-shaped piece of rusted roofing metal or a broken piece of asbestos, preferably in an irregular or triangular configuration. Once armed, we waded slowly and quietly through the mud, reeds, and shallows of the river until a school of fish were spotted near the surface, and then threw the kylies as hard as we could into the centre of the school. If luck and accuracy prevailed, those fish that were either stunned or killed floated to the surface. We then hastily lit a fire by the side of the river. The catch would have to be eaten as quickly as possible. If you were spotted cooking or eating the fish others would come running like blowflies to a cowpat.

To be a bedwetter at Boys Town was no more acceptable

than it was at Castledare. Those found guilty were humiliated in front of the entire dormitory. The beds of proven bedwetters had to be pulled back in the mornings and were inspected for "the stain". There were rumours of boys having cattle prods used on them to discourage bedwetting, but as far as I know, it was not undertaken in our dormitory during the time we were there.

Bob found a cat in the pine forest early in his stay at Boys Town and became quite fond of it. He tucked it down his shirt and took it everywhere. At night he smuggled it into the dormitory and hid it under his blanket. Giltrap, one of the older boys, was huge for his age, and a full-time farmworker. He forcibly took the cat from Bob one day and climbed to the top of the church belfry. He tied the four corners of a handkerchief to a single line, and that was then secured around the cat's stomach. He had made a parachute and announced loudly to the boys below that should it not open there was no need to worry because cats had nine lives and always landed on their feet. Bob pleaded from below for him not to do it. The parachute did not deploy! Bob was extremely upset but knew he would never win a stand-up fight with this boy. Our code demanded that you never "dobbed in" another boy to the brothers, no matter what. Bob simply bided his time.

Soon after, while mixing cement for one of the building projects that we were endlessly engaged in, Bob saw Giltrap heading his way and hid behind a low wall. As Giltrap passed by, he raised the long-handled shovel he had been working with and struck Giltrap with all his might across the back of the head and neck. A lay brother supervising work nearby rushed to the side of the still dazed and bloodied Giltrap to treat him as best he could before he was taken away to the infirmary.

Bob was also taken away, but not to the infirmary. The last I saw of him that day was being half carried by the neck of his shirt by one of the brothers. Bob never spoke of any physical punishment received. He did mention that after some time with the principal he was taken to the orphanage priest, to explain why he did what he did. A stiff penance was given, and Bob was left in the chapel to contemplate his actions, and to give his borrowed rosary beads a work-out. Nothing more happened.

Bob initially thought he had killed Giltrap, and therefore had committed a mortal sin! However, being an accomplished sinner was soon of little interest because he had now attained a new status, and no bully dared to confront him from that day on. Giltrap became Bob's subservient disciple and followed him everywhere in his self-appointed role of protector. Unfortunately, Bob did not consider that I should also be privy to this protective shield. This was a personal matter!

I cannot remember whether it was deserved punishment or simply being in the wrong place at the wrong time, but occasionally recruits were gathered together and lined up to receive metal buckets. The buckets were used in the hauling of raw sewerage from the very large septic tank that serviced the entire population of Boys Town, and then depositing the contents into 44-gallon drums on the back of the farm truck for disposal elsewhere, we did not care where! The most demanding part of this unpleasant exercise occurred during the final stages when we had to climb down a ladder and into the tank and pass the full buckets from boy to boy leading to and up the ladder. If you could, you avoided standing on, or at the bottom of the ladder! The stench was so bad that many of us contributed to the bucket loads by being horribly sick. It took long periods of time in the river and scrubbing with hard laundry soap to feel and smell cleansed.

In 1847, Benedictine monks arrived at New Norcia, which was approximately 126 km north of Perth, and while building and opening their monastery they simultaneously commenced their work as missionaries. Their goal was to provide education, housing, and general life skills to the local Aboriginal people, who may have also taught the monks a thing or two!

One of the monks, Dom Pedro Bede, visited Boys Town occasionally and was well-liked and respected by us all. He spent hours with our class telling us stories from his childhood in Spain, but most appreciated of all were his ghost stories. He would keep us open-mouthed, enthralled, and always pleading for more.

Two boys from Boys Town were selected each year to be Dom Pedro's assistants during the school holidays to work in the apiary and the olive groves at the monastery. I had the good fortune of being one of the two boys selected one year for the two-week stay there. It was the best experience I had in the years I was at both orphanages. We worked hard and were treated well by the monks. Once the hives had been serviced and the honey bottled, we moved on to picking olives for processing and eventual delivery by the monks to the restaurants and markets in the capital, and for sale locally.

We spent our free time later in the day roaming about the bush with the Aboriginal boys who were accommodated with their families in nearby rows of homes that had been built by the monks specifically for their large community. The Aboriginal Elders had great stories to tell us and appreciated the honey, olives and bread that we always brought them.

I have often thought of this kind monk over the years, and in late 2003 my wife Judith and I flew across the country to Western Australia to see family members and to visit New Norcia. Dom Pedro Bede would have passed away many years before our visit, but I wanted to pay my respects at his graveside and thank him for his friendship and compassion which was rare and special at a time when it was most needed. Alas, there was no headstone for this monk in the monastery's graveyard. I inquired as to the whereabouts of his remains and was referred to an older monk who advised us that Dom Pedro had returned to Spain in his final years to spend what little time he had left with family members in the village where he was born.

One of the older boys at Boys Town was found smoking in the dairy. He was marched to the front of the dining hall to be given his punishment in front of us all. We were told this was a mortal sin. Unfortunately for the culprit, he made the mistake of smiling when receiving his punishment. The brother delivering the punishment stopped, placed the dong on a nearby table, and without any warning, he spun around and delivered a king-hit to the big lad's head. It took four of us to pick up the prone body and remove it to the infirmary. We all learned a valuable lesson that day. Smoking was not good for your health!

The older boys at the orphanage would often meet for a smoke down by the river, or in the laundry, and when we small fry asked what they were smoking, we were told to mix dry cow manure, definitely not pig manure, with dry grass, and to roll it up in a piece of newspaper. They also suggested that if we had a problem with this routine, we should use a double roll of paper with lots of spit to ensure that the "fag" did not unroll. One day, after serving Mass at the nunnery at Boys Town, Bob and I retired to the rear of the chapel to try out this product, as instructed by the older boys. It was disgusting, and our coughing and gagging alerted an old nun to our activity. Another of her number was called to assist by giving us one hell of a hiding with a cane. We both learned another lesson that day. The dong was definitely preferred over the cane.

Perhaps the greatest mortal sinners were those involved in the storeroom raids. A small group of boys in our dormitory were involved in the raids. The raids progressed over a considerable period of time. Cans and jars of condensed milk, jams, pickles, and various types of canned meats and fish were the preferred targets. These were products we were never privy to in our dining hall. They were donated by various charities and businesses and stored for the annual fundraising fair to be used as prizes on the various spinning wheels and games of chance, etc.

Most of the raiders could not wait until morning to consume their individual shares of the booty and retired to a secluded spot such as the showers or toilets to ensure the contents were enjoyed, and as quickly as possible. Others, desiring a more sanitary disposal area, returned to their beds with the items, pulled a blanket over their heads, and devoured the contents without a thought for any of their fellow dormitory dwellers who were still awake and could only listen to the glutinous slurping, and burping under the covers. The remainder of the spoils and the empty cans and jars were stashed under the stage in the quadrangle near the bottom of our dormitory stairs.

The storeroom raids were over when a brother, for some obscure reason, looked under the stage and discovered the cache of both the unopened loot and emptied containers. 'Holy Mother of God!' the brother is reputed to have called out, and this would have to be close to the mark because he was after all an Irishman and a Christian Brother. Apparently, he kept repeating the same phrase over and over until finally he stood and blew his whistle. Other curious brothers joined him as scores of boys, guilty or not, peered apprehensively over the balcony, or slipped away to hide out until the furore had died down. It was quite a sight, several black-clothed bums sticking out from under the stage as the brothers pondered this sight on their hands and knees. This was definitely way up there in the mortal sin stakes.

The "Inquisition" ground gave way almost immediately. That fickle finger again pointed at our dormitory, with good reason. Everyone in the dormitory was lined up, and the guilty were ordered to step forward. There were no volunteers from the ranks of the guilty, so the brothers worked in teams to complete the task of giving a thrashing to us all. The brothers must have been exhausted towards the end of that task. It was a day of reckoning that some of us realised would come sooner or later, but at least for the guilty it was well worth it!

Attendance at Mass was a mandatory daily event for all of us, Catholics or pagans. If the Catholics had not taken Communion, they were highly suspect and must have either committed a mortal sin or not been to Confession to seek absolution. We of the pagan variety were ignored. We were considered to be in a permanent state of mortal sin. Latin was taught in the classroom, and instruction was given on the Catechism, which sums up the beliefs of the Catholic Church.

We had been instructed that Confession wiped the slate clean. This seemed like a good deal and made the self-gratification of sinning quite attractive! Sin by all means, and then come Saturday simply pop along to Confession, say your penance with as much sincerity as possible, receive Communion at Mass on Sunday, and all was good in your world again — until next time!

I was eleven, and Bob was ten when the brothers told us to prepare to become Catholics. We were not given an option. We had to stay behind after regular class hours, and on some Saturday mornings after our work assignments, to study the Catechism and Latin which would ensure we had a reasonable understanding of Catholic rituals. We were told that we had to select a godfather each of whom would be present during the ceremony of Baptism. We were given two names to choose from, Mr Joey Jackson, the part-Aboriginal bandmaster, and Mr Kadama, the Japanese cook. I drew Joey Jackson. Bob was a little upset to have drawn Mr Kadama, but later found it to be a blessing in disguise because his godfather would take food that was destined for the brothers' plates and set it aside for Bob to have during his kitchen duties. We were told to select a Christian name each. It could be any name so long as it was the name of one of the Apostles. I chose John. Bob chose John! Perhaps we could not remember any other Apostle's name.

Becoming Catholic was initially a most rewarding, but brief experience. Following the baptismal service, we were instructed to sit at the head of the dining hall at a special table near the brothers. We were then each presented with two fried eggs and two pieces of buttered toast for breakfast. We also received an apple and orange each and a handful of sweets. This was a privilege and a feast to be enjoyed. It had been years since we had even seen a cooked egg! While receiving these once-only bountiful gifts, the resident priest stood at the head table, and informed all present that we were now saved from the fires of hell, unless we misbehaved and committed a mortal sin. No problem for us, because we knew that we had Confession on Saturday as a great fallback should this happen, or more appropriately when it happened. It was difficult to enjoy the occasion because most of those boys staring back at us with a mixture of envy and disdain were already Catholics upon arrival at Boys Town and had already been saved. They had therefore also received all the rewards they were entitled to.

We were both confirmed as Catholics two days later on 7 September 1949, and at the end of this unrehearsed and long Confirmation ceremony, we were told to step forward and kiss the visiting Bishop's ring!

During the later stage of my time at Boys Town, I achieved the questionable position of training other boys younger than I in the fine art of becoming altar boys. However, I soon realised that my leadership qualities were sadly lacking. I lost control of my trainee group during one particular Saturday morning session while demonstrating the routine that should be followed in preparing and lighting the censer for the priest at benediction. We had engaged in this exercise outside the chapel, and across a narrow pathway from an expansive pine forest, as a safety measure. I had gone back into the chapel for just a minute or two when the bright spark, no pun intended, began swinging the censer around his head, increasing the arc until finally one of the brass chains anchored to the censer broke! Hot embers and incense sprayed out onto the pathway that ran alongside the chapel. The pine tree forest was only metres away on the other side of the pathway. In a frenzy, mats and Holy water were taken from the chapel and thrown at the flames, but without effect. The good Lord and everyone else in my training class had deserted me. The arrival of several brothers and an army of boys with buckets of water saved the day, but not my hide. The omnipresent fickle finger of fate was unreservedly pointed in my direction.

In addition to the fire episode, it came to light that someone had been sampling the altar wine and adding water to disguise the consumption rate! That was the final straw as far as the resident clergy were concerned. As far as I can recall, I did not gain legend status, even temporarily, but remember the hiding and dressing down I received. I had to bear the punishment in silence because as mentioned previously, it was "not cricket" to inform on your peers, and the culprit who instigated the wine-drinking alert had remained silent. Soon after, I was unceremoniously sacked from my role of an altar boy.

Bob was a natural sportsperson and won every race he entered. No-one could get anywhere near him. He admitted to me years later that he would bless himself with the sign of the cross and say a Hail Mary while preparing to get on his mark. He then asked Jesus, Mary, and Joseph to help him win, and when that whistle blew, nervous energy had him halfway down the straight before his competitors had barely left their marks. Bob should have let me in on his secret pre-race call for assistance from above. I desperately needed it.

Boxing was the domain of a select few who delighted in having us younger boys served up to them in the ring to practice on. The brothers often organised special days, when the Bishop, a senior police officer, or other visiting VIPs would be invited to attend the regular boxing event. Light-hearted entertainment was arranged for the visitors prior to the more formal boxing events commencing. Four or six of us sacrificial lambs at a time were herded forward and told to don voluminous leather gloves that we could hardly lift to cover our faces. We were then instructed to enter the ring where blindfolds were firmly tied. Older boys then spun us around in circles until we became giddy and disoriented.

If you were to last very long at all in the ring, you immediately started to swing your arms as fast as you could and hoped that you connected with someone before someone connected with you. The inevitable blow would catch up with you eventually, and you would be quite happy by then to crawl to safety at the edge of the ring. This brought the loudest howls of laughter from the audience because we were still blindfolded, and it could take a while to find the refuge we were seeking. The audience loved this blood sport. The last boy standing would usually be rewarded with a bag of sweets, or alternatively, he was told to kiss the Bishop's ring!

My saving grace from an inevitable slide into anonymity was a reasonable ability in the classroom. I was usually first or second in our class of at least forty or more boys. However, I would have preferred to win a race or two or complete good innings at cricket.

It was not an uncommon occurrence during those years for boys to attempt to abscond. Dissatisfaction with the orphanage management's harsh discipline provided added encouragement for the more courageous and adventurous element of our small community.

When a boy did a "runner", usually at night or early morning, he created a real problem for the staff. Police, the Department of Child Welfare, and other organisations had to be informed and involved in the process of recovery. The orphanage staff simply did not have the resources to allocate to the tracking of the boys. Their involvement began when the boys were returned to their care, usually by the police.

Scabies, boils, infected cuts, and Sandy Blight were constant accessories that we accepted as routine and rarely required assistance from the nun at the infirmary. The river, leeches, and our own homemade poultices usually sufficed.

We learned how to look after ourselves from earlier experiences at Castledare. One of my more painful experiences occurred when I had to be admitted to the infirmary with burns to my eyes after a wayward shovel of cement was accidentally sent my way. My eyes were washed out, treated with drops, and then bandaged for a couple of days before seeing daylight again!

Lime burns on our uncovered feet when mixing the mortar were also a common occurrence. The pain was extreme when sores or cuts were exposed, but we did not stop our work for fear of a clout across the head from the supervising brother. We developed a system of having a couple of buckets of water on standby to stand in to obtain some relief from the burning.

A group of boys were selected at least once a year to have their tonsils out. No-one knew what criteria were used in the selection process. Bob was one such candidate plucked from his class to have his tonsils out. He maintained he had not experienced any problems to warrant the surgery. Arguments or refusals were not considered. You simply accepted your lot and surrendered your tonsils! Each boy selected for tonsil removal was placed on a table, and a visiting doctor removed the "offending" tonsils with the assistance of a nun. Chloroform was used as an anaesthetic. Once the operation had been completed the patient was placed on a mattress on the concrete floor with his fellow patients to vomit, groan, whimper, and recover for a couple of hours. This situation did improve over time by transporting legitimate patients to the Royal Perth Hospital for treatment.

Soon after the Air Force handed back the facility to Boys Town in 1947-1948, a dentist visited and inspected every boy. However, after he had been at the orphanage for several days he was accused of interfering with a couple of the boys, and we never saw him again!

Soon after the incident with the visiting deviant dentist, the principal of Boys Town organised what would become the much-dreaded bi-annual visits of state government dentists. These were mostly student dentists, and we were the fodder. It did not take long before every boy knew when the dental clinic's caravan had arrived and proceeded down the long drive to the administration area. Some horrendous tales flowed from these visits. Extractions appeared to be favoured above all else by the young dentists. Rows of boys sat or lay about the courtyard spitting blood and nursing their jaws.

We tried other means of solving our dental problems if any of the boys were suffering from toothache in between the six-months visits. A long-standing procedure used to extract teeth was to tie a piece of string around the troublesome tooth and tie the other end to a door handle. This, we were told was the least painful and quickest way to take care of the necessary extraction. The "dentist", usually an older boy, counted to three and slammed the door as hard as he could. Sometimes the troublesome tooth was removed by this means, but more often than not it was a complete failure. No-one ever volunteered for a second try. One of the boys, who may have later gone on to become a dentist, prided himself on his ability to use the only tool in his possession, a pair of rusty long-necked pliers!

We were occasionally bused or trucked up to Bindoon, northeast of Perth, a remote boys farming community run by the Christian Brothers, similar to Clontarf. The Bindoon lads, despite their descriptions of the harsh discipline they received, were anxious to show us their work in building the huge main building and the surrounding farm buildings. We were paired off with our hosts, and once the tour of the building sites was completed our guides were either given other tasks to do or were selected to spend the rest of the day with us hunting rabbits or engaging in other activities.

A Maltese boy at Bindoon had a pet ferret, and he boasted to our small group of hunters of its prowess in getting the rabbits out of their warrens. The keeper of the ferret insisted on coming with us on our hunt. An older Bindoon boy borrowed a .22 rifle and a handful of cartridges from one of the lay brothers.

The gun-toting boy assured us that he had tallied up quite a score of hits with the gun on previous outings. Instructions were solemnly given by our gun-toting accomplice, and he repeated everything to ensure there would be no accident. He insisted that his routine was extremely efficient and would save a lot of time and effort because we would normally have to dig the rabbits out. The Maltese ferret master was to await the nod from the rifleman, and the silent "thumbs up"' signal from each boy standing at a burrow hole exit point with an appropriate weapon of choice, mostly shovels or large sticks, ready to dispatch the emerging bunnies. Thank heavens I had not read Richard Adam's book, *Watership Down*. I would not have volunteered for this exercise.

We all had positions behind and to the left and right of the gun, certainly not in front of it. The burrows to the front were restricted to the sniper's field of fire. Once the boy was confident and ready to insert the ferret into one of the openings everyone was on alert. Rabbits would be exiting at lightning speed and dispersing in every direction possible within seconds after the ferret went down.

The hunt was on, and everyone became silent and concentrated on the task ahead. The ferret went down what appeared to be the major warren hole. Breathlessly, our weapons of choice were raised, eyes peered into the dark mouths of the burrows in anticipation, and our own self-acclaimed marksman was ready to pick off the unsuspecting victims as they bounded out.

Only one shot was fired. I had no time to focus on that as I waited anxiously for my first victim to appear. It was all over in a few seconds after the shot. It really was unfortunate that the ferret came out first, and directly in front of the raised and ready weapon of our sharp-shooter. The scorecard of kills that day read Rabbits — 0, Ferret — 1.

The major income-producing event of the year for the Boys Town administration was the annual fair. Family, friends, and the general public were invited to attend. A variety of stalls, raffles, and prize wheels were in place to extract as much money as possible from those attending. We were each given two shillings to spend, our Sunday clothes and shoes to wear, and told to smile a lot. An inspection parade had to be passed before we were let loose among our visitors and the punters.

We had not had a visitor for almost two years at this stage, so we had to make do with the two shillings and rely on a little stealth and cunning to make the day a success. The gamblers among us were broke in no time at all and had to come to terms with what to do with the rest of what looked like a very long, thirsty, and food-free day. Those who were "savvy" casually strolled around the back of the stalls and game wheels where the prizes were stacked or lay in open boxes behind curtained-off areas, and once the "wheel of chance" was spinning and all attention was focused on the numbers, several of the boys swung into action, and casually "lifted" cans of condensed milk, and jars of pickles, jam, or whatever other consumable items were within striking range. These items were then tucked under shirts or rammed into trouser pockets and whisked away to the rear of the classroom buildings. The proceeds of crime were usually devoured on the spot, and as quickly as possible. You quickly discovered who your true friends were. This need for urgent consumption was necessary because you could lose the lot to a bigger boy who would give you a bloody nose rather than a 'Thank you very much, you little shit' if you did not hand over some or all of your loot. It was not unusual to see boys soon after their quite unusual feasts running into the toilet block and throwing up their various colourful concoctions.

Two of the brothers at Boys Town who appeared to enjoy

pounding a young body with a fist or "dong" were better known to the boys as "Killer" and "Thrasher". Both had been Irish policemen before joining the Christian Brothers and continued to ply some of the more physical aspects of their training on their young charges.

The fear and loathing of Killer finally got the better of a group of older boys who had been subjected to his beatings over a long period of time. Killer had a large black mongrel dog he used no imagination in naming Blackie. We referred to it as the "Black Bastard". These boys enticed the dog to the sheds behind the dairy, tied it up, beat it to death, and buried it. Killer never found out what happened to Blackie, but he must have had his suspicions. I always suspected that the same boys who killed Blackie were wholly or partly also responsible for killing a pup that Gran had received permission for me to look after at Boys Town.

One of the older boys grabbed me one day, and told me to go to the laundry, and take care of my dog. The pup had been thrown into a laundry vat of boiling water. She was in severe pain with skin blistering and swelling. She lay cowering in a corner, shaking, and whimpering. I tried to place a cold wet sheet over her, but that only made the situation worse. It was truly gut-wrenching to listen to her howl even louder, and not know what to do to ease her suffering. I could not cuddle her or touch her without inflicting even more pain. All the while I could not stop crying. She died soon after.

There were some caring and compassionate brothers

over the years, but they were few. One was Brother Patrick O'Doherty. He was my teacher at Boys Town from 1948 to 1951. Although strict, he was fair. He encouraged his students to excel in sports and in their academic studies. Every brother had a nickname, and because he was very tall, we called him "six-foot Dickie", or just "Dickie". He arrived at Boys Town at around the same time that we did. He was a graduate of a Christian Brothers seminary in Ireland.

I continue to retain considerable respect and admiration for Dickie's guidance, direction, and even his discipline, especially in his instilling the self-confidence that enabled me to continue to pursue an education later in life, and to contribute to meaningful aspects of my personal and professional life in military and public service to my country.

It was not my intention to denigrate or highlight the inadequacies and misdemeanours of some of the Christian Brothers and staff of the orphanages my brother and I were placed in, however, there were exceptions who were either too eager with their brutal punishments or had a penchant for preying upon those boys who were most vulnerable. These brothers were referred to as "fiddlers". Brother Lawrence Murphy was one such fiddler. He was the most feared Christian Brother that we would encounter during our stay at Castledare. I have found it extremely difficult to understand why it took over fifty years to bring him to justice. I wish to add, that Murphy and his like were a damaging distraction from the positive work that the majority of the Christian

Brothers had achieved over many demanding and difficult pre-war and post-war years.

We were too young to understand or appreciate the day-to-day difficulties being experienced not only by the general population of the country with food, and clothing rationing, but also by the Christian Brothers who were given so little financial or other assistance from the government.

The Western Australian Government formally apologised to all former wards and offered counselling and other means of rehabilitation and compensation to assist those who had been subjected to varying levels of physical, sexual, and emotional abuse. Yet another Royal Commission was announced by the prime minister in 2013, and it was expected to run for at least three years. Most of my generation will have either passed on or no longer have the strength, either mentally or physically, to retain any interest in any long-term outcomes.

It is most unfortunate that so many of the compassionate and genuinely devoted "men in black dresses" have been tarred with the same brush as those few who abused their charges with relative impunity. Those pathetic paedophiles who dressed in the guise of cassock and cross and preyed on helpless children would have to answer to the highest authority of all one day. That final judgement they cannot avoid.

There are so many other details relating to the way of life and experiences, both good and bad, that I could mention while at Castledare Boys Home and Clontarf Boys Town, but much has been written on this subject over the years and I do not wish to comment further. I think it best if I simply close this slice of my past by mentioning how I left Boys Town.

I have little recall of my last day at Boys Town and have had to rely on Bob and others for details of the events of that day. I was extremely ill in the morning. I had a high temperature and found it difficult to breathe, walk, and dress for breakfast. My nausea increased, and I had difficulty walking to the dining hall. Someone brought me my porridge and tea, but I could not eat or drink a thing.

The supervisory brother in the dining room prowled the rows of seated boys, as was the norm, to ensure that all the contents of the bowls had been emptied. He came up behind me and ordered me to eat my porridge, but it was impossible. I was fighting back waves of nausea and could not reply. The order was repeated again, but my non-compliance with his orders prompted him to hit me across the back of my neck and back with his leather dong. I was told later that he had continued to beat me until I fell onto the concrete floor. I had lost consciousness and was carried outside by my brother, and two other boys. They were told to leave me on the dining hall steps to recover, and then return to their seats. I was discovered soon after by a lay brother passing by. I was unconscious at the bottom of the steps. The brother called for assistance, and I was carried to the infirmary.

Bob had sat by my side for most of the day until an ambulance was finally requested in the evening, and I was taken away to Royal Perth Hospital. I was thirteen years of age. I was given penicillin injections while I remained in a coma for three days. I had double pneumonia and was apparently covered in bruises.

I have no idea why I had been placed in an adult ward. Smoking was allowed, if not encouraged in hospitals at that time, and once I had recovered enough to sit up and speak, a nearby patient asked if I would roll cigarettes for the fellows in the ward who could not do so themselves. The patients supplied the tobacco and cigarette paper, and later on they bought me a basic but effective cigarette rolling machine from the hospital canteen lady who wheeled her trolley of products around the wards each day. Packets of cigarettes were considered too expensive for most of the patients in my ward who were war veterans.

Bob was allowed to visit me in the company of one of the brothers every second week, and he really looked forward to this outing. I don't think it was the visit to see me that was the highlight of his day. The nurses made a fuss of him and ensured that he received a three-course meal during his stay. Before he left, they filled his pockets with biscuits and sweets. His dining experiences certainly improved for the better later in his life.

Bob was appointed Executive General Manager of Betts & Betts, Hay Street, in Perth. At that time this was the largest shoe store in Australia with five managers for the various sections, and one hundred and thirty-five staff. The company was also the largest footwear chain in the country with over two hundred stores. He travelled the world on buying trips every three or four months to select the next season's fashions. He stayed in the very best hotels and dined in the finest of restaurants.

During this period, I had been treated for double pneumonia and had my appendix out. Polio was suggested early on, but eventually excluded. Finally, the medical staff settled on rheumatic fever which may have been a desperate last diagnosis. I was treated like a guinea pig in a laboratory with countless tests made by groups of staff, and medical students, attending at my bedside almost every day, or at least it seemed that way. The most feared of all the medical tests was the long needle they inserted into my spine to remove fluid while I was curled up in a foetal position. I had at least three of those in as many months.

I have often wondered whether the staff kept me in the hospital as a safe haven, rather than sending me back to Boys Town. My reasoning for this suggestion is based on how I must have looked when admitted to the hospital.

A regular hospital visitor to another patient in a ward close by occasionally spent a few minutes with me before she left. After a while, she approached the Child Welfare Department to enquire if she could foster me out of the orphanage. I was unaware of this new development until the day they checked me out of the hospital and placed me in her care.

5

The Foster Family & Bess

1951–1954

My standing within this family unit was established very early. I was constantly reminded that I should be thankful for being rescued from Boys Town.

The foster mother advised that I was to be company for their son. He was a year older than me. Their second and older son was away in the Navy, and the family's daughter had just been married and no longer lived at home. I missed Bob and was told not to mention him again because they were my new family.

This rhetoric sounded very familiar and disconcerting! The father worked as a nurse at the nearby mental asylum. I had to serve Mass there with their son as an altar boy on Sundays. It was at times a quite terrifying experience.

I had missed several months of school while in hospital and had to repeat Year 8 at Christian Brothers High School (CBHS), Highgate, a suburb of Perth. I enjoyed my year at Highgate and made a few close friends there. We were all looking forward to meeting up again the following year, but that was not to be.

5 The Foster Family & Bess

I was told I would have to earn my keep and would be contributing financially to the household by being apprenticed to Abbott & Co, printers, in Hay Street, Perth. I was never asked whether I wanted to be apprenticed. I wanted to continue at school. It was the norm for boys at that time to start their apprenticeships at fifteen years of age. I commenced my five-year apprenticeship as a printer in late 1953.

I handed the envelope containing my weekly pay of three pounds ten shillings unopened to the foster mother, who then returned ten shillings to me to cover bus fares, lunches, and personal items for the next week.

The foster family received an initial lump sum from the Department of Child Welfare and additional regular payments followed. These contributions were supposed to be used to feed, clothe, and provide an education for me. My education had been terminated, and the only clothes I ever had come my way were those passed on from their son. Even the school uniform and sports clothes had been handed down from the son who had also attended CBHS Highgate.

Bob was allowed a half-day to visit the foster home after I had been there a year. He waited until we were alone to tell me that the following Friday evening our father, who had reappeared again, would be picking him up at Boys Town, and they would be going to stay at a caravan park in Mandurah, a seaside town south of Perth until Sunday evening.

I had not seen my father since his one visit to see us at Castledare Boys Home in 1945, when I was seven. Bob and I thought there was a good chance that we could all be getting together again as a family.

I told Bob to ask Dad if I could join them. The plan we settled on was for me to call the principal's office telephone at Boys Town from my workplace and ask to speak to Bob a couple of days prior to Dad picking him up. Bob could then confirm whether I could come with them. If so, we could also then discuss the location and time for the pick-up.

All went to plan, and we had a great time at Mandurah catching crabs, swimming, and vying unsuccessfully for the attention of our father. I naively imagined that if this was not to be the start of a family reunion, then perhaps there could at least be the possibility of a regular get-together. However, Dad's attention did not spill over to Bob and me. His complete focus was on his female companion, and we had little chance to spend any time with him at all.

Sunday evening came too quickly, as did my return to reality. I admitted to Dad during a session of questioning on the drive back to the foster home that I had not told the foster family about being with him and added that if I had told the foster family I would never have been allowed to see him.

I thought Dad was going to beat the living daylights out of me. The horrors of the past living with this violent man came back to haunt me in an instant. I was dropped off unceremoniously, and without a word, several kilometres away from my destination. There were no farewells. That was the last time I saw my father.

5 The Foster Family & Bess

Despite several searches of state records across the country, I have never been able to establish what my father did during the final years of his life, and where he may finally be at rest. Bob and I decided not to pursue the search any further.

I admit to having shown extremely poor judgement in not requesting permission from the foster parents to spend time with my father, but in retrospect, that weekend away in Mandurah changed the direction of my life for the better. I did not return to the foster home. Instead, I hid overnight under the bed of a school friend who lived nearby and left early the next morning before his family started to stir.

I needed refuge and advice on what I should do next. Gran was still working in New Zealand. Aunt Bess was the only other adult I could seek advice from. She was not really my aunt, but had been my grandmother's best friend, and I got to know her from the times she accompanied Gran on her monthly visits to Boys Town. Gran referred to her as Aunt Bess when she was with us.

I have no recollection of how long the journey took, or how I found Bess's home. I had only visited her home once previously with Gran when Bob and I had been allowed out of Boys Town for a weekend over a Christmas period. Fortunately, I remembered the address details.

I must have passed out from exhaustion at some stage after my long trek and lack of sleep. I awoke being slapped and shaken awake by two policemen in civilian clothes who thought I was faking a deep sleep. They explained to Bess that they had been searching for me for three days. I explained my situation and my earlier movements as best I could. I also told them I did not want to return to the foster home and would rather be sent back to Boys Town.

Bess stepped in and asked the police if they could check with the Child Welfare Department to see if it was acceptable for me to be placed in her care. This was quickly achieved, and I was given the front enclosed veranda sleep-out for myself. Bess became my guardian. I was to remain a ward of the state until I turned eighteen.

I could not have wished for a more caring guardian. Bess's husband, Harry, was a bookie at the Gloucester Park Trots, at East Perth, and although underage, I would often tag along, and work for him as a runner. The pay was excellent, and I always gave Bess half when I arrived home. Harry insisted that I should never bet on the horses as it was "a mug's game". Such advice from a bookie!

The five-year apprenticeship I had been signed up for was one of the longest apprenticeships at that time, but after almost two years of working in a basement, printing business cards one at a time by hand on an old foot-pedalled Platen machine, and attending technical college one day a week, I decided that this work was not my own life choice. I liked my workmates and the owner of the business, but I felt like a mushroom in that environment.

I became increasingly restless, and soon after having been taken up in a Chipmunk single-engine aircraft by one of the senior printers, a former Spitfire pilot, and put through a strenuous and gut-wrenching period of aerobatics, I knew that I wanted to pursue a career in the Air Force. This decision was made despite the horrible air sickness I endured during an hour of stalls, dives, rolls, and loops.

When we landed, I was told to carefully exit the aircraft without leaving any mess and to sit down nearby. An airfield fire truck pulled up minutes later, and I was told to step away from the aircraft, strip, and leave my stinking thick football sweater, shirt, singlet, and pants near my feet. The pilot had taken control of the hose from the duty airfield fireman.

No warning or further instruction was given before I was knocked over by the pressure of the water from the fire hose being directed at me and my items of clothing. He maintained the wash down until he was convinced that I no longer stank, and was completely devoid, externally at least, of the contents of my breakfast. I had pulled out my shirt and sweater and vomited inside them. Not a pretty picture, but it reduced the mess inside the aircraft.

I had to run around the tarmac area in my underpants, picking up my soaking wet clothes which had been blown some distance away by the chuckling pilot.

My supposed pilot friend had no doubt planned his energetic airborne manoeuvres and the arrival of the fire truck. He had expected and enjoyed the result he had achieved. It was my first time in an aircraft, airsick, and embarrassed, but I loved every moment of that flight and even the aftermath that followed on the Monday morning when I turned up to work. Everyone was in on the joke and they spent most of the day enjoying themselves at my expense.

I could not focus on anything else from that day on. A short time later I informed my employer, a WW2 RAAF bomber pilot who had earnt a Distinguished Flying Cross that I was going to apply to join the RAAF. At first, he was not impressed with this news, but he finally offered his support and a glowing recommendation to present to the recruiting office.

6

The Air Force & The British Nuclear Tests

1955–1961

I joined the RAAF on 2 October 1955 at seventeen years of age and was sent to RAAF Base Richmond, 50 km northwest of Sydney in New South Wales for basic training. I had no idea what I would be doing, but I naively thought that eventually becoming a pilot would be a great career choice.

I enjoyed the comradeship, the military discipline, and the tasks applied in basic training. I did not find the bellowing drill instructors, most of whom were ex-British instructors very intimidating at all, unlike several others in my intake. I thrived on the bivouacs, the exercises, the survival training in the bush, the weapons training, and everything else they threw at us during the months of "rookie" training.

The WW1 issue.303 Enfield rifle was still the weapon of choice for the RAAF in 1955, probably because it had only been ten years since the end of WW2, and it was the only service rifle available at the time. I was a skinny kid and found the weapon heavy and cumbersome. The recoil against my then bony shoulder was agony. I soon discovered that a pair of rolled-up socks were perfect for countering the recoil impact. My accuracy on the firing range also improved enormously.

The WW2 veterans on my course who had re-enlisted were treated with respect, at least by their fellow intake mates. While out on a survival exercise in the bush, I was instructed on the many uses one could apply to a can of baked beans by one of the older veterans who were on guard duty with me.

We had a particularly tough drill instructor with us on the bivouac, and after a couple of hours of staring into the dark and being bored silly, the veteran told me he was not an admirer of the British drill instructors and asked me to accompany him to the area where the instructor's tent was pitched. It was a few metres away from the recruits. The fire outside the tent had burned down to glowing embers by then. It was late, and the camp was quiet. I was told to stoke the fire with more wood.

The veteran went missing for a few minutes and when he returned, he produced a couple of very large cans of baked beans. He carefully placed them in the glowing embers. I thought this was to heat up the beans for our team on guard duty to have a late supper when the new team of guards relieved us. We quickly made our way back to our guard positions. He told me to listen, and not say a word.

A muffled explosion sometime later was followed by angry shouts and expletives. This appeared to delight the veteran. We both ran back towards the tent encampment acting out the role of concerned camp guards, to find a very unhappy drill instructor. His tent was covered in baked beans!

I turned eighteen during the period of my basic training. I was no longer a ward of the state of Western Australia. I was now on my own in a legal sense, but certainly not alone as a member of the Royal Australian Air Force.

A few of my intake could not handle the discipline of service life and went AWOL. The service police promptly located and arrested them. They were sentenced to serve a period of confinement to barracks before returning to their training or were discharged, because we never saw them again. I could not understand such behaviour. I considered basic training a holiday camp compared to the discipline dished out at Boys Town.

The instructors provided very innovative and unusual training in the art of throwing grenades. Munitions may have been scarce, or more appropriately in the hands of Army personnel, because our grenades were imagined objects, never real grenades! Perhaps Air Force personnel could not be trusted with such munitions?

The action in throwing the grenade was universal, it was just the absence of an object being thrown that was unusual, as was having to shout out loud the action being taken and counting (again shouting loudly) the seconds of each action — 'pull (pin) two, three, throw (grenade), two, three, (duck), two, three, boom' (shouted louder)! God help us, and our great nation, if we had ever been required to front up against an enemy force at that time! They would have surely died laughing!

Other than the baked beans caper the only incident I can

recall that was outside the normal training activity was in assisting the local people of the nearby township of Windsor which was approximately 46 km northwest of Sydney during a very destructive flood in early 1956. I thought I had filled and carried enough sandbags over a period of two days with little rest to hold back the Nile!

Dead animals, raw sewerage, and other assorted debris were a constant presence in the floodwaters during this exercise. We returned to RAAF Richmond once the sandbags and other assistance to the local Windsor community had achieved their purpose, and the flood waters had begun to subside.

Our ranks were already depleted by airmen being treated for dysentery, and the next morning while on the parade ground we had another recruit breaking ranks and shuffling off the parade ground in the direction of the closest latrines in short, but quick, paces.

Unfortunately, I discovered on returning to the barracks following the parade and laughing so hard at the events of the morning, that I too had contracted dysentery. The shower and latrine block had a lot of activity that day, and I had plenty of company that seemed equally hesitant in venturing too far away from the latrines. We had no medication provided. We were told that we would recover quickly from the effects in one or two days.

Upon completion of basic training, I was posted to the School of Radio in Ballarat, Victoria, west of Melbourne, where I commenced instruction in communications, telegraphy (Morse code), etc.

Our telegraphy course members were initially amused with the introduction of "singing classes". The entire class had to sing the Morse code in unison. We soon realised that this was absolutely necessary to memorise the complete alphabet in Morse code. Typing classes were initiated at the same time as the singing classes. We had to become proficient in both typing and the Morse alphabet before we could start the sending and receiving transmission classes and be trained on operating communications equipment.

During that Ballarat winter I complemented the two blankets that had been issued by sleeping in overalls, an overcoat, two layers of socks, and any other coverings that I could find. The showers before parade in the mornings with those freezing temperatures seem amusing now. Our bare feet pounded the paths to and back from the showers with only a towel to cover ourselves. Very bracing! There were no women on this course.

My first active posting was to the No. 3 Telecommunications Unit at Pearce Air Force Base in Western Australia. Top secrecy was imposed stringently in this unit. The *Official Secrets Act* had to be read and signed prior to the commencement of duties. Our unit was established in a remote bush area not far from the base. Soon after arrival at the base, I decided to go to the Child Welfare Department in the city to ask if I could see any of my brothers or sisters. I was advised that if I returned the same day of the following week at about the same time and stood on the other side of the street from their offices, I would be able to see my young sister, Kerry.

The following week I took a day's leave, drove to Perth, and stood in the position I was directed to by a child welfare officer. I waited for over an hour and was about to head back to the base when a middle-aged couple and a young girl about thirteen or fourteen came out with them. There was no mistaking that face. Kerry was our sister. She glanced over my way, but only for a second or so, and kept on walking with her foster family on either side of her. That was enough, just to see that she was well and appeared happy. Understandably, Kerry's new family had not wanted to be involved in the exercise.

I walked to the nearby Perth Botanical Gardens and found an isolated bench. I sat for a while feeling extremely sad, with thoughts of what could have been had we all been together and born to loving and responsible parents.

Kerry had another life that did not include Bob or me. I had to put such thoughts of a reunion out of my mind. Would this be the same reaction I would receive if ever I met up with the other siblings?

I persisted in contacting the Child Welfare Department for information on what had happened to the others. The results were not what I had hoped for. Andrew was not interested in meeting me, and William was still a small child with his new parents, and they were not keen on me coming into their lives either, which was understandable. Muriel was living and working at a boarding house at Northam which was some distance away from Perth, and I thought I would try to catch up with her later. That never happened, because I was posted soon after to the No. 1 Air Trials Unit, Woomera, South Australia, for the next two-and-a-half years.

I arrived at No. 1 Air Trials Unit in 1957. Our unit was involved in the testing of unmanned aircraft, more specifically, the "Jindivik". There was also a lot of activity further out from our base with international groups working on various other rocket programs.

I never gave up on my desire to fly, and I pursued my private pilot's licence training at my own expense at Parafield aerodrome outside Adelaide, and at other airfields over the next three years while on leave.

While at Woomera, I was always asking questions related to flying, principles of flight, navigation, etc. from a very helpful and patient Flight Sergeant pilot who helped me prior to sitting for my private pilot's theory exams. He had been flying the Meteor jet which was an aircraft that had been up against Russian-made MiGs during the air battles of the Korean War in the early 1950s.

A particularly sad event occurred towards the end of my posting when this same Flight Sergeant pilot was in the process of being cleared off the base on posting to a squadron in Queensland. He had received clearance to go up for one more series of "circuits and bumps", which is a routine of taking off, climbing to five hundred feet, circling the airfield, touching down, and powering on again with a take-off. While I was watching his practice runs, I could see that he was in deep trouble when what appeared to be flares started exploding out from the aircraft after he had made a turn to return for another "touch and go" pass. Seconds later, his aircraft exploded into a thousand pieces. A good man lost to family and the Air Force.

The majority, if not all, of the decontamination of the aircraft that flew through the atomic blast clouds at Maralinga's British nuclear test trials to the northeast of Woomera was conducted in our hanger at One Air Trials Unit.

The British personnel involved either in the decontamination or handling of their aircraft wore full protective clothing and went through a showering and scrubbing process after completion of the task. Our Australian airmen wore their normal dress of shorts and boots and showered as normal with their colleagues at the end of the working day! I was informed many years later that few, if any, of our RAAF personnel involved in the aircraft decontamination process from those tests evaded a cancer-related illness of some description. Several of us would often have morning or afternoon tea breaks sitting under the wings of these aircraft in the hanger. We were never briefed on possible nuclear radiation health issues.

The work at this post was interesting, and the friendships I made there have stood the test of time. However, I do not miss the choking desert sandstorms that hit us from time to time.

My next posting was back to No. 3 Telecommunications Unit at Pearce Air Force Base. I was only there for a few weeks before I was promoted and posted to the No. 25 Squadron, which was also at the Pearce Air Force Base. This provided me with the extra time to catch up with Bob.

While with No. 25 Squadron, I had several opportunities to bum rides in the dual-seat T35 de Havilland Vampire jet. My first flight in this aircraft was with a twenty-one-year-old pilot officer who had only just arrived from Advanced Flying Training School, also based at RAAF Pearce. He allowed me to take control of the aircraft briefly on a straight and level flight, probably against RAAF orders. He practised aerial manoeuvres that were great to experience but did not impress the aircraft maintenance crew when we landed because he had, as a consequence of the aerobatics, popped several rivets on the aircraft.

Figure 3. AOC inspection of 25 Squadron (City of Perth), 1957

After less than a year, I was transferred from 25 Squadron to RAAF Element, Maralinga Atomic Weapons Range, South Australia, to face even greater and more constant nuclear radiation exposure over a period of twelve months during the British nuclear test trials.

Maralinga was located in the Tjarutja Aboriginal country, bordering the Great Victoria Desert. We relied on our everyday supplies, food, mail, etc. to be railed in from Adelaide by the Indian-Pacific railway at Watsons Siding to the south. We called this train the "Tea and Sugar" run.

We were a small unit of twenty or so Australian Air Force personnel with similar numbers of Australian Army and Navy servicemen, and because of this isolated location, we were almost all single men. There were also approximately five to six hundred British servicemen, and many civilian scientists, also known as "boffins", at Maralinga at this time.

One of my more enjoyable duties at this base was to meet the twin-engine de Havilland "Dove" aircraft, which made occasional flights to Maralinga from Adelaide. Once on the ground, I escorted the female "hostie" up to the Officers' Mess for lunch or refreshments and later returned her to the airfield. There were always vehicles alongside the road leading to and from the airfield during these runs, with personnel pretending they had broken down. Others leant on shovels supposedly engaging in some make-believe roadside project. All of this activity was just to hopefully get a glimpse of a woman!

A RAAF Lincoln aircraft, an RAF Canberra aircraft (with RAAF aircrew), and RAF Valiants flew through atomic bomb blast clouds collecting samples at Maralinga. Four Dakota aircraft fitted with ionisation chambers and accompanied by scientists were also involved in air radiological surveys to determine ground contamination caused by fallout of radioactive dust.

During one test, "Operation Totem", nine out of the twelve Lincolns were found to have still been contaminated after their "scrub-downs". Four never flew again.

The Aboriginal people who originally inhabited the area were relocated elsewhere, and considerable efforts were made to keep them out of the test zone. There have been reports that those who either returned or remained close to the contaminated area have had an unusually high number of cataracts and thyroid cancers. Similar health reports followed the Kiribati nuclear tests conducted by the British and Americans.

In contrast to the extreme exposure at Maralinga and other nuclear test sites in Australia, Australia's general health staff in hospitals and clinics have always worn dedicated clothing covers. They must stand behind special screens when working with X-rays, MRIs and other equipment that require low-grade radioactive material in their procedures. Dentists and their staff, including my own daughter, operating X-ray equipment also take similar precautions, because they recognise that exposure to radiation, even at such minuscule levels, is considered dangerous.

Compare these examples to living 24/7 for at least twelve months, and often longer, in an extremely highly radioactive environment that has been created by nuclear test explosions incorporating plutonium and other such lethal materials never referred to publicly.

Figure 4. Enjoying breakfast at Maralinga, South Australia, 1960. Author 3rd from left.

In 2001, a researcher from the Scottish University of Dundee uncovered documentary evidence advising that service personnel had been ordered to run, walk, and crawl across areas contaminated in the days immediately following the detonations, a fact that the British government later admitted to.

The hazards included gamma radiation, neutron activation products fallout both on the ground and in the air, and the presence of heavy metal poisons — uranium, cobalt, and beryllium. The lack of availability of detection equipment for each of these hazards explains missed contamination statistics.

Most of our nuclear veterans have suffered horrific illnesses and deaths from various cancers, blood diseases, and other debilitating illnesses, doing their duty, without protective clothing, as they were ordered to, and most importantly, without being informed of the serious risk of exposure to the by-products of nuclear experiments.

These men have also been forced to leap through repeated and ongoing administrative and bureaucratic reviews, one after the other, filling out form after form, enduring appeal after appeal, and then having them passed on to yet another review which then ignores any resulting recommendations made! Families continue to assist with care, medical, and other expenses and cope as best they can.

I have been hospitalised several times over the years with life-threatening blood clots in the lungs and have been treated for many years with the anticoagulant Warfarin. Unfortunately, in my case, and a lot of others, the medication also caused a lot of internal bleeding at times. I was more recently prescribed a new anticoagulant Xarelto and will remain on this medication for the rest of my life.

The greatest fear and concern we few remaining survivors of the British nuclear tests have always had is whether we may have passed on damaged genes to our children and to other generations that may follow. My own children's health problems, which I am not inclined to mention here, are in no way unique or as severe as many others within the close fraternity of Australian and British nuclear veterans.

There may be light at the end of this nuclear tunnel. Some of our Nuclear Trials veterans, after sixty-plus years, are at last now receiving the Department of Veterans Affairs Gold Card which will be of considerable assistance in providing and accessing medical treatments.

As far as I am aware, the descendants of nuclear veterans have never been considered by government authorities as possibly having been subjected to the consequences of the British nuclear tests.

In 2005, several decades after our service in the area, the prime minister presented each nuclear veteran with a medallion and an accompanying letter co-signed by the Minister for Veterans Affairs. See below:

> This medallion acknowledges the dedicated and professional service of the Australian military personnel and civilians who participated in the British Nuclear Test Program in Australia. Between 1952 and 1963, the British Nuclear Test Program was conducted at the Monte Bello Islands off Western Australia, Maralinga, and Emu Field in South Australia. In bestowing this medallion the Australian Government thanks you for your contribution to the program and pays tribute to your service.

Unfortunately, the issue of a medallion did not provide a practical solution in assisting with the ever-increasing medical bills incurred by illnesses associated with such duty.

The New Zealand government obviously took the matter a lot more seriously and has provided long-term medical support to all participants for many years. The other two countries that have acknowledged their nuclear veterans are the United States of America and Fiji.

I remained firm in my decision to leave the RAAF in October 1961, despite the encouragement of my commanding officer at the time. I was twenty-three and there was so much more I wanted to do. My immediate goal was to matriculate and follow up with university studies. I knew that this action was essential if I was to be able to pursue a career in aviation or elsewhere. I also had another conflicting priority, I wanted to see the world beyond the shores of Australia.

I shall always be most thankful to the Royal Australian Air Force for the assistance given with my education, the development of various skills, and a discipline not normally provided in civilian life, and for the valued and continuing comradeship of those with whom I served.

7

Canada via the USA

1962–1963

Most young Australians travelling at this time were choosing England as their destination. If you were not a traveller, you saved, bought a quarter acre of land, got married, built your house, and raised your family. Life was relatively simple during those years.

Canada was my choice of destination, and the Royal Canadian Air Force was an employment possibility. I had contacted the Canadian High Commission in Canberra before resigning from the RAAF and requested advice on whether I was eligible to join and retain my RAAF rank. I was told this was possible on both points. That was good enough for me.

Bob was managing a boutique shoe store in Perth at the time of my leaving the RAAF in 1961 and successfully recommended me for a position as a trainee executive with Peter Kelly's Shoes in Perth. I did not have the heart to tell Peter Kelly that I would only be with him for three or four months, because I was booked on the inaugural sailing of the P&O cruise ship *Canberra* travelling to the United States via New Zealand and Hawaii in February 1962.

I shared a four-berth inside cabin below sea level with three farmers from outback New South Wales. They were around the same age as me. We quickly got into the swing of life at sea. Two New Zealand girls joined our little group soon after leaving Auckland.

Honolulu was our official entry point to the United States. My roommates and I hired a red Pontiac convertible and circled the island with the New Zealand girls, body surfing just about every beach that appealed to us in the time we had ashore.

We were so carried away with the excitement of the day's offerings and had displayed such gross ignorance of the driving time to the Port of Honolulu, that we almost did not make it back to the ship before sailing time. We drove the car onto the wharf and right up to the gangway in panic mode. I passed the keys to a rental car representative from another company and asked him to hand in the keys and the car for us. We all had to chip in a few dollars each to ensure that this was done. We had learned very quickly that Americans employed in any of the service industries depended greatly on tips to supplement their wages.

It appeared as though all the ship's passengers were observing the spectacle on the wharf with much cheering and clapping, while crew members at the other end of the ship's gangway were indicating that it would be pulled away if we did not board immediately.

We had a port call in Los Angeles and only had a few hours

there, so we hired a car, and with the help of a tourist map somehow found our way around the city and Beverley Hills. Our experience driving on the "wrong" side of the road in Hawaii helped enormously in Los Angeles. We hit all the top tourist spots before boarding *Canberra* again for the final leg to San Francisco.

Two days in San Francisco was not enough, but it was finally time to bid farewell to my shipboard mates at the Top of the Mark Hotel and board a Greyhound bus bound for Ponca City, Oklahoma.

I had accepted an invitation to stay with my sister Kerry's foster sister, Iris, her husband, Steve, and their thirteen-year-old son, Adrian. I enjoyed the pleasant hospitality and company of this family and their many "Okie" friends. Steve, a "Brit", was a senior executive with the Exxon oil company.

My stay in Ponca City was drawing to an end and the travel bug was biting. Steve and his family had previously lived in Calgary, Alberta for several years, and provided me with the address of a boarding house run by a friend of theirs that I could settle into, at least for an interim period, while I found more permanent accommodation.

I met some very interesting people during the long bus trip up and across the United States to Canada. It was over 3000 km from Ponca City to Calgary, Alberta. On the first stop at a roadside diner, I picked up my meal on a tray and sat at the counter. I had barely been seated when the diners on each side of me pointed to a glassed partition that had the sign Negroes

Only on it. Those on the negroes side of the partition told me in no uncertain terms to move to the white side. I tried to let them know that I was quite happy sitting with them, but they would have none of it, and once again they told me to move out of their dining area. The black diners may have reacted in the way they did because of the superior number of white diners who were watching them. The white diners were not happy with me either. This was not a warm welcome to the peculiar cultural sensitivities that existed in 1962.

I was sound asleep and enjoying the luxury of having an empty seat next to me to stretch out on, until I was shaken awake to find an unattractive red face with an accompanying vapour of stale cigarettes and strong liquor leaning over me. There were no words forthcoming, or necessary, only a stare and a hand movement to suggest that I should sit up and move over. We had stopped somewhere late at night in middle America, and had picked up a rather inebriated, mean-looking female Marine Sergeant.

The hand was extended again, but this time it was accompanied by a verbal introduction and glancing around I found the entire bus was now awake and interested in what was unfolding in my restricted part of the world.

Unfortunately, during the early conversation I mentioned my Air Force service and my nationality. This prompted the sergeant to suggest we had to share a few swigs of "Jack". A bottle of Jack Daniel's bourbon was produced from her service kit bag. She had obviously been well into it before boarding the bus. I dared not decline the offer. I had never heard of bourbon before and did not drink spirits. One swig was enough for me. It was a long night. The other passengers were either asleep or pretending to be, and I was careful not to start the sergeant on a loud rant again.

We all disembarked for a breakfast stop the next morning, and the sergeant disappeared into the toilets after she had eaten. Unfortunately, she did not reappear by the time the bus commenced to pull out. I called out to the driver, but he did not take any notice. My fellow passengers were also quiet, with a few turning around to stare at me with the obvious message of, "Shut up!" The rest of the trip up through the middle of America was enjoyable, with the Rockies finally making a grand appearance in the distance. Canada, at last!

I arrived in Calgary on the day before the commencement of the Calgary Stampede which is known as the Greatest Outdoor Show on Earth, at least by the Canadians, and I dare anyone to refute this in front of a Calgarian! The Stampede commences each year on the first Friday in July and runs for ten days of rodeo, music, dancing in the streets, parades of cowboys and Indians, chuck wagon racing, square dancing, etc. The party did not stop. Almost everyone wore a white stetson, and shouted, 'yee-ha'.

My first concern upon arrival in Calgary was to find the boarding house that had been recommended before leaving Oklahoma. I barely had time to meet my hosts and drop my bag in my room before two of the boarders, in their final year of university, hustled me into a car, and drove me into the centre of Calgary where the madness started, and the beer flowed.

The next day, adorned with a borrowed white Stetson, waving a vintage copy of a Davey Crockett musket, and riding in a supermarket trolley, I was shunted at the run down the city's main street, and through the batwing doors of the Royal Hotel. Unfortunately, the trolley's small wheels hit a raised door-stop at the entrance, and I was ejected at speed into a table full of beer and bodies. That's when the fight started! Suffice to add that I survived that period of ten days, of which I have only a fleeting memory.

Australians as a rule do appreciate a beer or two, and to say I was taken aback by the behaviour of my Canadian friends when they first introduced me to their beer would be an understatement. For example, upon receipt of a tray of the local seven-ounce glasses of the amber liquid, they would pick up a salt dispenser — there was one on every bar table — and proceed to shake the contents into the beer before drinking. This, so I found out later, was not to add to the taste but to provide at least a semblance of effervescence, something that we Australians expect to be the norm for a well-served beer that should always be served cold and come with a white collar or "head". I sincerely hope that their beer brewing prowess has improved over the years. At least it was a slight improvement over the British effort of dispensing their headless, flat, warm cans of beer straight out of a cupboard and not a refrigerator!

I do not recall whether it was the Stampede celebrations or the other necessities of life such as food and lodging, but my funds were reaching a perilously low level. I had to find a job, and fast. I had decided to delay my visit to the Canadian Defence Force recruiting office until I had sufficient exposure to their lifestyle. I could not set the standard I was hoping for solely by the experience of the ten days of the Stampede.

I read an advertisement for a shoe salesman in the local Calgary newspaper and called up immediately to advise them of my extensive experience in the world of women's fashion shoes in Australia. This was really not a complete untruth, after all, I had a brother in that field, and I had worked in that business in Perth for three months as a trainee executive! I was asked to come in the same day for an interview. I commenced work the next morning.

There were only three of us, four including the manager, in this small, exclusive, and very busy store that sold only expensive Italian imports. My Canadian co-workers did not wish to serve Americans, so I was left with a very lucrative clientele. Many of the women frequenting the store had husbands working in the oilfields in northern Alberta, and they were good spenders.

Three famous sisters, who were a well-known and very successful American Midwest singing trio at the time were by far my best customers. I cannot recall whether they were the Andrew or McGuire Sisters. If I sold a pair of shoes to one, the other two would buy the same. Despite my increased income, and the generous commissions, the Canadian staff still would not come out of hiding from behind the shoe racks to assist the American customers!

I eventually managed to scrape together a minimum deposit to purchase a 1959 MGA 1600 soft-top sports car and moved into an apartment with a musician and a barman.

I could not wait for my first winter in Canada. After all, I was a Western Australian and had never seen snow. The first snowfall was, therefore, quite an exciting experience. This excitement becomes more subdued over time, especially when you visit someone, park your car, and upon leaving, you discover that you cannot find your car, because the snow-clearing trucks, in an effort to clear the roads, have piled mounds of snow and ice over all the vehicles that were parked along the side of the road.

I joined the Calgary Sports Car Club which held regular rallies and weekends away. It provided a great social life. During the winter we competed in racing our cars on a frozen lake, and in summer we water skied at the same locations or competed in the club's car rallies.

I finally got around to visiting the Royal Canadian Air Force recruiting office to see what was on offer. I was extremely disappointed with the outcome. I was told that I would have to start from scratch again with a minimum salary and rank! This was not in accord with the information I had been given when I had enquired at the Canadian High Commission in Australia. I lost interest immediately. Now that was out of the way, I had to really start to concentrate on my future work choices and either return home to Australia or commit myself to a more settled life in Canada.

My roommates had become tired of the Calgary social scene and decided over a beer or two to take off for the more cosmopolitan Vancouver on the west coast! I was placed in the impossible position of meeting the rent bill by myself. I had no choice other than to resign from my workplace, which I had come to enjoy, and join the exodus to Vancouver, British Columbia.

My two roomies found casual work almost immediately and we settled into a log cabin just out of Vancouver facing an inlet with logs packed together on the water awaiting shipment. I took a little longer to find a job, but finally secured a full-time position in the women's shoe department of the Hudson's Bay Company, which was at that time the largest of the major retail stores in western Canada. That store today is simply called "The Bay".

The Cuban Missile Crisis in October 1962 was exacerbated by the announcements made by American President John F. Kennedy. There was a strong possibility of global nuclear war if the Soviets did not remove their missiles from Cuba. The American military and political leadership were acutely aware of the secret Soviet missile bases in Cuba that were only 145 km off the coast of Florida. The thirteen days that followed Kennedy's announcement marked the most dangerous period of the Cold War.

7 Canada via the USA

I am unsure how the general population in the United States reacted, but within hours of the media breaking the news in Canada, and more specifically Vancouver, all sugar, batteries, bottled drinks, and canned goods had sold out of the supermarkets and other food outlets. Much of these supplies went into the bomb shelters that many homes had been building since the mid-1950s.

"Black Saturday", 27 October 1962 started with the Cubans or Russians shooting down a U2 spy plane and killing the American pilot. Any misstep could have triggered a nuclear war. President Kennedy, in an effort to de-escalate the mounting confrontation that followed, sent a message to Khrushchev agreeing to remove their Jupiter missiles that were deployed in Turkey. By doing so, he managed to defuse the crisis late on 27 October. Khrushchev, without making that detail public, including to Castro, announced the next day that he had accepted the American proposal not to invade Cuba, and that he in good faith would remove all Soviet missiles from the area.

My roommates were once again becoming unsettled. Our rent was high, and the Vancouver natives were not nearly as friendly as the Calgarians. The musician was not getting as many gigs as he thought he would, and the other roommate was missing his girlfriend. We decided that we had made a major mistake in leaving Calgary. With cap in hand, I walked back into my former workplace in downtown Calgary. I started the same day.

My life in Calgary was not going anywhere. My social life was great, but I felt I was just marking time. I had to wake up to myself and grow up. I had to refocus on my education and a future path of employment.

I recalled overhearing a former commanding officer at 25 Squadron discussing his posting to Washington, DC in glowing terms, and decided to write to the Office of the Air Attaché at Joint Staff Headquarters (JSHQ), which operated under the diplomatic umbrella of the Australian Embassy in Washington, DC. I needed a job that would provide for the day-to-day living expenses and my educational costs. Calgary was a distraction from this plan.

I received a telegram from Washington within two weeks of my applying for a position. I was instructed to report to the Air Attaché the following Monday, which left me with only four days to present my letter of resignation to my less-than-impressed employer in Calgary, to pack my belongings — which did not take more than a few minutes — to make my farewells, and prepare the MGA for the fast and long drive of over 3600 km to Washington.

I left Calgary in the early hours of a Friday morning in the first week of July 1963. Another Stampede was about to start. I drove sixteen to eighteen hours a day for the next three days to arrive in Washington on time. My route plan had me driving from Calgary, down through Montana, the Dakotas, Wisconsin, Michigan, and other states to Washington. My experience rally driving and navigating with the Calgary

7 Canada via the USA

Sports Car Club assisted greatly with daily route planning and map reading.

I had driven the entire journey from Calgary with the convertible top down. Consequently, my face was severely burned when I arrived at JSHQ at 2001 Connecticut Avenue, Washington, DC early on Monday morning. It was the middle of summer in the United States. I had parked outside the main entrance two hours prior to the office opening and immediately fell asleep. I was shaken awake by a couple of Australian Navy Officers who thought I was lost after having seen my vehicle's Canadian licence plate.

8

The Office of the Air Attaché Washington, DC

1963–1966

My first day at JSHQ was taken up with form filling and preliminary briefings on my position and the functions of the Office of the Air Attaché and its relationship with the Australian Embassy, which was situated nearby. I was appointed as Contracts Officer in charge of purchasing electronics and communication equipment and parts from American suppliers. Work was well under way on the C130-A project, a real workhorse that has undergone several upgrades over the last fifty-plus years in the RAAF inventory.

I was introduced to the crew I would be working with and before the end of the first day, I had been offered a temporary place to stay by one of the other staff members at JSHQ until I could find my own apartment. The temporary digs were in Maryland near the naval shipyards.

In August 1963, a month or so after I had settled in, over 200 000 Afro-Americans and their supporters marched on Washington in continuous demonstrations for their civil rights. This was also the time that Martin Luther King and the Black Panthers were most vocal and active.

Tensions were high, and in the space of two months, our building went from all white to all black, except for us. We had decided to hang in and stay the distance because it was only a short drive to our workplace. We tried to let our fellow residents in the building know that we would show our solidarity by staying with them.

Unfortunately, the goodwill was very one-sided. The black tenants had no intention of letting us stay in the building. They quickly turned on the pressure by regularly dumping their garbage outside our apartment door, deflating the tyres on our cars, and crowding the stairs so that we could not enter the building without pushing, or being pushed. The final straw came when they slashed the front two tyres on my car. It was definitely time to go. Racial discrimination by black on white!

I had met Bernie Lowes, an Australian haematologist, at an official embassy function a few weeks earlier, and he mentioned that he had two other roommates, and they were looking for another person to share the rent with on a large apartment across the Potomac River in Virginia, not far from the Pentagon. The other two "roomies" were Americans. One was a Marine lieutenant working at the Pentagon, and the other was a Warrant Officer helicopter pilot in the US Coast Guard.

There were several airline flight crews in the building, and there were regular parties raging, mostly, it seemed, in our apartment. The good times came to an end a few months later when the Coast Guard pilot was posted to Florida, and the Marine lieutenant told us that he had applied for and been accepted into The Agency, the CIA, and would soon be off to the "Farm". He also mentioned later that he had been told not to disclose his new employer to anyone. Non-vetted aliens such as Australians were probably on the list!

Bernie and I could not afford to stay in the Virginia apartment after our two roomies left, so we found a small two-bed apartment close to Bernie's workplace at the DC General Hospital and not far from Joint Staff Headquarters.

Bernie had met a Pan American flight attendant while we were living in our former party house near the Pentagon and they were married a few months later. I did not want to let them off scot-free after leaving me as the sole tenant, but I was thwarted by the bride-to-be. She would not allow me to organise a bucks party for Bernie prior to the wedding. She had previously mentioned that I was a "bad influence".

I wanted to be fair, despite the angst displayed towards me by Bernie's new bride, so I gave them a three-day head start on their honeymoon to St Thomas in the Caribbean's Virgin Islands. I then flew to San Juan, Puerto Rico, and stayed there overnight so I could catch an early flight the next day on a local airline to St Thomas.

Bernie had unwittingly mentioned the name of the hotel they would be staying at, and I soon spotted them resting on lounges by the pool. I bought a pair of swimming trunks at the hotel's shopping arcade, and at an opportune moment, I stealthily slid into the pool at the far end and swam underwater near to where they were now sipping drinks. I surfaced and shouted 'Surprise!' I thought Bernie's brand new bride was going to either spill her drink or be horribly sick. She was also unusually speechless.

Bernie thought it was a brilliant feat on my part, and he could not be more enthusiastic about my sudden appearance, even at that most intimate stage of their honeymoon! Australian humour and mateship were momentarily at the fore, but sadly, unappreciated by his spouse.

However, the first stage of our reunion did not last long and I retreated to avoid the possibility of bloodshed, in this case, mine. Bernie and I decided to meet up later in the day for a couple of drinks prior to my flying back to Washington. True to his word, Bernie turned up at the nominated duty-free rum store on the pier at the agreed time of 4 pm. I could sense he had been given some sort of ultimatum to get rid of me as quickly as possible.

To cut a very long story short, we started at one end of the pier, and ended at the other by 7 pm after sampling too many of the potent free offerings at the rum stores. I thought Bernie could have handled the experience a lot better than he did, but then he did have a start on me with his cocktails by the pool earlier in the day. Our taxi had to stop at least three times on the way back to the hotel for Bernie to make horrible noises while kneeling at the side of the road and pleading for God's help.

When we arrived at Bernie's hotel, the driver and I took an arm each and steered Bernie up the hotel entrance stairs. We left him in a lounge chair in the foyer. He was out for the count and dribbling. It was not a good look! I asked reception to call his room and have his wife come down to assist him to their room. They were very eager to comply with this request, particularly as other guests of the hotel in the crowded foyer area were obviously not amused by the spectacle.

Both the cabbie and I retreated as quickly as possible, and I was taken directly to the airport to catch my flight out of St Thomas to San Juan with a direct connection to DC.

My next accommodation was with three workmates from JSHQ, a mix of Australian Navy and Air Force, thank heavens! The new accommodation was in an older building, only a couple of blocks from our office, and had several of our staff staying there in other apartments. Yet another "Party Central".

I did not have much in the way of personal belongings. That small suitcase I had left Australia with almost two years previously had not been replaced, and still adequately handled all I required for my simple existence. I was leading a disruptive and nomadic lifestyle with a rapid turnover of roommates, and I found the absence of chattels was, in fact, a blessing.

My new roomies and I benefited from having access to a nearby US Military post exchange for groceries, and duty-free liquor and cigarettes through embassy channels. Our favourite entertainment haunt was the Officers' Mess at Bolling Air Force Base. The Big Swing Band, Glen Miller style, provided affordable entertainment, dining and dancing with our dates on Saturday evenings. We survived very well indeed.

There was an endless merry-go-round of parties, weekend get-togethers at great beaches in Virginia and Delaware such as Rehoboth; sailing on the Chesapeake Bay; picnics in the Shenandoah Mountains; and of course, the obligatory military and embassy functions to attend. I have no idea how I initially managed this madness as it was combined with a heavy workload at the office and attending classes four nights a week from 6 pm to 10 pm.

I eventually came to the realisation that my studies had to take precedence over my social life, and that drastic changes had to be made. The new monkish life was akin to giving up smoking, extremely difficult at first, but it gradually became manageable. While attending classes, I was befriended by a fellow student whom I discovered was an Israeli Air Force officer attached to the Israeli Embassy. Warning bells started to sound when he drifted from the normal casual chatter of students to asking in-depth questions about my work. I reported the contact to my commanding officer, and he instructed me to keep him informed about any future conversations initiated by this Israeli that may be considered professionally inappropriate. I avoided this fellow deliberately, and he quickly got the message. He left the classes I was taking soon after, and I did not see him again. I learned from a close friend much later that friendships do not necessarily align with national interest.

The major event by far during this early period in Washington was the assassination of President John F. Kennedy. Washington was in turmoil, horrified, confused, and deeply saddened. Staff members in our office simply could not believe the first reports we were receiving.

Soon after President Kennedy was pronounced dead Lyndon B. Johnson was sworn in as the 36th president on board Air Force One, prior to flying him back to Washington, DC.

I observed the funeral parade with a small contingent from Joint Staff Headquarters, and later witnessed the low-level fly-past of Air Force One over Arlington National Cemetery during the final stages of the burial ceremony. This was an extremely sad time for the American people.

Most of our office personnel attended the Inauguration Parade for President Johnson. It seemed to run for hours with bands, troops and politicians from each of the fifty states. It all seemed so ghoulish to have such a ceremony so soon after Kennedy had been killed. The King is dead ... long live the King!

Several Inauguration Balls were held, and a few of us were invited to the US State Department for one of the balls that the new president and first lady were to attend around Washington that evening. President LB Johnson and party arrived with the usual security, pomp, and ceremony, and stayed for no more than a few minutes. I attempted to position myself where I thought I may be able to achieve a few seconds of fame dancing with the first lady, as was the routine if selected, but the wall of State Department Security Officers, and Secret Service Agents were impenetrable. We "aliens" were locked out. The selection of dance partners had already been established.

Several months later, in the midst of this frenetic Washington activity, Geoff Coverdale, one of my fellow roommates and co-worker, invited a new woman from the typing pool at the Air Attaché's Office to dinner at our apartment. She had actually volunteered to cook for us. Her name was Judith Boseley.

My life, as I knew and understood it to be, was about to change forever.

A little history of Judith Boseley's life prior to our first meeting may be of interest. Judith was from Wollongong, which is a coastal city approximately 50 km to the south of Sydney. She was the daughter of George and Alma Boseley, who had the Wollongong Hotel at that time, and were well-known and respected not only as publicans, but for several years George excelled as President of the Australian Hotels Association. He was also a well-known game fisherman with a couple of world records to his credit.

Judith was indeed fortunate in that she was raised within a loving family environment and never wanted for anything, including the best of secondary education at Rosebank College, a private boarding school for young women in Sydney. She studied music for several years and passed the Trinity College senior levels qualifications. Judith's mother was no novice on the piano either.

Judith abandoned business college in Wollongong after one year to follow a career as a fashion model. Some months at the June Dally-Watkins School were followed by a regular appearance in the *Illawarra Mercury*, which was the local daily newspaper servicing the Wollongong and south coast areas of New South Wales.

Judith won the Miss Illawarra beauty pageant and was entered into the judging for the New South Wales section of the Miss Australia pageant. I wish I could confirm that she won the coveted Miss Australia sash, but the judges must have been either blind or biased towards another!

Modelling continued to be Judith's choice of career path and she moved back to Sydney to join the Pat Woodley Model Agency. She remained with them for a couple of years. While working in Sydney and using her background as an "old girl" of Rosebank College, she was successful in being accommodated at Rosary Villa, a home for young ladies at appropriately named Darling Point. Male callers were vetted and restricted to a holding pen in the reception area!

Judith's parents wanted her to experience life and travel the world before she settled into married life with her then fiancé. An around the world trip was provided by her parents for her twenty-first birthday, and she left for England. The plan was for her to utilise her open return air ticket home via the United States when she had tired of Europe.

While in London, Judith lived at Sloane Square and was therefore referred to, in the environs of London, as a "Sloan Ranger". She worked in the cosmetics department of Harrods department store, and in the evenings, she worked at a second job in a restaurant as a waitress.

Judith made several forays as a tourist in Europe before she finally decided to return home. New York was to be the first stopover. The next stop was Washington, DC. Judith had only intended to stay with a girlfriend in Washington for a week or so but was encouraged to apply for a position at the Office of the Air Attaché because she wanted to stay on a bit longer and be able to afford to do so.

I will now return to the dinner that my roommate Geoff Coverdale had invited Judith to. I recognised her as the new girl in the typing pool and thought Geoff had invited her as a guest, but she had volunteered to cook us a roast lamb dinner! This news was initially received with some scepticism as none of the female visitors to our apartment in the past had ever asked where the kitchen was. We were always expected to entertain and feed them. It was the best meal any of us had enjoyed for some time and was certainly the best prepared from our kitchen. She was not only beautiful, and an excellent cook, but also had an engaging and outgoing personality unmatched by any woman I had previously met.

The Air Attaché called me into his office one day for a chat and asked me how we could improve our turnaround time in processing our aircraft operationally grounded (AOG).

Normal practice at that time for the Air Force was to ground all aircraft associated with an AOG order until the parts or equipment modifications required to have the aircraft safely in the air again could be provided. When we received a cable from Australia bearing this AOG header we knew that it was imperative that the task received the highest priority.

The Air Attaché (AA) asked me to provide a briefing on the current action that was routinely being taken at the office from the moment the AOG cable arrived. I provided the required information and highlighted the inadequate procedure of taking our handwritten contract orders to the typing pool where the work was prioritised by their manager, an intimidating and robust woman who you did not make demands of for fear of being silenced with a penetrating stare followed by your work being placed at the bottom of her in-tray! No words of admonition were ever necessary. Her narrowing eyes sent the message loud and clear! Aircraft would have to remain grounded if she damn well felt like it!

I seized on this opportunity with the AA to push for my own secretary because my section in the office was by far the busiest, and the equipment we needed to acquire was the most difficult to source from manufacturers and suppliers. I initially thought I had pushed too hard on this issue, but I eventually won the day. It was not long before the girls in the typing pool heard about the position of my soon-to-be-appointed secretary, and the games began!

Judith called the AA immediately to apply. She was in his office within the hour and started as my secretary the next day. I learned later that she had conned her way in by telling the AA that she had received another job offer, was college-trained in Secretarial Studies, and was a "whizz" on the typewriter. The AA suggested he would have to have a chat with the typing pool manager first to arrange a typing test and would let Judith know the next day if she was successful. This demure and beautiful woman, in a tight blouse and miniskirt, leant forward and said, 'I would love to, but unfortunately I have an appointment with another embassy for a similar position this afternoon.' He replied, 'No problem, can you start tomorrow?' Air Force Officers!

A desk, chair, typewriter, and other office necessities were all ready for Judith the next day, as were several files with contracts to be typed. She arrived on time, which was a good sign, but I thought she was a little overdressed for the occasion. She looked as though she was going to a modelling assignment, not an office desk. A briefing was provided by the typing pool manager and later by me. I asked her to focus on the urgency and the accuracy of the work to be completed, and to provide precedence to those files marked "priority". There was a lot of head nodding from my new secretary, suggesting that all was understood and would be complied with!

There was not a lot of work being done that first day, not only because of the obvious administrative shortcomings of the new secretary but primarily because of the constant parade of male civilians and military personnel passing by her desk. She was that distracting!

Judith spent the first hour or so of her work day talking to the girls in the typing pool. When a file was eventually opened and she was poised earnestly over the typewriter, I thought we were in business. Suffice to say, have you ever heard the expression, "waiting for the other shoe to drop"? That is what it was like that day, one key tap, long pause, another tentative key tap, and so on. The files in her "in" tray grew steadily throughout the day. The "out" tray was sadly devoid of any completed contracts.

The next day, with more files accumulating, and a general inactivity at my secretary's desk, I politely gathered up all the priority files, and pleaded with the typing pool manager for assistance. This charade continued for some time. I did not want to have Judith fired, especially as she got on so well with the other women in the typing pool. I could have had one very unhappy group of women had I requested Judith's removal. What was I to do?

I finally mustered up the courage to ask Judith out, and I confirmed within my own mind very quickly that this woman was unlike any other, and I wanted to get to know her better. It was not long before I realised that whatever path I chose to follow in the future, it had to include Judith.

The office staff was having a birthday celebration at our local watering hole, and I contributed to the conversation by mentioning that the Kentucky Derby was on that coming

Saturday. Judith and Geoff Coverdale and his date agreed that it would be a great event to attend. We requested and received approval to take off on Friday.

We loaded up my car and set out for Louisville, Kentucky, early on Friday morning. It was over 600 miles (965 km), and an estimated nine or ten hours of driving time. We arrived in Louisville without incident Friday evening and stayed at a southern mansion, a B&B, which could easily have been used as the main set in the film *Gone with the Wind*.

It was a fun day at the Derby the next day with a mint julep or two to further enhance the experience. You must have the obligatory mint julep before the big race, it was part of the local racetrack tradition.

The Kentucky Derby, the race of the day, was finally called, and everyone in front of us stood up with mint juleps raised. Sadly, we did not see a thing other than the back of hundreds of heads and big hats! Despite this setback, it was truly a memorable weekend enjoyed by us all.

Judith and I were rapidly becoming an exclusive couple until a minor hiccup came our way. Mary, one of Judith's roommates, and I had arranged some months previously before Judith's arrival in Washington to take a road trip to Acapulco in the southwest of Mexico. I had all but forgotten about this trip until Mary mentioned it in front of Judith. I did not sleep well that night. There was no need for my concern, however, because the two girls sorted it out themselves. They decided that they would both be accompanying me to

Acapulco! I was not asked for an opinion and made plans for the trip with considerable trepidation.

Our trip down to Mexico was via the Carolinas to the Texas border crossing at Nuevo Laredo, and then on to Monterey, our first stopover in Mexico.

We had a great dinner of the local dish, roast kid, in Monterey, washed down with one or two margaritas. On the way back to the motel, while we were waiting for traffic to let us cross the road, a police officer came up to us and offered to assist. Madness, or the tequila, must have overcome Judith, because she grabbed the officer's baton and charged across the street waving it about, attempting to stop traffic.

In the first quarter of the twenty-first century, and especially in Monterey, she would probably have been shot. Not so in the mid-1960s. It took a second or so for the cop, Mary, and I to grasp what had happened, before all three of us took off after her. No damage was done, and mercifully the policeman saw the funny side of it all and commented that I must be one hell of a guy to be travelling with two beautiful women. I humbly agreed.

Acapulco was everything we thought it would be, and more. Great food, great beer, great beaches, and the accommodation at the Boca Chica Hotel right on the bay was fantastic. Fortunately, Mary by this time had accepted the fact that Judith and I were a couple, and it was not long before she started joining other groups of hotel guests for drinks and dinner. She flew back to Washington early.

Judith was an excellent water skier, and on our first day there she was skiing up and down Acapulco Bay on one ski. I decided on a less exacting activity by positioning myself on a poolside lounge with a view of the bay. I watched Judith's first sweep by the hotel with one hand clutching the towrope, and the other waving excitedly.

I was half asleep on the lounge after watching Judith pass by a couple of times when the hotel's pool population started whistling, shouting, and running to the water's edge. I joined the throng just as Judith went proudly by on one ski again, waving wildly to her admiring audience. I think it worthwhile mentioning that her bikini top was at that moment not where it should have been, it was around her waist! I am not sure to this day whether she was unaware of her provocative showing, and the impact it was having on the "Bay-side Screamers".

Judith told me later that she thought everyone was applauding her skill on the skis. Someone in the crowd must have been more than impressed though, because early the next morning we had an intruder enter our room while we were asleep, and the only item stolen was her bikini!

The trip back to Washington via Florida, and up the east coast through Louisiana and the Carolinas was an uneventful trip, except for the live baby alligator in a cardboard box I had been given at a petrol stop when I bought a pack of cigarettes. We named it Ali.

I cannot recall why on earth I accepted the reptile. I had taken it into the motel we had stayed at that evening and thought it humane to leave it in some water in the bathroom's hand basin. Alas, I had added too much water to the hand basin, and it escaped during the night. An early morning visit by Judith to the bathroom was immediately followed by unearthly screams. Ali was loose, somewhere in the room and had to be disposed of if I was to get any peace and avoid a visit from the motel manager. The swimming pool was the only disposal area I could think of!

We booked out before the sun came up, so I have no idea how the early morning swimmers reacted to my little toothy mate who was probably doing laps in the pool by then.

Judith had to resign from her position at the Office of the Air Attaché (JSHQ) when she accompanied me on the trip to Mexico. She had not been employed long enough at JSHQ to acquire any holiday leave. She had to set about finding employment as soon as we arrived back in Washington. There was nothing available at the Australian Embassy or at JSHQ.

Networking was the way to go in Washington during those years when seeking employment with diplomatic missions, United Nations Organisations, the World Bank, or the International Monetary Fund. These establishments covered their locally engaged staff with a B2 visa, which had no restrictions on the time allowed to reside and work in the United States.

Judith was successful in finding a new position within a few days with the Embassy of the United Arab Republic. She was

8 The Office of the Air Attaché Washington, DC

appointed secretary to the Commercial Minister. His name was Farti Bahig.

Farti had invited us to his home on a couple of occasions and insisted we use first names. He and his family were wonderful people who enjoyed telling us about life in Egypt and the Middle East, and more specifically of their home in Alexandria. When Judith left his employ, he presented her with a beautifully carved box and a large plate with pearl shell inlays.

Soon after our relationship had become more serious, Judith's fiancé, Peter, flew into Washington. I was not at all impressed! This was the first I had heard of her long engagement to someone from her hometown of Wollongong.

Judith invited me to meet Peter a couple of days after his arrival. We arranged to meet on a Saturday morning at a cafe on Connecticut Avenue. I must admit to feeling very confused, angry, and ready for battle with her, her fiancé, or both of them. All was politeness and smiles for a while, but I soon became annoyed with this little game Judith appeared to be playing. I did not consider the consequences of the action I was about to take. I simply told Peter that I thought it would be a great idea if he would 'bugger off, and go home'. Both he and Judith sat still, quite stunned at my outburst, and said nothing. I stood and left the cafe without another word.

The next day Judith asked me to meet her for lunch. I sat in silence in the restaurant and waited to hear what she had to say. Judith looked as though she had had very little sleep, and told me that she had apologised to Peter, and had told him she wanted to be with me and that it would be best for all of us if he went home.

The breakup must have been very hard on both of them as they had been together for over three years. There is a saying, "opposites attract", and if ever two people came from quite different worlds, Judith and I did.

I had been concentrating on completing a class assignment on a Saturday morning and was late getting to a lunch and drinks function. I found Judith in the toilet kneeling on the floor embracing the commode and making indecipherable utterances of despair. I tried to console her, and being the gentleman that I was, and continue to be, I held her hair out of the commode, but she was too far gone and continued with her intermittent crying, spraying, and groaning. I waited for the right moment to say something to distract her. The only thing I came up with was a question that required an answer, "Will you marry me?" It worked! The crying, groaning, etc., stopped immediately. The silence was followed by a lifting of her head slowly from the commode and the stare. A scary emotional outburst with more crying was accompanied by damp arms wrapped around my neck, and those lips got closer and closer. Too late for me to renege, and impossible to disappear with her dead weight hanging around my neck while trying to leverage herself from the floor.

In Judith's defence of the condition that I found her in, she had contracted hepatitis A after dining at a restaurant in Noumea when she was eighteen years of age, and nearly died. It took many months for her to regain a reasonable level of health. Her liver was still not in good shape, and over-indulgence that evening had made her very ill. By suggesting over-indulgence, even two drinks will be enough to reach this result.

I have never regretted my unorthodox proposal. Within a week or two Judith had a new fiancé (me), and a ring she considerately helped me to select. I was penniless for some time!

Another experience that had to be faced was even more daunting. I had to phone Judith's parents, Alma and George in Wollongong, and go through the formality of asking for her hand in marriage, as was the custom at that time.

Judith's parents must have been brought up to speed by the returning ex-fiancé, and quite possibly by Judith too, because Alma and George were most gracious, very positive, and accepting of me, which must have been extremely difficult for them especially considering they had never met me.

The blessing from Judith's parents was important to me, but I was prepared to tell them that we were going to get married anyhow. I had rehearsed that little speech in my mind earlier. There was a lot of crying from mother and daughter. I cannot remember much of what her father had said to me, only that he approved of his daughter's decision.

Figure 5. The engagement, Washington, DC, 1965

The wedding date was set for 2 October 1965, with a Nuptial High Mass to be held at St Ann's Cathedral on Connecticut Avenue, in northwest Washington.

I heard on the grapevine that a new position of personnel officer and supervisor of embassy security staff would soon be promulgated within the locally engaged ranks of the embassy. I immediately submitted a letter declaring my interest in the upcoming position and mentioned that I had a Diploma in Personnel Psychology. I was asked to quickly send in my application. It was approved within a couple of days.

It was with mixed feelings that I left the Office of the Air Attaché. I knew I would miss the great friendships that I had made there, but I had finally found a career path that I wanted to pursue.

I hoped the personnel officer position at the embassy would assist as an introduction into the Department of External Affairs (later re-named Foreign Affairs), but that would require completing my studies in Washington, our return to Australia, Public Service examinations, interviews, selection processes, and final appointment to my department of choice before that could be achieved.

One of my first tasks as a personnel officer was to appoint a new receptionist at the entrance foyer in the embassy's Chancery. Judith was a perfect fit for the position. She had been very happy at the Embassy of the United Arab Republic, but it did not take too much encouragement to get her back into the fold. She looked great sitting behind the enormous mahogany desk greeting visitors and staff.

Judith's parents were unable to attend the wedding because of their business commitments, and therein lay a problem. Who was going to walk Judith down the aisle? Our Communications chief, Jim Duncan, one of the older and more reliable members of the embassy staff came out of his den nearby. We called him over, explained our predicament, and asked him if he would do the deed. He agreed wholeheartedly.

The nuptials were to be followed by a reception at the apartment Judith had shared with Nell, her American roommate, who worked at the Washington office of the Peace Corps. Nell was the niece of Dean Rusk, who was the US

Secretary of State from 1961 to 1969, and one of the most powerful men in Washington. We discovered later that Judith had been thoroughly vetted and security cleared by the FBI. Nell often asked Judith along to Dean Rusk's family dinners at his home.

Several members at JSHQ and the embassy organised a surprise bachelor's party night for me the evening before the wedding. It was a cruel set-up, with a card game organised later in the evening for me to lose nearly every hand and have to down a shot of gin at each loss. Suffice to say, gin of any description has not passed my lips since that pre-wedding evening of 1 October 1965.

My less-than-compassionate friends ejected me from my bed after only three or four hours of restless sleep and presented me with a plate of greasy eggs and chips. I have never ever been as ill as I was that morning, and nor have I been since.

Intermittent trips had to be made to the bathroom to assist in expunging the impurities of the previous evening. The hilarity of my escorts to the wedding was not appreciated, especially when they continued to recount their escapades and conspiracies of the previous evening.

I arrived at the cathedral just before Judith's white Cadillac pulled up bedecked with white and cream carnations. The Nuptial Mass was due to start at 11 am. My Best Man was trying to frog-march me up the steps, but I could not resist a quick backward glance. Judith looked absolutely gorgeous, as did Nell and the accompanying bridesmaids who had been recruited from the Peace Corps office and the Office of the Air Attaché.

Fortunately, the young priest officiating at the wedding had been briefed on my previous evening's over-indulgence and extremely fragile condition, and when it came time during the Mass for the priest to pass the chalice of wine to me, I nearly gagged when I lifted it to my lips. He whispered, 'pretend'. I did so, gratefully.

Following the lengthy Nuptial Mass, we moved to the registry to sign the marriage register. I started to feel worse by the minute. The priest halted proceedings, and hastily led me to the side door, and into his rose garden where I embarrassed myself, Judith, and those witnessing the registry signing procedure by discharging the remnants of my greasy breakfast over his once red, pink, and white roses.

The only memory I wish to recall of the reception was Judith, still in her wedding dress, on the phone talking to her mother in Australia. I believe I was a sorry-looking sight, and unable to even raise a glass of champagne or any other alcoholic drink to the toasts being made. Water was my choice of liquid refreshment for my wedding day.

We learned later that the priest was the last to leave and had thoroughly enjoyed himself. He was no doubt enjoying himself recounting my behaviour in his rose garden.

Nell had our bags packed, and as soon as we made our farewells, we ran for our car with a howling crowd pursuing us throwing rice and confetti. We set off on our two-week honeymoon with our first overnight stop at Gettysburg, the site of one of the bloodiest battles of the American Civil War. A nice start to a marriage!

Figure 6. Leaving the church on the wedding day, 1965

We made our way up through New York State and booked into the highly recommended Honeymoon Hotel on the American side of Niagara Falls. The hotel had been made famous at that time by an Elvis Presley movie. Not my idea. Never an Elvis fan. It was the most garish building I had ever seen, with pink paint on every exposed part of the building. Had we taken a wrong turn and ended up in Disneyland?

To add to my woes, I found the TV was not working and it was almost time for the daily evening news. One must stay informed, honeymoon or not! I hurried back to the reception foyer and found a bus load of tourists waiting to book in. I went straight up to the Duty Manager, explained the situation, and quietly asked for a working TV. In full voice and with a ready audience in the foyer, he replied that the TV set in the Honeymoon Suite had not worked for years, and no-one had ever complained! The attentive audience, following the example of the manager, burst into shrieking laughter which accompanied me as I retreated back to our suite.

The next day we boarded a tour boat and cruised through the picturesque Thousand Islands that separate the United States of America from Canada.

After a few days in this area, we set off on our way back to Washington, DC, enjoying stopovers in several small towns in upstate New York. The weather had turned very cold by the time we arrived back in DC to our tiny studio apartment on N Street. The first snowfalls were due in a couple of weeks.

Judith usually picked me up from my evening classes during the hot, humid months of the Washington summer, and we would park by the Potomac River to have a sandwich or salad on the parkland shore. I would then hit the books again if time and enough light allowed, or until the evening cooled sufficiently to return to our apartment that wasn't air-conditioned.

By the time we had paid our rent and my tuition fees there was not much left of our combined wages. We could not afford to eat out so we made our own sandwiches when we were out for the day.

We had decided while on our honeymoon that we would

return home to Australia within the next six months or so. That was the easy decision. Our careers, where we would live in Australia, and so many other matters had yet to be decided upon. All in due course. We were young and in love, and that was all that mattered at that time.

We ensured most of our Sundays were free even though I was still studying and attending classes most nights and Saturdays. We went on picnics not far from Washington whenever the weather allowed. We did not require or seek the same level of social activity that we had had in our previous single partying lives! We also had to really make an even more concerted effort to save whatever we could for the approaching return home to Australia.

My new responsibility as a husband required a change of mindset. I had to seriously consider a career move that we would both be comfortable with. We decided it was time to return to Australia to meet my in-laws and to pursue employment with the Department of External Affairs as soon as our lease was up on our apartment. We made our farewells in Washington and returned to Australia in mid-1966.

9

Return to Australia & Meeting the in-Laws

Mid-1966

Our first few weeks back in Australia were spent assisting in the family's hotel, meeting Judith's many relatives and friends, deep-sea game fishing with my father-in-law George Boseley (GB) and spending a few days in Canberra sitting for Public Service examinations and interviews that were a requirement prior to selection for a Public Service position. If I passed the necessary requirements, and my request for a position with the Department of External Affairs was approved, I had to then wait to hear from the staffing people at the department.

GB would often point out many of his regular customers while I was helping out at the family's hotel and give me a brief summary of their backgrounds. One day, he directed my attention to one of the regulars at the Public Bar who apparently always sat on the same stool at the end of the bar, and seldom engaged in conversation with the bar staff or other patrons. GB thought he was rather strange but was no trouble.

I thought I would attempt to get to know him and see if we could cheer him up a little. It did not take long for him to disclose that he worked for the Australian Government. I told him of my own plans that were in progress in seeking a career with the Department of External Affairs. He mentioned that he was with a security organisation within the government and suggested that I may be interested in speaking to his people before accepting any other appointment within the Public Service. I was very curious and agreed to supply him with my CV. I thought this would also fill in a little time while awaiting a call from Canberra. It could also be a possible fallback position should I be unsuccessful with the Department of External Affairs.

A few days later I was advised that arrangements had been made for me to be interviewed at a location in Sydney the following week. I was to come alone. Nobody, including my wife, was to know of the meeting, or where it was to be held. The whole exercise was getting quite spooky!

On the day of the interview, I mentioned to Judith, out of necessity, that I had to meet some people about possible employment. She became very determined to discover where, when, and with whom this meeting was to take place, in case I was going to be late for our lunch together. I caved in after being interrogated for a few seconds, but not completely. Some spook material I was! I told her where I was going to meet with people from a government organisation about a possible position, but not who they were. I insisted that she

9 Return to Australia & Meeting the in-Laws

not come to the meeting location and stick to our plan of waiting for me at the restaurant.

Upon arrival at the designated building, I was met on the third floor, and taken into a small conference room. I was introduced and seated facing two formidable-looking gentlemen who looked as though they had been to the same tailor and had chosen the same pin-striped material. There was some diversity with the ties! My escort into the room was younger, and a little less formal in his attire and attitude. He sat behind and to the side of the more mature twosome.

We spent some time on questions and answers, they were asking and I was answering. I thought the interview had progressed well. I was finally asked to confirm that I had not mentioned the meeting to anyone at all. I declared that I had not. I was told to expect a call within the next couple of weeks and was excused by my escort who was instructed to see me safely off the premises.

Cloak, dagger, and self-imposed imagery of the new James Bond flew out the window immediately after we stepped out of the interview room. There was Judith, resplendent in her kangaroo-skin coat, seated, unsmiling, and looking at her watch to indicate that I had been a lot longer than the hour I had given her to meet me for lunch.

A slammed door and a loud cough caught my attention, and I turned to see my escort standing outside the closed interview room with palms outstretched, and head moving ever so slightly from side to side indicating, wordlessly, *what the hell is she doing here?*

I thought I had briefed Judith well on the need to stay away from the building, but it had obviously made no impression on her at all. In her defence, I should add that I had not been completely honest with her on just what organisation I was to be interviewed by.

My recruiter turned up at the hotel a few days later and advised that I should stick with my plans to join the Department of External Affairs. I have no regrets.

10

The Department & A Baby

1966–1967

A letter dated 8 May 1966 from the Commonwealth Public Service Board arrived soon after to advise that it was pleased to offer me a permanent appointment to the Department of External Affairs with a commencing salary of A$2793 a year. It sounds like a pittance today, but in 1966 it was a reasonable income with secure employment and offered an interesting career.

We only had a couple of suitcases of personal belongings between us, so our move to Canberra, the nation's capital, had been fairly uneventful. We were assisted by the department in finding a small house to rent in the northern suburb of Dickson.

We had just settled in Canberra when Judith broke the news that she was pregnant. We had been so busy in Washington, moving back to Australia, meeting the family, and finding a new job and a home, that the possibility of becoming a father had not even entered my mind.

Words cannot express my feelings upon hearing the news for the first time. I seriously doubt whether any man is ever prepared emotionally for parenthood, at least on the first occasion. Life until then had been all about us. Now there was someone else joining the family mix! I was ecstatic.

I felt utterly useless during Judith's pregnancy period. She appeared to be prepared, looked even more beautiful during the pregnancy, and her mother visited often for most of the final months, so that was comforting for Judith and of course for me. Alma was a great cook and left me casseroles and other dishes that would ensure I would not starve whenever Judith stayed with her in Wollongong.

My big break came the day I discovered my true paternal mentor, Dr. Spock! We fledgling parents-to-be referred regularly to the good doctor's advice. His book was to be our bible and major reference tool in the years ahead on overseas postings where we had either very little or no assistance, especially in bringing up our first child from 3 months to two-and-a-half years of age while on our first posting overseas.

The other reference tools that we often referred to while serving overseas were *The Family Medical Handbook*, and the *Modern Medical Counsellor*, a revised 1954 Australian copy I discovered at a garage sale in Canberra. It was a cumbersome, 960-page reference tool that I believe was at one time used by a final-year medical student.

My major responsibility during this period of the pregnancy was to be on call 24/7 to produce, as quickly as possible, another dozen Polly Waffles. For the uninitiated, a Polly Waffle was a chocolate-covered light wafer filled with marshmallow. Sadly, it has been missing from supermarket shelves for years.

Judith's parents took her away to Shoal Bay, north of Sydney, for a couple of weeks' break over Easter 1967. At this stage, Judith was approaching her final stage of pregnancy, and as agreed earlier with the family, I drove up to Shoal Bay for three days prior to the end of their holiday to drive Judith back to Canberra. When we first arrived in Canberra, we bought a 1958 red Mini Minor that was probably approaching the end of its life, but was within our price range, and met our short-term needs.

The drive back to Canberra from Shoal Bay was supposed to take us five hours, or thereabouts. It was a very hot day, and I had pushed the Mini too hard trying to get Judith home as quickly as possible. There was no air-conditioning in the car. The engine head blew when we were just south of Sydney with another 270 km to Canberra. Hitch-hiking back to Canberra could not be considered, and it was too risky to leave the car by the side of the road for too long and so far from Canberra.

I was extremely concerned for Judith. She was having difficulty with the heat and being so close to her delivery time did not help. She sat in the Mini with the doors open and windows down, while I stood on the side of the road with my thumb extended. After quite a while of experiencing rejection, Judith pleaded with me to sit in the car out of sight, and she would have a go. We were picked up almost immediately by a most obliging elderly man who went out of his way to drive us directly to Judith's parents' home in Wollongong, which was only 40 km away.

There was no other alternative than to leave our car by the side of the road. It was of secondary importance at that stage.

It took two of us to get Judith out of the car when we arrived in Wollongong. She did not look well at all. We were all on edge expecting a premature arrival. The in-laws had only just arrived an hour or so before us and helped with the climb up the stairs into their home.

I could not thank the elderly driver enough for his assistance, and with our sincere thanks, he was soon on his way with a contribution of beer and whisky for his trouble. He had refused any monetary offerings.

We made it back to Canberra three days later and much poorer after having the Mini towed and repaired. Judith had recovered quickly from the ordeal and was almost back to her normal pregnant self.

Soon after returning to the capital, Judith knew it was time for her to go to Canberra General Hospital for the birth. She went through a lengthy and painful time during the pre-birth period and eventually had to have a caesarean section.

Our first son, to be named Adrian Alexander, arrived just after midnight on 24 May 1967. A bundle of joy with a mop of red hair, brown eyes, and what I took to be a wide smile, was handed to me soon after. What a wonderful feeling, like none other.

I had knowingly broken a long-standing family tradition. Every first son back through the family lineage had been named George.

I did not realise that it was even remotely possible to feel so much love for Judith and this little baby boy. I recall having read somewhere, "What else could anyone want from life than to give it?"

The in-laws were ecstatic to hear the news. Adrian was their first grandchild. Alma drove down to Canberra the next day. I respected and loved Alma dearly and always welcomed her into our home, no matter what country we would later be posted to. There may not have been any further requirement for the search at all hours for Polly Waffles but catering to the care and needs of a new baby kept us all occupied, as every responsible parent would appreciate.

11

Posted to the Australian Embassy, Moscow, USSR

August 1967

Twelve months after joining the department, and a month after Adrian's birth, I was called into the office of the Head of Staffing and asked how I would feel about a posting to Moscow. I did not hesitate in accepting. I had expected to receive specific training and briefings that related to the duties of an Attaché (Consular & Administrative), during the pre-posting period, but there appeared to be either a sense of urgency in my getting to Moscow or a serious lack of understanding of just what training I should receive. For example, When I mentioned during my final pre-posting briefing that I had not received any training in consular duties I was told, 'No problem, there is a copy of the *Consular Instructions* at the embassy that you can refer to!'

The Australian Embassy in Moscow from 1967 to 1969 only had one Second Secretary (Consular & Administration), and one Attaché (Administrative) and vice-consul. Our area of consular responsibility in Moscow at that time covered Russia, Poland, Ukraine, Armenia, Georgia, the Baltic countries of

11 Posted to the Australian Embassy, Moscow, USSR

Latvia, Estonia, Lithuania, as well as Outer Mongolia, and the various "Stans", which meant ostensibly our diplomatic and consular area of responsibility covered approximately one-third the earth's surface.

A post report was prerequisite reading as soon as notification had been given of a posting. It was usually first read by the officer proceeding overseas, and then passed on to the spouse to assist and prepare them for what lay ahead. We were very much on our own in seeking additional advice and researching whatever general reading matter was available.

It was suggested that we contact officers and their spouses who had previously been posted to Moscow for advice on matters such as the level of language aptitude required, and the other basic requirements, such as banking, accommodation, clothing, schooling, medical facilities, food supplies, and any other needs of the family unit for the duration of the two-year posting.

One old-timer was readily forthcoming with general advice and recommendations, some of which I thought may have been passed on to see how I would react. For instance, I was told to pass on to my wife and close family members that from time to time we may have to cope with a wide variety of difficult and dangerous local conditions which we could never imagine prior to leaving home.

Another veteran officer advised that many foreign service families and single staff were exposed to extreme security hazards, violent political upheavals, health risks, trying climates, living in compounds under guard, and being subjected to overpowering harassment and repressive surveillance.

My experienced colleagues continued to advise that we should expect to experience a loss of a lot of other normally accepted activities, pleasures, and cultural opportunities that most of us had taken for granted at home in Australia prior to serving overseas, such as having access to English language TV, theatre, concerts, daily news via newspapers, radio, and magazines, visits to the beach, sporting activities, and the ubiquitous Australian family barbeques. Schooling problems, a lack of medical facilities, and language difficulties should also be expected along the way.

We would also be missing the birthdays, anniversaries, weddings, and funerals of friends and family, and as we were a dual-income family at home in Australia, we should expect to revert to one income.

I was briefed by a couple of officers that had been posted to Moscow earlier, and they warned that it was an extremely difficult post with many of our officers subjected to constant surveillance and living under the strain of knowing their every utterance was monitored by Soviet security personnel within the confines of their accommodation, and in some cases even their cars. They also suggested that similar treatment, possibly more overtly, was applied when travelling outside Moscow, and throughout the Soviet Union.

Thank heavens all of this information was dispensed in

11 Posted to the Australian Embassy, Moscow, USSR

small doses over a period of days. Otherwise, I think I would have been extremely concerned about what I was about to unleash upon my wife, and how she would cope with life in such an environment. There was also the three-month-old baby to consider in the mix. I discovered very soon after arrival in Moscow there was no need for concern about Judith's ability to manage the many difficulties she would be confronted with.

I was handed a sixty-five-page book called the *Guide Book for a Diplomat's Wife* during the pre-posting preparations which had originally been sourced from the Foreign Services of Canada, Great Britain, and Sweden by the Department of Foreign Affairs Wives Association in Canberra, the members of which provided additional input of their own. I was asked to pass it on to my wife to read prior to departure. I was also told that there should be a copy at the embassy for wives to refer to when necessary.

The book set out the requirements for the behaviour of young diplomats' wives. It would have proven difficult for most young Australian women in the twenty-first century to follow, at least without breaking into hysterical laughter. Many of the guidelines would be deemed archaic and laughable in today's world. For instance:

> The wife is warned to watch her place, and not to be unnecessarily pushy, where her husband is concerned. She is told that while older or senior people can without giving offence, ask her questions of a somewhat personal kind, it

is advisable for her to restrict questions to senior people as queries (rather than questions) such as, 'Did you have a good journey?'

The prospective young diplomat's wife is told that she can solve almost any problem by consulting the booklet's index, that is, overcoming shyness, handling servants, developing a sense of humour, or learning how to curtesy correctly and appropriately. The booklet is persistent with its advice to the young wife that she should know her place, for example:

> So far as possible, it is best to entertain people of your own age and rank. The reason for this is a practical one. Flattering though it may be for a young couple to entertain senior and distinguished people, by the time your husband is himself in a senior position these older ones will be either retired or dead.

Another little piece of advice from the book that would not go down well today is as follows:

> Should the wife have a tendency to talk too much, it is suggested that she and her husband develop between them a secret 'warning phrase' which the husband can drop whenever the wife starts getting carried away.
>
> The phrase should never be disclosed to colleagues or friends.

I can only imagine what the reply would have been if I had even hinted to Judith that such a phrase be used if she was "starting to get carried away".

Judith never had a problem with her guests, or in following the basic protocols of diplomacy. We had already been exposed to the procedures and protocols to be followed in entertaining guests at dinners and cocktail parties in Washington, while at the Office of the Air Attaché and the Embassy, prior to joining the department. Common sense was also a great benefit to fall back on. Finally, the booklet suggests:

> Protocol unfortunately has come to have for some people a connotation of all that is snobbish, stiff, and pretentious. In fact, life would be a great deal more difficult in any international society if there were no rules. It would be a little like driving on a highway without any road signs.

On that note, I will close the *Guide Book for a Diplomat's Wife*.

A matter that many Australians in this twenty-first century, in and out of government service, may not be aware of is the principal reason for the relatively few women at the top levels in the department until the late 1960s. It was because women were obliged by Public Service regulations to resign upon marriage. So many potential and talented female ambassadors and high commissioners were lost to the foreign service as a result.

I had no Russian at the time, and as I had studied Spanish while at college in Washington, I had hoped for a posting to a Spanish-speaking country. That would come later.

A Russian language tutor was eventually sent from the Department of Defence to provide language training twice a week for a short period, which provided only a very basic understanding of the extremely difficult language. I was encouraged to continue with my language studies in my own time and was given a Russian handbook to assist me in doing so. Wives received no language training at all. Thorough medical check-ups were completed and included a variety of inoculations.

Diplomatic passports were issued. Australian diplomats of that period travelled with diplomatic passports with "British Passport — Australia" printed in gold lettering on the red leather cover. My first diplomatic passport was issued in August 1967 and was probably one of the last diplomatic British passports issued to an Australian citizen. The photograph shows the outer corners of the passport are clipped because my posting had been completed. The words "British Passport" were removed later in 1967, but the Crown was retained. On today's Australian passport, "Australia" appears immediately below the Crown, followed by the Australian Coat of Arms.

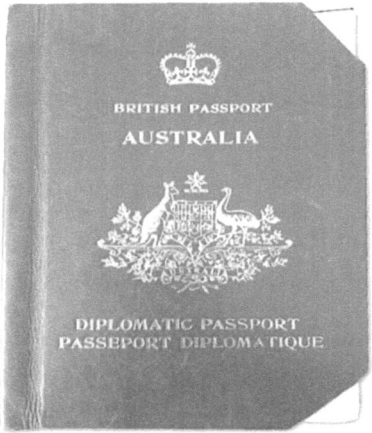

Figure 7: Diplomatic passport, cancelled, 1967

11 Posted to the Australian Embassy, Moscow, USSR

Air tickets were in hand; our personal effects had been packed and uplifted; and finally, we were given three days' leave with Judith's mother and father in Wollongong. At that time officers and their families, particularly with young children on long-distance flights to hardship posts, flew First Class.

The in-laws drove us to Sydney Airport. There was much sobbing, hugging, and indecipherable chatter between Judith and her mother while I stood silently aside with her father. I felt as though I was tearing the family unit apart.

I think the in-laws were more than a little concerned for our wellbeing. This period in the 1960s was during the height of the Cold War, with the Soviet Union as the bastion of communism. Its Kremlin masters were at the centre of the enemy encampment that we were about to be thrust into in Moscow! The Cuban affair and the close call of the Cold War heating up to World War Three were still reasonably current in most minds at the time.

The feeling of foreboding that I was receiving during these last few minutes with family members prior to boarding was such that I could not wait to get on that plane!

Judith's tears abated a little upon boarding our flight. Flowers and a chilled glass of champagne arrived from the Qantas staff to ease her distress. I was more focused on the end game and eagerly looking forward to my first overseas posting. Judith had just turned twenty-four, and I was twenty-nine. Our son, Adrian, was two-and-a-half months old!

London was to be our first official stopover for the required three-day Foreign and Commonwealth Office briefings, and shopping for supplies, especially for the baby, who was no trouble at all during the long flight to London.

London in 1967 was vibrant, with great stage shows, and much to see and do. This was the age of the Beatles, Mary Quant, and miniskirts. The youth were more interested in making love than war. Not that there is anything wrong with that! It was quite a different scene to that of Australia where our involvement in the Vietnam War was impacting heavily, particularly on our young, with conscription adding to civil unrest.

Unfortunately, we had little time to enjoy the few days in London. Judith spent most of her time shopping at Marks & Spencer (aka Marks & Sparks) for all the baby gear, including clothing, nappies, food, bassinet, stroller, cot, etc., which would have to last for at least the next twelve months. We had been told that most, if not all of these items, would not be available in Soviet Russia.

We had been to our Commonwealth Bank of Australia (CBA) branch in Canberra prior to departing Australia and had set up an account for my salary and allowances to be paid into because there were no banking facilities for us in Moscow. Our CBA banking representative was located at Australia House in central London at the time, and they were most helpful in providing an advance to pay for our supplies.

I had been instructed prior to departure from Australia to

report to a London location for special briefings, and practical instruction on the operational methods and equipment that were used by the Soviet intelligence organisations against foreign diplomatic personnel.

Judith and I had a pleasant evening together in London following the end of the briefings with a room service dinner followed by a night out at the theatre across the road from our hotel to see the stage show *Oliver*. The tickets had been booked for us by the Australian High Commission. The only setback was that one of us had to remain with the baby in the hotel. We solved the problem by each enjoying one act and then dashing back to the hotel to let the other go. It worked logistically. We made the best of what we had with the time that we had.

We had one free day prior to departing for Moscow and had decided to get out of London and into the countryside. Judith had spent a year working at Harrods in London in 1964 and lived at Sloane Square, Knightsbridge, in central London, so she was a great guide.

Australia House staff were most helpful in arranging a hire car, and we set off to the Cotswolds, Bath, and Stratford-on-Avon, the tourist mecca for anything Shakespeare. A day of relaxation we desperately needed.

Our flight to Moscow from London the next morning was on a BOAC Super Constellation. We thought we had the small first class area to ourselves, but it was not to be. Just prior to take-off a BOAC staff member and an Australian

High Commission courier boarded, approached me, and asked to see my passport. I was told I was to be the courier for the several diplomatic bags that were deposited and strapped into the seats around us.

The flight itself was pleasant but filled with apprehension about what was awaiting us upon arrival. There was one event during the flight that was a distraction of sorts. A fellow in white coveralls strolled into our closed first class section an hour or so after departing from Heathrow Airport, and without a word, he set about pulling up a section of the flooring in front of us and immediately outside the aircrew cabin. He disappeared down into the belly of the aircraft with a torch and what looked like a toolbox. He eventually re-emerged, without the toolbox and replaced the flooring panel. He made no eye contact or comment and left our area. Just prior to landing at Moscow's Sheremetyevo Airport, he again followed his previous routine down into the area behind the aircrew cabin. He reappeared a short while later with his toolbox, and retreated quickly from our area, again without acknowledging our presence. Was this the operational forerunner of satellite intelligence gathering, or perhaps a simple repair job by an aircraft technician?

12

The Australian Embassy Moscow, USSR

1967–1969

Figure 8. Presentation of Ambassador's credentials, Moscow, 1968. The author is standing in the back row, first on the right

Upon arrival at Moscow's Sheremetyevo Airport in late August 1967, we were cleared through Border Control without any problem and met by the officer I was replacing. This officer also cleared the diplomatic bags while we retrieved our luggage. We were on our way within minutes to the diplomatic "Ghetto" at 45 Leninsky Prospect, southwest of the Moscow CBD, and shown to the small apartment, No. 7, that would be our home for the next two years.

There were several of these massive grey buildings spread around Moscow officially designated for foreigners only. The entire city appeared to be devoid of paint of any colour. In addition to the diplomatic corps, our building also housed foreign business representatives, journalists, and military personnel attached to various embassies.

The entrance to our building complex was through an archway at which visitors had to stop and identify themselves to the uniformed militia guards. We were identified by the diplomatic plates on our vehicles. The militia alerted the "watchers" of the KGB's Surveillance Directorate who were responsible for reporting on the movements of the building's occupants, and for keeping the local population from contacting us.

No matter how hard we tried to imagine what our accommodation would be like, it could not even come close to what we were presented with. The apartment was at the top on the seventh floor and consisted of a bedroom with enough room for a bed which was a cross between a single and a double bed barely wide enough to hold two slim adults. The only other piece of furniture was a free-standing wardrobe which we used as a barrier between our bed and Adrian's cot.

Another space available was a small kitchen that could only accommodate one of us at a time when the baby's highchair was in use. The lounge area had a two-seat sofa, a lounge chair, several dining chairs of varying age, colour, and design, and an ancient dining table with three legs that belonged, and one that did not! The apartment had previously been occupied by single officers since Australia's first diplomatic representatives arrived in 1943!

We discovered very early in our stay that we had other unwelcome occupants living with us in the apartment. A plague of large, black cockroaches! We were advised to just get used to them as efforts to rid the apartments of them only produced a brief respite because they followed the water pipes out to a neighbour's apartment when spraying was conducted, and then came marching back when they deemed it safe to do so! We found that idea difficult to deal with, especially with a very young baby. We could never successfully cull them to a manageable level.

The elevator, circa the late 1800s, in our section of apartments at 45 Leninsky Prospect seldom worked. When it did, the metal cage frightened the daylights out of newcomers. It was extremely noisy, rattled and swayed in its movements up or down, and had a mind of its own, stopping at times between floors for some considerable time. We rarely ever used this facility. Furniture or other large items had to be carried up as the maximum load the lift could hold was three average-sized people, and nobody wanted to tempt fate by adding any additional weight.

Personal mail was sent to Canberra via London by diplomatic bag and passed on to Australia Post for distribution to our families. The turnaround for the "snail mail" could take up to three or four weeks to receive a reply.

There were no computers, Skype, Zoom, email, social media streams, or smartphones to communicate with family and friends during the 1960s and 1970s. Patience was definitely a necessary virtue during that period, particularly at posts such as Moscow which did not even use telephone services, for obvious reasons.

The Australian Embassy was located at 13 Kropotkinsky Pereulok and consisted of three buildings dating back to the early 1800s. The main building, called the Chancery, was a two-floor structure housing the residence of the ambassador, and the large entertaining room, the *Bolshoi Zal,* on the ground floor. On the upper floor were the offices of the ambassador, Australian staff, the archives, and the Secure room. The Secure Room was something akin to a pod or shipping container on stilts, a room within a room. It had its own power supply, and when powered up it was surrounded by an electromagnetic field.

The ambassador's deputy, the counsellor and his family resided in a smaller two-floor building in the embassy grounds. The garage for our official cars and drivers was between the counsellor's building and the consular area.

The consular section was housed in what had once been the stables at the rear of the embassy grounds and was separated from the Chancery by a small garden area and the parking area. The embassy's reception area, translators, and general clerical staff were also located in the consular area.

There was a large room in the basement of the Chancery which I later turned into "The Down Under Club". We opened this area up on Friday evenings after working hours for our staff, the staff from friendly embassies, and any visiting Australian visitors. Our two Federal Police officers provided our embassy security and were also accommodated in the basement area of the Chancery.

In Moscow, all embassy staff lived under the strain of knowing their every utterance was being monitored by Soviet security personnel. If ever Judith or I wished to discuss a matter that we considered personal or work-related, we had to walk down the seven flights of stairs, and out of the building, and even then, you had to be guarded with your conversations. During the winter months we had to first don our coats, muskrat fur hats, felt boots, gloves, and scarves before exiting the building which meant the conversation had to be worth the effort. The arrival of winter was usually accepted when the first snow fell in mid-November, or soon after spotting the salt-spreading trucks parked in the side streets. The general mood of new arrivals, especially those who had never experienced or seen snow previously, eventually matched the rest of those who had already experienced a long Moscow winter. You could also sense the changes in the inhabitants of Moscow not long after the first snow fell. General lethargy and a more sombre mood seemed to become increasingly pervasive as winter settled in. The winters were long, cold, confining, and grey, with leafless trees lining the streets, dark skies, dark clothing, and dark everything, including shorter days.

The organisation that we had to use as our initial point of

contact for all matters relating to services to the diplomatic corps was the UPDK. The initials UPDK were the Russian letters referring to the Directorate of Services to the Diplomatic Corps. We simply referred to the organisation as UPDK or The Directorate. This organisation was an arm of the KGB apparatus. They were also the issuing authority for diplomatic identity cards, referred to in Russian as a *katoshka*, for each new arrival at the embassy

Figure 9. Diplomatic ID cards, Moscow, 1967

The organisation's other responsibilities included providing diplomats with accommodation, and the appointment of all locally engaged Soviet staff at the embassy, such as translators and interpreters, drivers, clerks, cleaners, and our personal domestic staff such as a maid or nanny. They were also the authorising body that approved, or not, our travel to destinations that exceeded 25 km from the centre of the city of Moscow, or when leaving and re-entering the country for any reason at all — official, medical, holidays, shopping.

We applied reciprocity to the Soviet Embassy in our own capital city in Australia, Canberra on all such restrictions placed on us in Moscow. Reciprocity was a word regularly used and applied by both sides at that time.

To elaborate further on the restrictions, any request to venture on approved roads outside Moscow for a picnic or visit to a special destination such as a friendly embassy *dacha* or country house required at least a week to two weeks prior to submission for approval to the Directorate. In addition, we had to apply in writing at least forty-eight hours in advance for permission to go to a restaurant or other social outings.

Our diplomatic car plates commenced with D-16 which immediately identified us as Australian diplomats. D-1 and D-2 were allocated to the USA and the British. D-3 to D-15 identified the other NATO countries. We came after the NATO countries.

Technical staff from Canberra, or others we brought in via London, made occasional visits to sweep the embassy for bugs and ensured the Secure room and its surrounds were impenetrable from directional microphones, underground built-in listening devices, and cavity resonators, among other interesting equipment. A few devices were found in the roof of the Chancery, and in its stairwell on one of the sweeps during 1969. The technicians were only given very short visit visas, so they did not linger in Moscow.

The Canadians brought in their own sweepers. Their Consul-General advised me that they had been successful in finding several devices. Most of them were installed in window ledges!

The American Embassy found small transmitters had been installed in the typewriters used by staff in their Secure room, which they referred to as "The Yellow Submarine". It was generally accepted that the transmitters had been installed when the shipment of typewriters had been intercepted while being shipped to Moscow. The American communications traffic from their secure area had been transmitted direct to a nearby KGB electronic listening post for a short period before the Americans located the intrusion by the Soviets.

Suspicions were held for some time within the small diplomatic community that there may have been health problems stemming from over-exposure to electromagnetic field and microwave penetration, but as far as I know, no research or investigation has ever been initiated on the health of any of our staff who had been posted to Moscow since we first opened in 1943. I do know of three senior officers with whom I served in Moscow who passed away with brain tumours. There may have been other staff affected before and after my postings in Moscow that I am not aware of. That may be a file best not opened.

Our staff and their families had to rely on the periodic visits to Moscow of a British doctor. If the matter was serious, we would be evacuated to either Helsinki or London. We could not visit Soviet doctors, or hospitals, for treatment because of the personnel security policy in place at the time. There was an exception during 1967 and 1968 when the pregnant wife of one of our staff members had to be taken to a Moscow maternity hospital as a matter of urgency.

We had only been in Moscow for a year when Judith and Adrian became very ill. I followed soon after with severe headaches, nausea, diarrhoea, and high fever, and we could not bear any light at all. The British doctor was called but advised he had to leave for London that evening and would not be back for two weeks. His cursory consultation over the phone provided the advice that he was unsure what our problem was. He left us a packet of antibiotics and quarantined us for several days. We looked after ourselves with aspirin after the antibiotics ran out. All ended well on that occasion, and a reference to our family medical adviser book indicated that it was likely that we had experienced salmonella.

American Embassy personnel had unexplained problems with hair falling out, tumours, and other illnesses. Excessive microwave bombardment of their embassy was purported to have imposed long-term adverse physical impacts on many of their staff members over the years. Leukaemia was another such suspected by-product. American staff voiced their anxiety and concerns to Washington, and soon after the report was released a special mesh was mounted on the outside of all windows of their embassy in Moscow and others around the world to counter this perceived problem.

I believe that the hardships experienced by our spouses were generally far greater, and more demanding, than those imposed on the officers. For instance, spouses and their children were removed from family and friends for years at a time. With little or no language training, they were thrust into foreign, isolated, and at times extremely dangerous environments. In comparison, the officers worked in a relatively secure environment within the confines of the diplomatic mission and were occupied by the demands of their work.

Families that were dual-income earners at home in Australia would have to revert to the one income of the officer. Many spouses had to sacrifice their careers.

There was no need for any concern about Judith's capability to adjust on her own in such a foreign environment. She excelled during the settling-in period, and in dealing with the lot she had been dealt. She was blessed with an outgoing personality, was extremely positive and confident, and became involved in every activity possible within the embassy and the diplomatic community generally. Thankfully, she been raised by hard-working parents in the hotel industry which gave her an edge on how to behave as a host, and what guests expect from a host. She was also occupied with a baby, which as any young parent knows keeps you very busy indeed. If Judith was ever in doubt, there was plenty of reading and excellent advice from books such as the *Guidelines for Foreign Affairs Wives, Dr. Spock*, or the *Family Medical Adviser*.

Life could also be extremely difficult for the single staff, particularly the female secretaries, who on some postings regularly worked long hours, and six or seven days a week if required to do so. There was no backup staff to call upon to assist them when workloads got very busy, and unlike our married staff they also had to deal with the added impact of isolation and loneliness as best they could.

Judith and a few of her friends from the American and Canadian embassies kept busy by holding family functions for children with outings, birthday parties, and school projects. Our children of school age all went to the American embassy's Anglo-American school. Some of the younger wives, including Judith, joined the "Second" Bolshoi dance classes, which were especially promoted to the diplomatic wives' community.

Sport of any kind was an outlet and a distraction from the restrictive environment within which we lived and worked, and I immersed myself in every sport that was available to us. For instance, I joined the Canadian Embassy's broomball team, the Moscow Maple Leafs, during the winter months. The team consisted of a Swiss businessperson and an Australian (me), but the rest were Canadians. Broomball was similar in a rather strange sort of way to ice hockey, except that we did not wear skates; we played on a frozen tennis court; we used a small hard rubber ball instead of a puck; and instead of a hockey stick we used a short straw hand broom that we taped at the end into a curve, soaked it in water, and rammed it into the wall of snow alongside the court to accelerate the freezing process. Therefore, it was not really similar at all, other than it was a game that was played on ice with instruments designed to draw blood, and it was invented by Canadians, or at least I think it was!

The Finnish Embassy was next door to our embassy, and during the winter months their tennis court was cleared of snow and used as one of the destinations for the broomball competitions. The real fun bit came when the game was over and the battered bodies of friends and foes disrobed and crowded into the Finnish Embassy sauna. The beer did not stay cold for long so you had to drink it fast before running out and diving into the snow. I only did that once!

The Canadian Embassy staff had some excellent and experienced hockey players. One of the most outstanding was Aggie Kuklowitz, the Air Canada manager. He previously had a successful professional career with the New York Rangers. A group of local Russian players would always be on the rink when Aggie and his multinational ice hockey mates turned up. A game would be quickly negotiated. I watched.

Aggie asked me to accompany him on one occasion to a

major international invitation ice hockey game between the Soviet Union and Canadian teams. The two of us tried to make as much noise as several thousand avid Soviet fans, and at times the atmosphere got a bit heated with their supporters, culminating when the Canadians won. Aggie suggested we leave quickly because the crowd did not appear to be in a congratulatory mood. He was right. We just made it to his Air Canada VW bus with an unfriendly crowd in pursuit.

The Soviet fans kicked and hammered on the side of the van, which displayed a large red maple leaf on both sides. One of the locals was still hanging onto the windshield wiper supports and had a foot-hold on the front bumper as we drove off. There was no more ranting and abuse from our anchored passenger, just an undulating scream mixed with Russian expletives, and pleading for us to stop. Aggie braked suddenly. Our passenger was ejected onto the rough gravel of the parking area near the exit gate. It turned out to be an interesting and very enjoyable evening, despite the dents in Aggie's vehicle.

There were no supermarkets for food supplies, dairy products and baby food, etc., in Moscow like we were used to at home in Australia, and there were no other suppliers closer than Helsinki, which was approximately 1200 km away. Even if you wanted to do a quick trip to Helsinki you could not in an emergency, because of having to get approval from UPDK a couple of weeks in advance.

At that time, we were way ahead of the current growing

interest in online shopping. We placed orders for canned goods, sweets, biscuits, cigarettes, liquor, and other non-perishables from Ostermann-Petersen in Copenhagen. Milk, baby food and whatever fruit and vegetables were in season were ordered from the Stockmann department store, in Helsinki. New Zealand lamb and some other meat products were requested from our people at Australia House, London. Clothing, shoes and other items were ordered from a Sears, Roebuck and Company catalogue — if you had a friend at the US Embassy who invited you to use that facility.

On the rare occasion when our meat orders from London had not arrived, and word had filtered down through the embassy wives' pipeline that a local market or store had received supplies, there would be a mad scramble to get there as quickly as possible.

When we received approval from the UPDK to visit a particular restaurant we had to be there at 7 pm. We were also expected to stay until at least 11 pm, which was usually just prior to when the main course was served! It was deemed a privilege to be allowed or approved to dine out in a Moscow restaurant, and therefore diners were expected to stay for the duration.

A routine that we learned very early after arrival in Moscow was to always eat something before arriving at a restaurant, and to avoid, as much as possible, mixing of grape and grain (i.e. vodka and wine, or brandy and beer). Black bread was usually the accepted sustenance to keep you seated at the table, but new staff would usually not partake of the bread because of its coarseness and sour smell.

Thursday night was poker night at the Marine House which was located in the American Embassy compound, and I was the only non-American invited. The American government, through its military officers, State Department personnel and others contributed favourably to my income.

During my first year in Moscow, I heard that the Marine detachment were about to upgrade their "Marine Bar" and that all their old gear was going to be tossed out. I suggested that if they did not have other plans for their antiquated bar, they may like to donate it and any other equipment to our fledgling "Down Under Club" in the basement of our embassy, instead of having the Soviets (UPDK) getting their hands on it. The Marines happily obliged. They not only delivered the lot, but they also installed it for us. I offered the Marines honorary membership in the club. All staff, especially our secretarial female staff, thought this was a brilliant idea.

I received a phone call from Vatican City in late 1967. It was from Brother Patrick O'Doherty from Clontarf Boys Town in Western Australia. He had been invited to Rome to receive an award from the Pope. He called to wish me well, and to say that he was extremely proud to have one of his "old boys" serving Australia in its foreign service. His call was made from the Pope's staff office. I asked him if he could put the Pope on the line, and after a short period of silence, I had to tell him that I was only kidding! This was arguably the darkest period of the Cold War, and phone intercepts, particularly of international calls to foreign diplomats were a reality of life. I must have really impressed their Security Service, or not!

I received another surprise phone call in early December 1968, this time from my former Australian roommate in Washington, Bernie Lowes. Bernie, a haematologist, had married an American woman, and was now working at Miami General Hospital. I have mentioned in an earlier chapter an experience not appreciated by Bernie's wife while on their honeymoon in the Virgin Islands. I told Bernie it was snowing in Moscow and was extremely cold. He suggested that we hop on a flight, and get over to Miami for a Christmas catch-up, and to soak up some sun.

I discussed Bernie's idea of taking a break from the Russian winter in Miami with Judith, and two weeks later we had joined the Finnish-American Society and had flown to Helsinki to join the Society's charter flight to New York. No questions were asked whether we were Americans or not.

Unfortunately, we had a disruption to our departure flight arrangements from Helsinki because we were snowed in, and all flights were cancelled until the following day. We accepted a kind invitation to spend the night at the home of an American fellow passenger with whom we had been sitting and chatting for some time in the departure lounge. A Lincoln Town car arrived at the airport and drove us all to the American's palatial home on the outskirts of Helsinki. He added that the airport would call him as soon as a departure time had been set for our flight. We had our hand luggage, and that would suffice.

We had no idea until we arrived at the American's home that he was the CEO of the Ford Motor Company in Scandinavia. His wife met us upon arrival and had prepared a hot meal. It was an enjoyable stay with great hosts who had turned what could have been an extremely difficult and uncomfortable overnight stay at Helsinki airport with a sixteen-month-old child into a memorable encounter with the warmest hospitality.

The charter flight's entry point was New York, and we had to then catch a flight to Washington, DC where we had arranged accommodation for a three-day stopover to catch up with several friends who were still at the Office of the Air Attaché, and at the Australian Embassy. Upon arrival we rented a car, booked into the Marriott Hotel not far from the Washington National Airport, and did a little sightseeing for the rest of the day.

We had trouble confirming our seats on a flight to Miami so we decided that we would drive to the airport and see if we could solve the problem in person. There was no parking available at the airport so I decided to circle the perimeter while Judith and Adrian went into the terminal to get our tickets sorted out. No problem, we finally had our tickets, and drove back to the hotel, where I dropped Judith and Adrian off. We were very tired by this stage, so I went looking for takeaway dinner.

Mission accomplished, I had our dinner and parked the car in the underground carpark. When I stepped out of the elevator on our floor, I was grabbed by two men in dark suits, thrown against the wall of the corridor opposite the lift, and held there. My airline bag with our passports, and a bag with our dinner were taken from me and thrown down the corridor. I had one arm twisted behind my back and held against the wall while one of the assailants identified himself as FBI. I immediately felt some relief, and just to make sure they were indeed FBI, I asked for their IDs. They ignored me and kept on calling me a name I was unfamiliar with. One question flew after the other while I was held against the wall. I was confused, concerned, and in some pain with my arm being pressed back at such an unnatural angle. Their IDs were eventually produced, but only after I had made several additional requests. I had no idea what they were talking about so I finally used some well-honed Australian expletives, and shouted at them to retrieve my airline bag, and told them they would find two Australian diplomatic passports inside. This was done, and after a short period of mumbling and whispering, the apologies started. The agents picked up my belongings and walked with me to our room. Another agent opened the door, and I found Judith and Adrian sitting on the bed with a female agent standing nearby.

The story that unfolded from the lead agent was that Adrian's look-alike was the subject of an interstate kidnapping. He was the same age as Adrian, and also had red hair. Judith's shoulder-length dark hair apparently looked similar to that of the woman who had kidnapped the child. My driving around the airport several times, while Judith picked up our flight tickets to Miami, was the clincher for the agents to move on us. They advised that they had been following us for some time during the day.

An agent left the room while we were receiving the explanation of the day's events and returned soon after with bags of takeaway food, and a couple of cold six-packs of beer. Our meal had been destroyed in the process of the initial contact with the agents when I stepped out of the lift. This incident could have become a serious diplomatic problem for these agents, and the Bureau. We all relaxed, and I told them of my earlier experiences in the Soviet Union, and how I thought they were the bad guys. All ended well, and they went on their way to further their search for the real villains.

I never thought of it at the time, but I must have used my still current Washington, DC driver's licence from my time with the Australian Embassy in Washington when I completed the paperwork with the rental car company. The FBI must have checked our car's licence plate with the rental company as a priority to establish my personal details, and there would not have been a record of a diplomatic passport as an identification requirement.

The next day, we met with old friends with whom we had served a couple of years earlier at the Australian Embassy, and at the Office of the Air Attaché, and the following day we flew to Miami to catch up with Bernie Lowes and his family. The remainder of that enjoyable stay in the United States was concentrated in nearby Fort Lauderdale. The return to a freezing Helsinki, and an even colder Moscow several days later on the charter flight was fortunately uneventful.

I had been working six and often seven days a week with long hours most days for several months, and applied for three weeks' leave. The leave was approved, and we proceeded with planning for our road trip to Europe.

Departure day finally arrived, and we had barely travelled more than two hours from Moscow on the first leg of the trip to Helsinki when Judith suggested I try to get some sleep on the back seat, while she drove and her mother, who had recently arrived to visit us, moved into the front passenger seat with our son, Adrian. I had not slept much at all the night before departing because I wanted to clear my desk of outstanding matters and had the final preparations for the trip to take care of.

Alert militiamen, who were stationed at one of the intermittent checkpoints, had obviously failed to see me while doing his headcount as Judith drove past, and had given chase. Judith did not understand what was happening when the motorcycle with another officer in the sidecar swerved in front of her waving a baton to indicate that she should pull over. I sat up just as one of the Militiamen peered in to do a head count. I startled him. He did not look amused. Superficial requests were made for an inspection of our documents, and to keep the militia officers happy I returned behind the wheel for most of the remainder of the trip to the Soviet-Finnish border.

We were behind schedule so once we were across the border we bypassed Helsinki, drove straight on to the port, and caught the overnight ferry to Sweden with only an hour to spare. Then it was another ferry to Copenhagen from the southern end of Sweden, and a couple of days later we left Denmark for West Germany. Judith's mother potty-trained our son in the back seat of our VW Beetle. Never a dull moment.

Germany was still divided by the Soviet East and West, so we were restricted by time and the route we were to follow through much of Europe before we had to turn north again and retrace our journey back to Helsinki. We had plenty of time to complete our shopping for supplies in Helsinki that would hopefully last for the next few months.

Once the shopping was completed the next day, we loaded up the VW and headed off on an easy one hour's drive to the Finnish township of Porvoo for an overnight stay, and to allow for an early morning start the next day to Vyborg at the Soviet border. Porvoo's close proximity to the border provided time to get through the Soviet border procedures, refuel in Leningrad (now St Petersburg), and make it to our halfway point at Novgorod in time to book in to the only hotel we were allowed to stay overnight, and have a meal.

We should not have been surprised with the outcome of our accommodation booking at Novgorod. We had checked and received confirmation on our Novgorod Hotel reservations before leaving Moscow, and in Helsinki the day before, but we were still met with blank stares upon arrival in Novgorod. We were told that they had no knowledge of a booking for us. We were also told there were no rooms available.

We were not amused. We had been driving from dawn to nightfall on a road that appeared to have more potholes than bitumen, and we were exhausted. We were told to keep driving the approximately 600 km to Moscow because there was no other approved hotel accommodation we could stay at between Novgorod and Moscow. It was a waste of time and energy to attempt an argument. Judith and Alma were rugged up, and already approaching their need for sleep. Adrian was sound asleep.

The highway was unlit, the night was dark, and the hour was late. I was almost asleep at the wheel. We had not seen another vehicle since we left Novgorod. I could tell there was no way I was going to last much longer without a rest. We came to an intersection, and I decided to turn off the main road, and park for a couple of hours sleep in the car. At that stage, I did not give a damn if the militia came looking for us. Everyone else was sound asleep.

I had driven just far enough along the side road to avoid other vehicle lights flashing into the car or have an alert militia officer asking us to move on and had been following a slight curve in the road when the VW's headlights shone on a high wire fence and row upon row of aircraft and military vehicles directly ahead of us. This could have been a storage or graveyard facility, or an active Soviet Air Force base. I only had a couple of seconds of visual contact at most. One thing was sure though, I was in an area that I should not have been. I immediately turned my vehicle's lights to low beam and did a three-point turn very slowly on the narrow road and headed back as casually as possible in the direction of the main road to Moscow. I felt extremely uneasy and would not have liked to guess what my heart rate was at that moment. Judith had woken during my turning of the vehicle. There were no sirens, or other lights, which would have been expected under the circumstances, if we had been seen. I almost shouted with relief when we were out on the main road again, hopefully with nobody having witnessed my transgression. I was no longer tired!

The consequences, if we had been apprehended would have been awkward, to say the least. Not necessarily just for me and the family members in the car, but for the embassy and consequently the Australian Government. I expected one of the many checkpoints to pull us up for questioning, and I spent some time during that drive south trying to put together a viable explanation for deviating from the main road. However, there was no need for such concern because we completed the remainder of the journey without any checkpoints showing an interest in us.

We had only been back in Moscow a week or so, when our Third Secretary knocked on my office door, and asked whether I would like to join him on a little outing. It was a Saturday morning. I gladly accepted the break away from my office, if even for an hour or so. We drove in the Third Secretary's car, a black Volga used widely by the Soviet bureaucracy (*apparatchiks*), but with the distinction of having diplomatic plates identifying it as owned by an Australian diplomat. I was briefed on the way to our destination. Soviet demonstrators (a rent-a-crowd) were marching on the Chinese Embassy in great numbers. We were going to be observers only and join in the ranks of the demonstrators.

There had continued to be extremely strained relations between the Soviet Union and China over some border riverine islands on the Amur River. Trouble had been brewing for some years between the two countries and was now escalating to dangerous levels. There had been a series of military clashes along this Sino-Soviet border area in the late spring and early summer of 1969.

We parked in a side street and watched the demonstrators exiting from long lines of buses, with many of them being given placards which bore quite hostile signage towards the Chinese that would no doubt further inflame tensions between the two countries. We walked towards the vocal marchers with the intention of blending in with the crowd as they headed towards the Chinese Embassy. Unfortunately, just as we were about to join the ranks of the demonstrators, we were hustled out of the line, and escorted back to the side street in which our vehicle was parked. We had been spotted from the outset.

Our embassy numbers at that time were such that we could not have two officers away together at any one time. We had no option but to travel with diplomats from other friendly nations. The Brits kept mostly to themselves. The Canadians also rarely had someone available to travel with us, so I more often than not joined my fellow Thursday night poker players at the US Embassy who I thought I could trust to behave themselves. This trust was often overrated.

I regret being repetitive, but our embassy staff had to be aware at all times of the situations that they could be subjected to from those with an adversarial interest in us. With this in mind I will recall just some of the other instances of "attention" that had been applied to my family and myself during the first posting to Moscow.

Several months after our arrival in Moscow, Judith and I were invited to join an American diplomat and his wife on a trip to Leningrad. Two British Military Attachés and their wives were also staying at the Baltiskaya Hotel and joined us at dinner. During the course of the evening, we accepted an unlabelled bottle of what appeared to be vodka from a group of male Russians at a nearby table. One of their number stood, pointed in our direction, waved to us, and raised his glass. In accord with local custom at least one of us was expected to stand, while we all raised our glasses accepting the gesture, and then send a bottle of our choice back to them.

I learned the next day that both the American and British officers had the same adverse experiences which later that night left me semiconscious, nauseous, and disoriented. We had been far from intoxicated when we left the dining room and could only conclude the next morning that the contents of the bottle, we had received in good faith at dinner had contained something in addition to the vodka.

I read much later of other officers from western or NATO countries who had travelled to Leningrad, but without their wives. Some of them also had similar experiences to ours but had not been so fortunate. Luckily, Judith and the wives of our dining companions had not been involved in the "toasting ritual".

An incident that was of concern, at least initially, occurred when we were in a crowded underground railway station in Moscow waiting for a train with our son Adrian (then eighteen months old). Judith had hold of Adrian's hand, and without any warning he was pulled from her grasp and picked up by a fellow in a uniform who tucked him under his arm and took off. I threw my bag on the ground near Judith and ran after them. I lost sight of them both for a brief moment in the crowd. A Soviet Air Force Officer and Adrian reappeared from behind an ornate marble column, and as I approached, they both stood before me with wide smiles. Adrian had his hand outstretched to show me a handful of sweets. The officer had obviously been celebrating and was not a real threat at all. He was probably on his way home on leave to see his own family. I took his extended hand and nodded to the officer that I had no problem with him, although Judith had joined us by this time, and let him know, thankfully in English, that she was not amused. The arrival of our train put a timely end to any further comments or complications.

We also experienced three extremely interesting events over three days from 18 to 20 August 1968. Firstly, Judith and I were invited to dinner at the American Embassy compound by a US Air Force Military Attaché on August 18th. Our host was in the throes of completing his posting to Moscow and was preparing for deployment to Vietnam to take over a United States Airforce (USAF) Command near Da Nang. Judith and I left the American Embassy compound late in the evening to head back to our apartment, and as soon as I drove onto the *Sadova* (Moscow ring road) I became aware that we were in the middle of what appeared to be a major movement of military vehicles, with many of them driving with either no lights or dimmed yellow lights. Street lighting on the *Sadova* provided enough illumination to keep the vehicles moving.

Priority must have been given to the military vehicles because traffic in our lane had stopped. One of the countless personnel carriers with fully armed troops pulled up alongside us. They had kit bags at their feet and were sitting back to back on an open platform. We were only a metre or so away looking up into the eyes of one line of these troops, and I could not resist winding our car's window down to ask what was going on. Not a good idea. If looks could kill?

The staring game and silence only lasted a moment or two before they started to move away and were replaced by several more vehicles of the unsmiling troops. This activity went on for some time, with variations in types of vehicles and military personnel. At first, I thought it was an exercise, but the longer I sat in their midst the more I was convinced something really big was in progress. I finally concluded that as they were passing so close to the American Embassy, they may have been using the late hour to reduce their visibility and movement. It was well after midnight at this stage so I briefed our counsellor the following morning.

Secondly, late in the evening of August 19th, I was working late when one of our guards, a federal police officer, entered my office and advised that a Russian "walk-in" had entered the embassy grounds, and wanted to speak to me. Me? I accompanied the guard out to the poorly lit garden area within the embassy grounds, and he left me standing with a stocky, middle-aged fellow wearing a black coat, and to add to the attire's blackness, the visitor had black hair slicked back, and a thick black Stalinist moustache; he was possible a Georgian. My immediate impression was that perhaps he was a dress-up fan of the mid-1960s TV series *The Addams Family*.

I did not like the look of the "walk-in", and all I could think of was how did this fellow get my name. I introduced myself as the vice-consul. He wasted no time in getting straight to the point. He said that he wanted me to take him to the American Embassy in the back seat of my vehicle. I was to cover him up in the well of the back seat and drive him into the American Embassy grounds without stopping at the entrance for inspection by the militia guards, as was the norm for foreign (non-US Embassy) diplomatic vehicles. I had an uneasy feeling that I was being set up, and just wanted to get rid of the fellow as quickly as possible. I told him that what he proposed would not be possible and added that he should find his own way to the American Embassy. He repeated his request, and I repeated my answer. He was not at all happy with me and walked away. I watched him walk out of our embassy driveway entrance and disappear around the corner at the end of our street. We did not have Soviet militia guards at our embassy entrance at that time.

I met the guard in the embassy's car park while on the way back to my office. He had stayed nearby to ensure there were no problems with the walk-in. He advised that the fellow had initially asked to speak to the Senior Intelligence Officer in the embassy urgently because he had extremely important information. The guard had no choice other than to pass him on to me because I was the only officer still working. He also advised that the walk-in had not asked to speak to me personally, which was a relief in so many ways, or so I thought. I briefed the counsellor the next morning.

I had a very difficult time with the Soviet spooks (KGB) after that experience until I left Moscow on my next posting to Santiago de Chile late in 1969, and when I returned to Moscow six years later as First Secretary and Consul in 1975.

I had obviously been erroneously marked as an Australian Intelligence Officer by the Soviets.

Thirdly, the Soviets invaded Czechoslovakia late the next day, 20 August 1968, with approximately 200 000 troops, 5 000 tanks and mechanised vehicles!

Border Guard personnel patrolled the frontiers of the Soviet Union, and during the late 1960s and early 1970s, they bore the brunt of the conflict with the Chinese along the Sino-Soviet borders. Their officers also served as advisers in Hanoi during the Vietnam War. Their major responsibility was to keep the Soviet population caged within its borders and to guard against infiltration. It had an elite Army and Navy of hundreds of thousands of personnel and was equipped with the latest weaponry.

My consular duties ensured that I had occasional contact with the border guards at Sheremetyevo, Moscow's major airport. The initial advice of Australians having been detained would come directly from the Soviet Ministry of Foreign Affairs.

Very early in my first posting to Moscow, I was fortunate in meeting one of the more personable border guard officers at Sheremetyevo International Airport who would be of great assistance with some very trying and difficult consular cases that followed in the years ahead. This man was Captain Yuri Knox, my surname, and he suggested that my Christian name was also the same as his so we soon established a rapport that was deemed improbable, if not impossible at that time, particularly because the Soviet border guard officers were known to be seriously lacking in charisma and were an integral part of the KGB organisation. They also had a notorious reputation for their ruthless efficiency.

I was at first surprised that a Russian would have a Scottish name, but after a few simple questions were asked of Yuri, and some research of my own, I discovered that the Russian Czar, Peter the Great (1672– 1725) had recruited hundreds of Scots to undertake the building of a great Russian naval fleet. One of those Scottish shipbuilders was named George Knox. He and many of his fellow Scots married Russian women and settled permanently in Czarist Russia. Yuri was a product of one such union.

We were all extremely conscious that the Cold War presented barriers at that time that demanded that the correct protocols were understood and observed at all times.

Yuri's English was at best mediocre, as was my Russian, but between us, we were able to communicate well enough to get our respective points across without too much difficulty.

Other than the ticketed passengers with boarding passes at Sheremetyevo International Airport, no-one else was allowed past the passport checkpoint on the way to the aircraft, and this included diplomats; but Yuri assisted me, without asking, in escorting the departing Australian Ambassador, John Rowland and his wife and young children, out on to the tarmac and onto their aircraft. Yuri had led the way to the aircraft, but naturally, he could not board it, and nor should I have! An aircraft of foreign nationality is treated as a sovereign part of that country, and therefore, as occurred in this case, by stepping into the British aircraft I had left the Soviet Union and was outside Yuri's jurisdiction! I was completely unaware of my infringement of protocol procedure.

At the time of writing, I continue to work for the Department of Prime Minister & Cabinet, and Department of Foreign Affairs and Trade (DFAT) as a protocol officer in Brisbane, and that experience with boarding the BOAC aircraft in Moscow has served me well. When I now say farewell to a departing royal, foreign president, prime minister, or foreign minister, I ensure that neither I nor any other official accompanying me does not put a foot onto the departing aircraft.

After ensuring the ambassador and his family were settled, and having said my farewells, I moved to the aircraft door and waved to Yuri who was standing at the bottom of the boarding steps on the tarmac. I shouted something asinine (in Russian) like, 'Good-bye Yuri, see you in London!' He was not smiling! Aussie humour was not understood or appreciated. I quickly left the aircraft and joined him for the walk back to the terminal.

There was a surprise coming. Yuri ushered me past the entrance leading back into the lounge area, which immediately caused me some concern, especially when we were out of sight of the concourse area. Had I gone too far in putting his trust to the test with my naive performance in boarding the British aircraft? Just prior to rounding the next corner, I heard the sound of what I recognised from my own military service as a group coming to attention with a lot of boots stamping on the ground in unison. At that stage I was becoming even more anxious about Yuri's intentions, he was after all a KGB officer of the Soviet border guards.

We rounded the corner, and there standing at attention with automatic weapons clutched against their chests, in what I assumed was a Soviet "Present Arms" stance, were at least a dozen border guards in a single row. They looked a formidable lot. To say I was extremely concerned at this stage would be putting it mildly! We continued past the line, and into a passageway that led to another entry into the departure lounge.

The only words Yuri spoke after walking past his border guards were 'My men, good?' I got the message, loud and clear. This was his turf, and he had trained and armed men to take care of business.

I had a disturbing incident in Riga, Latvia, while travelling with two American diplomats. I had left my travelling companions to do their own thing, and during the course of the day I had unintentionally lost my surveillance team, or more likely they lost interest in me and pooled their resources onto the two Americans. At least that is what I thought at the time.

I was visiting the city's cathedral that same day and noticed a tour group assembling nearby. I joined them with no problems. Most churches were not places of worship at that time, and there were no pews or other items of furniture or religious artefacts that I could see on display. The cathedral was a place for tourists to visit. It was majestic in its structural appearance, but sadly lacking in purpose.

The tour came to an end, and the group started to follow the guide outside. I should have left with the group but thought it would be easier to leave from an exit on the other side of the cathedral. I had not intended to avoid any possible surveillance. I had earlier planned to visit the old part of the city which would be much easier to reach from that exit. I had only taken a few steps from the rear of the tour group when two solid middle-aged men also detached themselves from the departing tour group, grasped both my arms, and anchored themselves on each side of me. They unceremoniously walked me backwards while I was wedged firmly in between them until we were behind a huge pillar. They turned me around, pushed my face hard against the pillar, and held me there. I waited for the blows, but nothing happened. They released me soon after, and casually walked away. Not a word had been spoken during this encounter, and they did not physically engage with me again. They exited through the side-entrance that I had originally entered.

I finally calmed down and used the same exit from the cathedral as my "escorts". They were standing across the street smoking and chatting, without a glance in my direction. We all got back into step for the remainder of that day as if nothing had happened. A message had been given. 'Behave yourself!'

My first trip to Kyiv early in 1968 was also eventful. Once again, I was accompanied by two officers from the American Embassy. The senior officer was accompanied by his wife. The junior officer was a regular at the poker game evenings. Their primary reason for the visit to Kyiv was to witness one of the most important days on the Ukrainian religious calendar, the Easter service.

There were other items on our agenda before we were to take part in the Easter rituals of the Ukrainian Orthodox Church, which had a submissive relationship with the Russian Orthodox Church. I believe that simply on the basis of unity the Russian followers would have preferred that the Ukrainians had aligned themselves under the banner of the Russian Orthodox Church.

The first day of this Kyiv visit was to be an easy familiarisation tour of the city, and the plan for the junior officer and myself was to tour the catacombs just outside the city. The senior officer and his wife were to visit the planetarium, and then we would meet up later in the afternoon.

Our escort for the day was waiting for us in the foyer of the Dnieper Hotel. They were also being quite obvious in casually deploying behind us as we exited the building. We could only assume that they were definitely letting us know that they would be with us for the duration. Their dark grey suits, white shirts, dark ties, and mid-length black or dark brown overcoats, along with military-style close-cropped haircuts appeared to be the standard dress code for the majority of these KGB operatives in Kyiv as well as in Moscow. They were hard to miss.

While in the catacombs I became separated from my American companion when I veered off into a dark side chamber, and our escort of two at the time went by without noticing me. They were most likely more fixated on the American than me, although we played such asinine games at times to confuse our "escorts". I stayed where I was, to see how long it would take for them to realise I was missing, or if they would even bother coming back for me at all. After only a few seconds I heard hurried footsteps returning, and one of their number nonchalantly fell in behind me as I re-emerged into the main corridor pretending not to notice his obvious presence.

You can only spend so much time lingering in the tunnels of the catacombs. The smothering effect of our escorts was also intrusive and annoying. We decided to return to the hotel. On exiting up into the daylight again we hailed a taxi from a nearby rank and watched our escorts sit patiently in their vehicle, waiting for us to make the next move.

Our taxi driver had obviously been partaking of a few vodkas with like-minded fellow drivers while they were waiting for a fare. He was delighted to hear his passengers were an American and an Australian, and without hesitation, he regaled us with anti-Soviet jokes. My American companion was a fluent Russian speaker having been raised within a migrant White Russian family in the USA, and he thought the jokes were hilarious. Regrettably, I could not understand the jokes. The American was translating, but I was focused only on survival and was hanging on to whatever I could to avoid ending up in the footwell of the vehicle as we sped down several narrow alleys bouncing over chunks of broken and discarded ice on our way back to our hotel.

I had become too occupied to notice that the taxi driver had lost our escorts somewhere along the way. We pulled up with a hard-braking slide outside the entrance to the hotel. Just prior to entering the foyer of the hotel I turned around to see the taxi driver was still laughing as a couple of new faces hauled him unceremoniously out of his taxi and hustled him around the side of the hotel, and out of sight.

In every hotel, usually on the mezzanine or ground floor, was housed the Service Bureau. It was the resting or waiting area used by the surveillance crews operating out of hotels.

The following morning, I called my American travelling companion from my room, and we agreed we should make a booking for lunch at a recommended rustic Ukrainian restaurant. It was generally taken for granted that every hotel room we were ever allocated would have a live radio that could be turned down, but never switched off! The Service Bureau, therefore, had overheard our discussed plans for the day and would have been well prepared long before we had even exited our hotel rooms.

As we left the breakfast dining area and were passing the office of the Service Bureau on our way to the front desk, we heard a female voice mentioning our names. We stopped to listen to what may follow. The woman, at a desk just inside the Service Bureau, and with her back to us, was relaying our proposed movements for the day, including the lunch stop. The American, I thought unwisely, stepped up to the office entrance, and said, 'Thank you very much' in Russian and quickly exited to rejoin me. She would not have been amused by the American's remarks.

The planetarium, high up on the banks of the Dnieper River was extremely interesting, and I thought it was well worth another trip when I next visited Kyiv. Our tight schedule had us out the door within an hour, and into the city again. We also had the restaurant booking for lunch that we could not be late for.

Our lunch had been a disappointment, but not so for our escorts nearby who were ordering up big-time on both food and liquid refreshments. They appeared quite annoyed when we suddenly stood and left after settling our account. Our escorts appeared to be treating the day's work as a fun day out, a game, with a nice meal, on the office.

We all boarded the electric train together for the return to the Dnieper Hotel. The American and I had already discussed a strategy that we were about to implement, having no doubt been emboldened after a couple of Ukrainian beers at lunch. The surveillance group had split into teams of two on the train, and had manned doors further to our left, and to our right. We lined up behind other passengers in the middle of the carriage as the train approached the station we were to exit on. Both their teams stepped onto the platform and headed towards the exit at the end of the platform while we held back, and politely continued to encourage other passengers to step in front of us to exit the train. We then sat down again as the doors slammed shut. The Ukrainian/Russian foursome were left standing on the platform and stared at us as our carriage moved past them and on to the next station. The American seemed quite pleased with himself, and I thought he may have tried this manoeuvre previously. If the high-five slapping of another's hand was in vogue at that time, we would have been enjoying that moment.

The train had been so fast, and the distance so great, that our lunchtime "escorts" could not possibly have had another team dispatched in time for our arrival at the next station, but they must have anticipated our pathetic antics in employing such a tactic. They were well ahead of the game, and waiting for us, or perhaps this was their standard "Plan B" routine! We were encircled by four new faces when we reached street level and separated.

The American received a couple of body pushes, possibly in an attempt to unsettle him. I was almost ignored except for a mild elbow nudge, and a body block to assist in separating me from the American. It was not a situation where you started to laugh! They certainly appeared threatening. I was concerned because I was unable to ascertain what was going to happen next. We would have to take what was coming for being so stupid in playing a game that we should have anticipated would result in retribution of some sort.

The surveillance crew had not said a word during this unfriendly pantomime, and casually walked back to their car, sat, and waited, which was a huge relief.

I found my fellow traveller only a few metres away, around a corner of the station's exit gate, sitting on a bench in the small park area. He did not look perturbed at all. He took time out to tell me how lucky we were to get off so lightly and commenced to elaborate by telling me the story of two British Assistant Military Attachés, who had tried a similar caper in their car. They had been pulled over by two KGB cars in Moscow that they had eluded earlier, and were dragged from their vehicle, beaten severely, and left on the ground. The KGB officers then got back in their vehicles and waited for the Brits to recover and fall back into formation all the way back to the British Embassy!

We walked to a taxi parked nearby with a driver holding its door open for us. The American raised his eyes to indicate that this was most likely a vehicle belonging to our escort. We sat quietly all the way back to the hotel.

The tour of the catacombs in Kyiv, including our lunch and train surveillance experiences, was a precursor for the Ukrainian Orthodox Easter service to follow that evening.

The Ukrainian people had a close religious bind with their Church prior to the revolution of 1917, and there was a general belief that there was still a substantial underground following of believers waiting for the day their Church would surface again, without the shadow of the Russian Orthodox Church hanging over them.

My travelling companions had mentioned on the way to Kyiv that there were so many questions to be answered on just what the general health of the Church was, and the level of involvement of its Ukrainian followers during that period. Did distance from the seat of power in Moscow dilute control over the Church? How did the once religious Orthodox Ukrainians cope with Moscow's control over their Church? Were the Ukrainian people in the main supplicants waiting for the clouds of communism to clear, or at least start to fade away? It was quite possible that so much of the Ukrainian psyche could be in conflict with the Soviet system of rule and could therefore be exploited.

We had decided to meet at the Dneiper Hotel's restaurant early so we could enjoy our dinner together prior to what could be a busy evening to follow. Our "escorts" entered soon after and sat nearby. They pretended, overtly, to ignore us, and this made the situation quite ludicrous. The senior American Embassy officer suggested the performance was simply to put us on notice.

During the latter stages of dinner, I could not stand the overt nonsense of the surveillance crew any longer so I approached their table and presented each of them with a kangaroo pin, by personally placing the pins in one of their coat lapels. They were delighted, and the fellow we had earlier decided was their chief half nodded with a smile. I felt as though I had at least won the first round of the evening. The Americans just sat with opened mouths, with Junior shaking his head. The smiles and chuckles from the Soviet side were unexpected.

I did the same thing with the kangaroo pins a couple of times during that posting. The pins ensured we had no problem later in the evening spotting the people in the crowd who were keeping an eye on us.

We set off with our entourage in tow an hour or so before the service was due to start. Our taxi dropped us some distance from the cathedral. There were rows of buses spilling out thousands of eager recruits from factories and farms in and around Kyiv who were gathering together in groups with varying printed placards which were held high above their heads. The sea of people slowly walked in the same direction as us and appeared to be out for some serious entertainment.

The Orthodox followers, many of whom waited near the cathedral entrance, were already being jostled and ridiculed by the crowd. We started to push our way towards the entrance as the time for the commencement of the service grew closer, and the crowds grew thicker and quieter.

The normal procedure on such an occasion was for several clergy, and other religious attendees carrying incense dispensers and large ornate wooden crosses to exit the front door chanting or singing a hymn, and then proceed around the building three times. Once the circuits had been completed, the procession of the faithful would re-enter the church. That was the plan, but sometimes plans come unstuck. We finally made it to the wall of the cathedral, and close to the entrance on the side, the clergy would exit. We would have by then theoretically blended into the ranks of the believers. However, seemingly at a given signal, the outer ring of the rent-a-crowd commenced to surge and continued to press the hopeful churchgoers and ourselves up against the walls of the church. It was a human wave that rippled back and forth pressing harder each time until several people including the senior American's wife cried out and appeared in some distress. The surveillance crew that had initially surrounded us on the way in swung into action immediately. They formed a flying wedge with us in the centre and aggressively pushed their way out into a clearing. They walked away as soon as we were clear.

We decided that the night's exercise was over because the clergy could not even exit the front door to start the ritual. The wife of the American Embassy officer had also become increasingly unsteady on her feet afterwards. She showed us her coat. It had most of the buttons torn off in the crush! The rent-a-crowd that had been bussed in for the occasion had won!

We had a midnight train to catch back to Moscow and had to make sure we had time to collect our bags from the hotel and get to the train station.

An unusual closing episode worth mentioning on this visit to Kyiv took place as we were pulling out of the railway station. I dropped my travel bag off in my compartment but had not taken off my winter gear. My fellow travellers were busy getting themselves organised for the overnight journey, so I walked through to the last carriage and stood out on the small open platform at the rear of the last carriage to have a cigarette and reflect on the activities experienced in Kyiv.

I had the platform all to myself, and just as the train began to slowly move away from the station, I noticed a small group of our "escorts" who had been accompanying us over the previous days, identified by dress rather than features, standing in the semi-darkness. A solitary figure under the last of the platform lights saluted, at least I thought it was a salute! I did not see the finger! It took a moment to react to this totally unexpected farewell from Kyiv station. I returned the salute. That was one of the most theatrical moments that I had experienced from that organisation during the entirety of that posting. These were probably Ukrainians after all, and perhaps not tied so tightly to the dogmatic Soviet dictates and disciplines of the distant Kremlin.

One of the more interesting narcotics cases I had was when a group of eight "mules" were apprehended by the Soviet border guards in 1969. We received a call from the Soviet Ministry of Foreign Affairs to advise that an Australian had been among those arrested at Moscow's Sheremetyevo Airport. The eight mules had flown in from Bangkok on two separate airlines and were waiting in the transit area for a connecting Alitalia flight to Rome when they were apprehended. There were no Brits or citizens from other

Commonwealth countries among the group, but there was an American.

I contacted the American Embassy to see if their duty consular officer would accompany me to a holding room at the airport transit area. The officer I was connected to said he was too busy, but someone else may be going out later in the day! I was extremely disappointed with that reply, but I discovered later that drug bosses in France and America had put a price on the head of this former undercover DEA officer. He had been keeping a low profile at the US Embassy using the cover of an American vice-consul, but he could not get involved in any of the consular workloads! He simply hung out at the Marine House Bar and chatted up the female staff members!

I approached the border guard commander on duty at the airport and asked if he could provide any information on what technology or techniques had been used so successfully in discovering the heroin among the different nationalities apprehended, that is, electronic devices, informants, or dogs. Narcotics reporting also fell within my area of responsibility.

The commander advised that it was a very simple discovery. One of his officers had made a random selection of one of the passengers and invited him to the inspection area of the transit lounge, where he asked the passenger to empty his bag. Once empty, the inspecting officer picked up the bag to move it to the side and found it was still unusually heavy. A search of the sealed bottom section was made and a kilogram of heroin was discovered.

Another of the assisting border guard officers on duty had noticed that several other transiting passengers seated around the transit lounge area had the same type and colour of bags and reported this to his superior. The tops were all green, and the bottom sections were red. Several officers were deployed to quietly round up the other transiting passengers with the specific green and red carry-on bags and take them to separate interview rooms. As simple as that!

The story given by those apprehended on such occasions was usually the same. The mule is befriended in a bar, hotel foyer, or some other place in Bangkok, and once it became known that he or she was booked on a flight, and in this particular case to Rome, the approach would be made with the story that a friend had left his bag behind. The passenger would then be asked if the bag could be delivered to the friend who would ensure he or she would be looked after while in Rome.

Another noteworthy and demanding consular case occurred towards the end of my first posting to Moscow when we received a telephone call from the Soviet Foreign Ministry to advise that a tourist bus carrying several Australians and other nationalities had been involved in an horrific accident, and the surviving casualties were in the process of being taken to a nearby village medical clinic near the Polish border, over 1000 km from Moscow. The only information forthcoming from the ministry at that time was that several Australians had been injured. I had to go, because the consul (my boss) was away in Helsinki with his wife who was having a baby.

I briefed the ambassador on the little information we had been given by the Foreign Ministry. He agreed that I should go, and quickly. The ambassador told me to take his Head of Mission vehicle. I requested, and the ambassador agreed, that Yuri Mishin should be my driver, rather than his own driver who was as dry as a burned piece of toast and would be of little assistance other than to drive.

I regarded Yuri as the best of the drivers we employed. I had watched him on several occasions handle his comrades with quiet authority, and this would be a necessary attribute in avoiding lengthy delays at militia checkpoints should we be pulled over for questioning by militia who may not have received advance notification from UPDK that we had to travel urgently. There would also be the officials at the village clinic to contend with; stops in Minsk at a hotel and the security overnight of our vehicle; knowledge of refuelling locations; and other logistical and unforeseen circumstances that would require Yuri's assistance. We were to leave early the next morning.

An immediate concern expressed by the ambassador was in my not having another officer available to accompany me, particularly as this journey could entail at least two nights' stay away from Moscow. Official procedures for all of us travelling away overnight dictated that we should be accompanied by our wives, another officer from our embassy, or someone from one of the friendly countries. Judith could not accompany me because we had a very young baby and the early stages of winter had set in.

Consular officers from other countries that had casualties were eventually sent from their missions in Warsaw, which was a lot closer to the crash site. Diplomatic and therefore consular responsibility for Poland still fell under our embassy in Moscow's area of responsibility.

Both Judith and I called our friends in the British, Canadian, and American Embassies, and gathered together bags of cosmetics, shaving gear, toilet paper, two cases of beer, several bottles of spirits, a variety of packaged food and anything else our little group of donators thought would be required by the injured tourists.

I could not foresee any possibility on such a mission for anything untoward to occur, even though I knew Yuri was a KGB major. I had seen his official KGB ID red card previously when he assisted me by producing it for a difficult restaurant receptionist I had been attempting to communicate with. The receptionist's acknowledgement of Yuri included his rank, and therefore his standing in the embassy's Soviet staff hierarchy.

We left early the next morning and overnighted in Minsk, the capital of Belarus. We arrived at the village clinic close to midday the next day. My first duty was to call on the Clinic Administrator to establish details on any deceased and injured. Fortunately, there were no deceased Australians.

While I was with the administrator, Yuri loaded most of our bulky bags, bottles, and the beer onto the lower trays of two gurneys and to reduce speculation and questions he used some of the other items to cover the liquor. We carried the remaining items in a couple of canvas diplomatic bags. That little red card of Yuri's came out with a flourish on a couple of occasions before we were finished that day, and to ensure there were no other problems with clinic staff he remained with the gurneys and bags.

I would have loved to have been able to photograph the look on the faces of the patients as soon as we entered their ward and mentioned I was from the Australian Embassy in Moscow. I had arrived before the consular officers from other nationalities based in Warsaw.

Men and women were packed like sardines in one large room. The small village clinic was struggling to cope with this sudden influx of patients, some of whom were in very bad shape.

I asked the Australians to identify themselves and handed out paper and pens so they could provide me with their names, home addresses, next-of-kin phone numbers, the nature of their injuries, etc. Once that task had been completed, I asked for volunteers among the Australian patients who were able to do so, to assist me in collecting information on the seriously injured Australians and the other foreign nationals so that I could pass this on to their respective embassies in Moscow, and to our consular section at the department in Canberra who would then inform the relatives.

When I had completed the official side of the visit Yuri ushered any medical staff out into the corridor, closed the door and stood guard as I wheeled the gurneys in, and pulled the sheets away. Most of the contents of the bags and cartons were quickly distributed, and the remainder were stuffed under the beds closest to the walls. There was a rush of conversation and a few tears, especially from an elderly couple who appeared to be in worse shape than the rest.

I understood later, as I was leaving, that the tight grips and the tears were more for the fact that one of their own had come all the way from Moscow to assist them, and more importantly that their family and friends could, at last, be made aware of their circumstances. It was not easy leaving, but I felt that we had achieved all we could at that stage, and it would be best for all concerned if I returned to Moscow as quickly as possible to get a full report back to Canberra.

It was moments like this that made me feel I was really doing something worthwhile and truly representing my country abroad. I am reasonably sure that consular officers of any nationality would no doubt identify with this comment.

An extremely sad item of news was offered later as we were preparing to leave the village. One of the clinic's two ambulance crews that had attended the bus accident had been in the process of loading a casualty into an ambulance when a drunken taxi driver came over a hill behind them at excessive speed, killing a nurse and the patient, and severely injuring the ambulance driver. The taxi driver sustained only minor injuries from the crash, but these were further compounded by the beating he received from local police.

We stopped at a nearby truck refuelling station with a café for a meal prior to proceeding on to Minsk for an overnight stay. We had not eaten since an early morning coffee and pastry. The truck stop was very noisy when we entered with most of its customers in full voice singing songs that Yuri advised were local peasant ballads.

One of the merry groups sitting next to us sent a small carafe of vodka to our table as soon as we sat down. Yuri thanked them and told them I was from the Australian Embassy in Moscow and explained the purpose of our visit to their area. Several tables of workers then stood up and raised their glasses to toast us. I had to return the initial toast with my classroom Russian language to the amusement of Yuri.

Yuri had not gone past a sip in reply to the labourer's toast because he had to drive on to Minsk which was still a couple of hours away. We had a meal of boiled meat and potatoes before leaving just in case we had any problems when we arrived in Minsk.

We started out from Minsk early the next day to ensure we would make it back to Moscow before dark, but the single-lane roads were so congested with military and farming vehicles that it took almost twelve hours to cover the remaining 700 km to Moscow.

I continued to be involved in this case for several days after my return to Moscow. The technology of today would have been of considerable and immediate assistance with such cases back then.

It was quite amusing to stand outside the American Embassy during the May Day celebrations, and mix with the people gathered on the *Sadova*, and look up at their embassy's top floors while Soviet military hardware passed by on the way to Red Square for the May Day parade. Figure 10 below shows a photo of this event. Curtains moved aside on the top floor just enough for a camera to make an appearance. Once the photos had been taken, the camera quickly disappeared behind the curtains again until the next piece of military equipment that may be of interest came into sight. The Soviets had to be aware of what was happening. That only added to the whole comedic performance.

Figure 10. Missile on way to Red Square for May Day parade, 1968

Our Russian nanny was Adrian's constant companion, and with our approval, she took him home with her sometimes to play with her own children. They attended a Soviet kindergarten with Adrian three days a week. There were no other English-speaking children. The kindergarten adjoined our diplomatic block. Adrian, like most children, absorbed language like a sponge and enjoyed the company of the Russian children his age at the kindergarten.

The care and attention provided in the kindergarten was first class. The children were given hot meals, their own bed for sleep periods, and during winter the staff ensured all children were wearing their felt boots, fur hats, and thick winter coats, scarves, and gloves before they were allowed out for walks or play periods. We observed the children from our apartment windows when they marched out of the nearby building holding each other's hands for walks in the snow and playtime. They looked and walked like a conga line of little penguins bobbing along a path with their headwear just showing above the heaped snow walls.

It became apparent that Adrian's indoctrination had begun while enrolled at the kindergarten. The day I mentioned to him that we would be returning to Australia soon and that he would be meeting his grandma and grandpa for the first time, he attempted to correct me by suggesting that he had two Grand Pa-Pas. One was the Pa-Pa (in Australia), and the other was Pa-Pa Lenin! Yes, it was definitely time to be leaving the USSR behind.

Judith had to be medically evacuated from Moscow back to Australia in early July 1969 and was hospitalised in Sydney for a short period following complications from another miscarriage. Fortunately, her mother had been visiting us at the time and assisted her on the flight home. The department also assisted with her immediate transfer from the flight upon arrival to a hospital in Sydney.

An incident occurred in my final week prior to my departure from Moscow in late August 1969 that would have involved our Soviet hosts. Most western embassy staff were well aware that a specialised group of expert and highly mobile surveillance teams were utilised in especially sensitive operations, such as the entrapment of diplomats, business people, and visitors to the Soviet Union with innovative routines, methods, and equipment. These activities, employed with skill in designated hotels, were usually referred to as "honey trap" operations.

Our counsellor had discussed and warned me of the possibility of such an attempt. I was therefore prepared for any eventuality. My replacement and his wife had arrived in Moscow and had settled into our apartment. The embassy had requested UPDK book me into a hotel and the one allocated was the National Hotel. The knock on the door of my hotel room, and the seduction attempt never happened. However, the Soviets had planned another caper that we had not envisaged or prepared for.

The move to compromise me was made by someone I had considered a friendly airline representative. I will not mention the name or nationality of the airline. I only had a few more days to go before I was to return to Australia.

I was invited to one of my last farewell dinners at the apartment of the airline representative and mentioned that I no longer had transport, but he arranged to pick me up from the hotel and also confirmed that he would return me to the hotel after dinner. I had been told that there would only be his wife, himself, and myself for a quiet and early dinner, which appealed to me. To my surprise, two uniformed attractive female flight attendants were also guests that evening.

After dinner, my host said he would drive me back to the hotel after he had dropped the flight attendants off at their hotel, but instead he drove us all to the apartment of a military officer of his own nationality, who he said was away on holidays. I asked what was happening, and how long would we be. There was no reply other than to request that we all get out of the car and follow him into the apartment because he had to locate an item in the apartment for his friend, to have it repaired. He added that it may take a few minutes to find it. No search for the item was made. The flight attendants and I were shown directly into the lounge area. Drinks appeared, music was turned on, and the airline manager started to dance with one of the flight attendants. I was encouraged to do the same. I sat with my drink and felt very uneasy. Moscow being what Moscow was, the thought of it being a blatant attempt at entrapment won over.

The situation seemed quite ridiculous with the airline fellow trying too hard to promote a party. I put my drink down, stood, and suggested that I had to leave, because I was extremely tired, and had a busy day ahead of me. I was again encouraged to relax and stay for a little while longer. I remained standing and stated my sentiment to leave once again, but more forcibly, suggesting I did not wish to put a dampener on the evening so I was going to call one of our embassy officers who had an apartment in the same block, and ask him to give me a lift back to the hotel. We all left the apartment without another word, or a search for that item that had to be repaired, and with a continued and strained silence he dropped his female guests not far from the Central Post Office.

I cannot recall any worthwhile conversation while on the way to the National Hotel to drop me off. I reported the event to the counsellor the next morning and provided a written report for the embassy's records.

The last days just flew by after the honey trap episode. I completed the arrangements for my return to Australia, and the handover routine with my replacement.

This matter would be raised again five years later when I was on posting to the Consulate-General in Chicago and had been asked to fly to Washington to have a chat with the ambassador prior to my returning to Moscow on another two-year posting.

13

Moscow to Santiago de Chile

1969–1972

A fellow officer based in Beijing had arranged for me to stay with him for a couple of days on my way home to Australia, but a severe earthquake hit two weeks before my departure in August 1969, and the Beijing staff including Ambassador Stephen Fitzgerald had to leave the unsafe embassy building, and camp outside in the grounds of the compound. There would be no visit to Beijing.

I had also received an invitation from a good friend and fellow officer, Graham Noonan, at our embassy in Teheran, and he encouraged me to visit. I accepted Graham's most kind invitation and had a really interesting three days in Iran.

The Shah of Iran, Mohammad Reza Pahlavi, referred to by some as the Emperor was still in power and would remain so until his exile in January 1979. He was the last Shah of Iran.

We rode up into the mountains on Graham's motorcycle, and around the city of Teheran every day. One tour he took me on was to the Ali Baba bazaar which was filled to overflowing with people, spices, and products the likes of which I had never seen before. I ended up with a couple of

Royal Household Cavalry swords. I declared them to Customs upon arrival in Sydney, and they were confiscated!

My second and last stopover on the way home to Australia was Hong Kong, which was crowded with US troops on leave from Vietnam. I also had time to catch up with another Department of Foreign Affairs (DFA) friend, John Osbourne, who was on posting as consul in Hong Kong.

For an Australian who has been away from home for a considerable time there is nothing so uplifting to one's national pride as flying over Sydney Harbour, the bridge, and the Opera House prior to landing on home soil. Peter Allen had not yet released his emotional song *I still call Australia home*, but it cuts to similar heart strings. Judith had recovered by the time I arrived back home and was waiting at Sydney's Mascot Airport with the in-laws. We were quickly on our way to Wollongong for a long-awaited break away from anything to do with overseas government service for at least a week before commencing language training which had been arranged for me at the School of Languages, University of New South Wales. I had my own tutor, which was great because it meant that I could drive to and from the campus every day from Wollongong, and stay with Judith, Adrian, and the in-laws, rather than be tutored and accommodated at a hostel by myself in Canberra.

Language study, pre-posting briefings, and the reading of the Post Report were completed along with the obligatory round of health checks, and injections. Our personal effects were packed and uplifted, and passports and airline tickets were in hand.

George and Alma must have been very patient and capable of great love and forgiveness for their first grandson, Adrian, after his many attempts as a two-year-old, to destroy their home during this brief interlude before leaving for Santiago.

An unappreciated, but eventually forgiven, event occurred early on the day that had been set aside for our farewell BBQ lunch with family and friends. The lunch would be an early family Christmas get-together, because we would be away in Chile. Adrian had opened one present, a Matchbox fire engine, and forgetting everything else he ran around the house until finally he dropped it into the main bathroom toilet while attempting to fill the fire engine with water and flushed it! It took a couple of plumbers, a bricklayer, and a lot of money to put the house back in order before family and friends arrived for the Christmas lunch. I think the in-laws must have been relieved when we left for Santiago a couple of days later.

I had very little knowledge of Santiago, and what I did read led me to believe that it was looking like a pretty weird place to be spending the next three years. Geographically it presented as a narrow strip on the map approximately 90 km wide and 4300 km long with the Andes mountains stretching along the length of the country separating Chile from Argentina.

Another item relating to Chile that I found strange related

to the uniforms of the Chilean Armed Forces. The naval uniforms were based on the British Navy; the Air Force uniform was based on the USAF; and the Army uniform, including the helmets, were exactly like the WW2 German uniform. The Army had even adopted the German goosestep parade marching style. Very strange indeed.

We had two stopovers on the way to Santiago. The first stop was Hawaii, and although we had a booking for a one-bedroom apartment at the Illikai Resort, we were upgraded at no additional cost to a penthouse apartment. The General Manager was an Australian! This was a blessing, because we discovered Adrian had contracted mumps soon after arriving in Honolulu, and we had to stay on for several days longer while he was being treated and was well enough to travel again. The next stop was Mexico City for a day stopover. Then it was a nonstop flight to Santiago.

The flight from Mexico City to Santiago was quite spectacular as it tracked along the Andes mountains most of the way. The daytime flight provided time to gaze at the snow-capped Andes and ponder what may lay ahead of us over the next three years. In my wildest dreams, I could not possibly have conjured up the future events that we would experience and endure in Chile.

14

The Australian Embassy Santiago de Chile

1969–1972

We arrived in Santiago in mid-December 1969 with Adrian who was now almost two-and-a-half years old. We had been booked into the Carrera Hotel, opposite the Presidential Palace on the Plaza de Armas. We discovered on our first night in the capital that Chile is situated on active tectonic plates and is often rocked by earthquakes. Adrian thought it was fun watching the glass of water on the bedside table bouncing about before falling to the floor. Once the shaking had eased, I looked out into the corridor to see if there was any emergency routine or evacuation in play, but it was all business as usual.

We got used to the tremors after a while and would rarely even notice any movement or swaying unless the tremors were announced by the Chilean staff running past my office. They appeared to be more conscious and concerned with the tremors than we were.

Two officers had been sent to Santiago to conduct the initial opening of the embassy. The officer I replaced left a couple of days after our arrival, and Cavan Hogue, our First Secretary, who was acting as the Australian Government's official representative in the absence of an ambassador, left a month or so later when he was replaced by Ian James, another First Secretary who had arrived from his last post in Bangkok. The ambassador was not due to arrive for another few weeks or months. He had been ambassador to Cambodia. We continued to operate our "embassy" out of the Carrera Hotel for some time.

The first few weeks kept us busy finding a house to live in and clearing our container of personal effects with Customs from the seaport at Valparaiso. Chilean Customs at that time had a notorious reputation in that they usually took for themselves at least twenty to twenty-five per cent of what you brought in. That was part of the local folklore. They were a little more circumspect with most foreign diplomatic staff's personal effects. However, a hole had been smashed in the side of our wooden container and we were lucky to just lose a few items that could be easily replaced.

There were occasional exceptions to the perceived rule of "hands off" of a diplomat's shipment by Customs personnel and others involved in the shipping of the consignment. For example, after a few months at the post, I had ordered one hundred cases of Swan Gold lager from the Swan Brewery in Western Australia for official entertaining purposes. Customs in Santiago advised that only eighty cases arrived!

I first became aware of what must have kept the crew

happy on whatever ship brought the beer to Chile, and perhaps the Chilean Customs Service upon arrival in Chile, when I poured a beer for a Canadian Embassy officer after a gruelling afternoon of tennis and he complained of it being flat. He also suggested that the smell and the taste were also not quite what he was expecting after my enthusiastic and patriotic pitch of Swan Lager being one of the best beers in the world! I was asked to take a sip to establish that he was not being fussy. I only needed to smell the liquid to identify it as human urine, or to put it more plainly, piss! No tasting necessary.

The Canadian took off for the toilet, but his wife was using it, and with only one toilet in the house he had to make a dash outside for a mouth rinse job with the garden hose. I had to live with the bad beer jokes every time I came across the Canadian or any of his colleagues.

The Swan Lager had obviously been consumed somewhere along the freight line from Western Australia to Chile or at Customs. The bottle was then refilled with the end product as described above. The gold foil and caps were replaced and repacked back into the carton for delivery to the Australian Consul, me, to entertain guests on behalf of the Australian Government! Suffice it to say that it became an anxious routine for quite a while when someone asked for a beer at our place. I was not upset when we finally ran out and reverted to the local brew.

Our next task was to order a Ford from New York and

have it shipped down to Chile. The Ford, a Mach 1 Mustang, became our vehicle with diplomatic plates. We had earlier bought a Fiat 500 which had regular Chilean plates. We used the little Fiat a lot more than the conspicuous Ford so no-one would identify us as belonging to a diplomatic mission during the periods of political turmoil, assassinations, curfews, and riots that occurred a few months after our arrival in Santiago.

We spent several weeks living in the Carrera Hotel, while Judith continued to search for accommodation. She finally found a fully furnished house we could call home for the next three years at 88 Malaga, north-east of the city with the snow-capped Andes as a backdrop. We later discovered that a Soviet Embassy First Secretary had moved into 888 Malaga! He never received any mail delivered to our address, and no doubt if ever there was any of ours delivered to him it never made it back to us. Such was life!

Judith enrolled Adrian in the Little Prince kindergarten soon after settling in. Unfortunately, he was not enrolled there very long. The headmistress invited us both to a meeting a few months after his enrolment, during which she advised she wanted to discuss the reason for the expulsion of our almost three-year-old son.

Adrian and Juan, his three-year-old Chilean friend, had become separated from their group while on a kindergarten-sponsored trip to a chicken farm. They were eventually discovered in the large chicken coop.

The chickens were on the loose and running in every

direction after being chased out of the coop by the two little delinquents. Many of the escaping chickens had tried to make a dash for freedom across a busy major road. Unfortunately, not all made it to the other side, which brings to mind the question often asked, "Why did the chicken cross the road?"

The screeching of cars braking had drawn a small crowd to the area, and they joined in the chase of the fleeing chickens. Very few of the fowls survived or were returned. I had listened to those details while the headmistress was explaining her case for the expulsion of Adrian.

The headmistress was in full voice when I had to apologise between intermittent coughs and chuckles and abruptly left the headmistress and Judith. I sat on a bench outside the building until I could regain control. My laughter had reached such a level that I was incapable of speech, and tears were running down my face.

That day did not end well at all. Judith had received a scolding from the head of the kindergarten alone. I had embarrassed Judith and upset the headmistress with my lack of understanding of the seriousness of what had occurred with our son's role in the "chicken breakout". On the plus side, I still had a happy little three-year-old to talk to, but on the minus side, I had to make a considerable cash payment to the kindergarten who hopefully passed it on to the chicken farm. The next task on our list was to employ a nanny for our son. He had been expelled from the only kindergarten anywhere near where we were living.

One of the American Embassy officers with whom I had travelled in Kyiv and played poker with at the US Embassy in Moscow had also been posted to Chile a month or so before we arrived. The regular Thursday night poker game at the American Embassy was alive and well in Santiago, as it was at many of their overseas posts around the world.

Life in Santiago was relatively stable when we arrived in late 1969, but there were undertones of growing dissent and division that were becoming more vocal and disruptive as the general election of 4 September 1970 grew closer.

Salvador Allende Gossens' ascension to the Presidency of Chile as head of the Popular Unity Coalition was not expected or received well by his Conservative opposition, in particular the National Party, who feared he would usher in a pro-Soviet communist government. Allende and his party were elected with 36.6 per cent of the votes. It was a three-way election result with the Conservative candidate Jorge Alessandri and the Christian Democrat Radomiro Tomic splitting the other 63.4 per cent of the votes. Allende was inaugurated on 3 November 1970.

There should not have been any expression of surprise from the Nationals, because Allende campaigned quite openly on a Marxist-Socialist platform. His major pre-election promises and post-election follow-up included the introduction of that ideology to Chile. He had promised farm and land takeovers for the farmworkers, and the nationalisation of many companies, in particular the copper mines of northern

Chile. These, and other such announcements displeased the banking, industrial, commercial entities, and especially the many American business interests in Chile at the time.

Henry Kissinger, the US Secretary of State under then President Richard Nixon may have seriously doubted the ability of the Chileans to fully understand the importance of the issues facing them at that time and be responsible enough to avoid letting the country turn into another communist state.

Chilean non-indigenous land owners and foreign business executives were lining up outside my office from daybreak to sundown seeking visas to leave the country. We had to finally request extra assistance from Australia for immigration officers to be sent as quickly as possible to assist with the processing of the long lines of people fleeing the country. Others were applying for visas as a "Plan B" and were not making final arrangements to leave until, or in case, a worst-case scenario evolved.

The situation certainly evolved, and quickly. It was not long after the Allende government came to power that riots in the streets of the city centre increased and became the norm. As soon as the noise level in the street below our offices started to rise, we ensured that all windows were closed as the tear gas from the street fighting below would waft into and through the embassy, resulting in our mass evacuations of the building. Gas masks were supplied to the embassy sometime after I had left Santiago.

Early reports started coming in about landowners being

shot, injured or thrown off their properties, and of foreign-owned business offices being raided, looted and burned.

I had been returning to the embassy on foot one afternoon when a running battle between students and Carabineros or paramilitary police surged up from the plaza in my direction with tear gas and water cannons following those involved in the riot. It was pandemonium. I took shelter in the doorway of a closed office entrance. Several students had the same idea and were followed by gas-masked and helmeted Carabineros with shields in one hand and raised batons in the other. The students took the brunt of the attack. I only received a couple of partial blows that were shared with the students. I could not move, see, or say anything because of the tear gas. I covered my head and crouched as low as I could to lessen the chance of more blows and waited for the crowd of Carabineros and rioters to move on.

I was told later by a Chilean ministry official that if I had held my diplomatic identity card up for the Carabineros to see there would have been no problems. That was the last thing I thought of during the melee in the street, and I seriously doubted whether the Carabineros would have taken any notice of a card being waved in the air by a cowering male in the midst of protesting students.

The water cannons used were extremely effective for post-mop-up operations by the Carabineros. They mixed green dye with the water, and simply drove around for a couple of days later picking up anyone with green hair or skin. Some people referred to this as the "Martian hunt". Fortunately, I had not been hit by the water cannons.

I had an appointment that I had to keep at an official luncheon during this period of street rioting and had waited for several minutes for the smoke and tear gas outside our building to ease. An embassy vehicle was waiting with my driver, a former Carabinero, frantically waving at me to get in the car. A tear gas grenade came bouncing down the street, and hit underneath the back of the vehicle, immediately spilling out and encompassing the entire vehicle just as I opened the door. I received a good lungful, and do not remember much after that, other than the driver dragging me into the rear seat.

I do recall being thrown around in the vehicle with the horn blaring nonstop as the driver drove through the crowded streets. He stopped several blocks away and pulled me out onto the footpath. I was having trouble breathing, and I was dry-retching uncontrollably. People gathered around and tried to assist. As soon as I had settled down and could breathe normally again the driver drove me straight home for a shower, a change of clothes, and a lot of cool water. I never made it to the luncheon.

Maria, our first maid, was an attractive blonde with a not-so-pleasant disposition and a tendency to pocket any small amounts of money left lying around. She was not only light-fingered, but as we would soon discover, she was also extremely generous in entertaining military guests in her accommodation at the back of the house late at night or when we were out.

Maria's considerable skills and range of entertainment came to light one evening when we had several guests to dinner. I had a British Embassy officer barking in my ear nonstop about the ongoing political demise of the country. He had asked for a gin and tonic before he had even reached the rest of the guests sitting in the garden area. I thought I would assist in getting him on his way earlier than he may have anticipated by pouring a very liberal gin with only a little tonic.

I was about to continue on our way out to the garden area when the Brit had a sip and asked if he could have a little more gin! No problem, I poured half a glass of gin with only a dash of tonic to ensure his request was met and waited for him to taste it. He did, and he grimaced. He asked for the brand of gin because he could not taste it. I poured a small amount into a glass to taste. I hated gin and had not even tasted it since my pre-wedding bachelor's party five years previously. I immediately realised this was no laughing matter — it was 100 per cent water!

I had already experienced enough friendly and some not-so-friendly abuse about my Swan Lager beer which some would-be Canadian comedians referred to as "Aussie Piss". Now I would have to suffer through another barrage of jokes and insults by the British after serving up water and trying to pass it off as gin! I blamed the Customs officers at the port. I was getting good at that.

I was successful in distracting the Brit from entertaining the other guests with his story of a no-gin gin and tonic by introducing him to a table with a recent arrival at our embassy who had a party trick he had performed at a previous dinner. He did not disappoint. Shortly after, I could hear voices being raised, and knew he would be accomplishing his unique talent of drinking the last of the wine in his glass, and then eating the glass! No further comment necessary. We discovered soon after the watery gin episode that Maria had been entertaining the Chilean soldiers who had been guarding the telephone company next door to us. They came over the wall at the back of the house where the maid's quarters were and had a great time with the help of Maria and our liquor supplies, including, I hope, some of the bottles of our now infamous "Aussie Piss".

Late one evening, I heard hesitant footsteps moving along the passageway past Adrian's room and heading towards ours. I had a pump-action shotgun under the bed. I injected a shell as noisily as possible in the darkness, while at the same time shouting a warning to the intruder. The footsteps stopped for a brief moment, and then picked up pace to a run out of the house with me shouting as loud as I could as he disappeared over the high brick wall into the neighbouring telephone company's property. The intruder had obviously not been given clear instructions on where Maria's accommodation was. I called the local Carabinero station to report on the intrusion into the house. A lieutenant and two of his men did not arrive until early the next morning, because there was a curfew. Anyone on the streets after 1 am and before 6 am would be shot. I explained what had happened and asked what would have happened if I had shot at the intruder and hit him. 'No problem' was the reply, and he added that if anything like that did happen in future, I was to drag him back inside the property, and if he was dead, I was to take off my watch, and put it in his hand. I posed another question for the lieutenant, 'What if the man was still alive?' The reply was, 'Again, no problem, drag him back inside your property, shoot him again, this time in the head to make sure he is dead, follow the same routine with your watch, and then you should call me'.

A fellow officer at the embassy advised that he had a similar experience after he had disturbed an intruder. The Carabinero on his case simply said, 'Shoot him, no questions asked'.

Maria was sent on her way soon after her free bar and entertainment facility were discovered. Our new maid, Graciela, a middle-aged indigenous Mapuche woman with few teeth but a pleasant disposition, was welcomed to our home. Graciela was briefed on the reason for Maria's leaving, which ensured there were no more strays coming over our wall.

Graciela was a constant companion for Adrian. She became more of a nanny than a maid, because of the demands of so many invitations to official dinners, national day events at other embassies, and cocktail parties, that had to be attended.

We almost dismissed Graciela when we discovered the reason why women walking their children along our quiet, wide, and leafy street would cross over to the other side of the road or walk faster past our house. Graciela had no English language at all and had been teaching Adrian what we thought was the Spanish language as taught in Santiago's schools. That was only part of the tuition from Graciela. Her forte included a rather more explicit and blasphemous range of the Spanish vocabulary that Adrian used innocently when calling out to those unfortunate passers-by with young children who were about to be initiated with his uncouth greetings.

We had been completely unaware of what was happening until a Chilean mother living a couple of houses away dropped by one day to explain that Adrian's well-delivered Spanish content was more suited to the criminal elements!

I cannot recall Judith's reaction to this neighbour's visit. My Spanish was textbook, and therefore I was completely unfamiliar with Adrian's range of expletives. I was tempted to get some tuition from him to expand my own vocabulary for possible future use.

Graciela was safe for the time being but had to endure a lecture from me and promise that her language in front of our son should be more in keeping with his age. Despite her minor shortcomings, she remained with us to the end of our posting in Chile.

One of the consular cases which I found quite different than most occurred on this posting to Santiago. I received a phone call from a judge's office near the university town of Concepción which is approximately 500 km south of the capital. I was advised that an Australian couple had been arrested for the possession of narcotics.

Local law enforcement said they had found backpacks on the bank of a river, and while searching for identification they found two bags of marijuana, some pills, and passports for two Australians. The two young Australian tourists were discovered swimming nearby and were arrested.

The judge said she had interviewed the couple and was impressed with them. She tended to believe their story that the drugs did not belong to them and added that she would not like the matter to become more complicated and that perhaps I could listen to what she had in mind. The plan, which I agreed to, was to separate them and place them in solitary confinement overnight to scare the daylights out of them. The next day they would be driven to our embassy in Santiago and handed over to me for transporting to the airport to catch the earliest flight out of the country.

The alternative was for the judge to have to impose a prison sentence which would have to be served in Concepción. I agreed to the one night's discomfort for the couple. They arrived at the embassy the next day under police escort, but too late in the afternoon to get them on a flight.

I made sure that they understood how lucky they were with the decision made by the judge. They were most thankful and mentioned that they were too scared to mention it while in Concepción, because the two officers who had found the drugs had suggested that a fine of US$100 would ensure they would be clear to go on their way. The couple refused to pay, mainly because by doing so they would be admitting they were guilty. They were convinced, after being arrested, that the two officers involved were the ones who had placed the drugs in their bags.

I called Judith and explained the situation to her. I used their open return tickets to Mexico City to make their bookings for a morning flight out of the country. The couple had to stay in my charge until departure, and therefore we fed and accommodated them in our home overnight.

An unusual duty that I would not normally be involved in while in Santiago or elsewhere, was to join our ambassador, Noel Deschamps, and Sal Djemal an Immigration Second Secretary at a meeting with Chile's LAN Airlines representatives to establish whether it was commercially viable and politically agreeable for both the Australian and Chilean airlines to fly to and from our respective countries via the South Pole. Shortly after that meeting, Sal Djemal and I were sent to Tahiti via Easter Island for a week to continue discussions with Qantas, and to relay the substance of the meeting we had with the LAN Airlines representatives in Santiago.

I have no idea of the final outcome of those discussions because little was achieved in Papeete with no advice on when or if senior representatives of either airline would be arriving. After three of the seven days set aside for the meetings in Tahiti, I had achieved little to nothing, and following discussions with Sal, my travelling companion, I was on a plane heading home to my family in Santiago. I was anxious about Judith. She was in the final stages of her pregnancy, and after her experiences with two miscarriages in Moscow, that to me was of a higher priority than wasting my time in Tahiti eating frog's legs and snails while waiting for Qantas representatives to arrive for talks, most of which had already been confirmed in Santiago.

Judith could not contact me, or her gynaecologist, when she was about to give birth to our second child. We had both been playing golf — together! One of the club's office staff took a call from the hospital, and a golf cart was sent out to collect us when we were halfway through the first nine holes.

We drove ourselves as quickly as possible to the hospital to be with Judith who was in labour and not at all amused by this stage, particularly as we continued to talk about our interrupted game while at her bedside.

During a break in our conversation Judith took her time, in between moments of discomfort with contractions, to berate me because she had to drive herself to the hospital, and the hospital staff spent ages trying to locate her gynaecologist and me of course. She was not happy with either of us.

Upon reflection later, I have to admit she was justified in expressing herself so candidly, and loudly. If I learned anything at all from this experience at the hospital's maternity ward, it was that you should never try to be funny or tell pathetic jokes when your wife is in the throes of delivering her child.

Judith had her second caesarean section to deliver another

red-headed, brown-eyed little boy, Adam, on 2 March 1971. Adrian loved the new addition to the family. We could not have been happier with our expanding little family.

This was an occasion when Graciela excelled and ensured Judith had as easy a recuperation period as was possible after the caesarean.

Judith's mother and her brother, Brian, arrived not long after Adam's birth for a month's stay and were a great help, and excellent company for Judith.

A severe earthquake of magnitude 7.5 hit Santiago on the evening of 9 July 1971. We were both out. Judith had been invited to a function held by embassy wives, and I had been at the home of a US Embassy officer for a poker night.

Minor quakes were a regular occurrence in Chile, but this one was scary. Eighty-three people were killed and 447 were injured, with over forty thousand left homeless.

The poker group had just taken a break when the earthquake hit. I stepped out into the backyard and had difficulty standing. The ground was rippling, and it sounded like an express train was roaring underneath my feet. No-one said anything at first, but as soon as the quake eased, we ran to our cars and headed for our homes.

There were no house, street, or traffic lights. Debris littered the roads, and at times hindered progress. People in theatres and public buildings panicked and trampled others in their desperate flight out of the buildings to safety. Thousands of people were stranded without electricity, drinking water, or telephone service. Several communities were cut off by landslides that blocked roads and railroads.

Judith had arrived home just before me, and we found Graciela sobbing and terrified with both our sons still outside with other people in the street. Graciela had rushed outside with Adrian in his pyjamas and the baby in his bedclothes. It was July and as in Australia, it was the middle of winter. Graciela refused to return to the house, even though the severity of the aftershocks was easing by then.

We retrieved both children from Graciela and moved as quickly as possible back into the house to tuck Adam into his cot, which we had placed by our bedside. He was asleep within minutes. Adrian was no problem, and we put him into bed with us. The aftershocks continued during the night, and into the early morning.

A couple of days later Adam was coughing and appeared to be in some distress breathing so we called Judith's obstetrician. He recommended that we call a doctor friend of his to make a house call and check on Adam. The GP advised that Adam should be kept at home under supervision rather than be taken to the hospital because he would receive much better treatment at home.

There was to be no apportioning of blame. No-one could have forecast the events of the earthquake. Adam's removal by Graciela from his crib to the relative safety outside the home was the accepted practice when severe tremors or earthquakes hit.

Four days after the quake, while Judith was preparing Adam's bottle and a warm bath, she noticed his cough was becoming more constant and congested. He had a temperature that was not subsiding following the doctor's visit the day before.

Judith decided against his usual morning bath as a precaution, and when she returned with his morning bottle, she found him still and quiet. She thought at first that he had gone back to sleep, but on closer inspection found that he was not breathing, and immediately started mouth-to-mouth resuscitation. Her efforts were not proving successful, so she wrapped him up, and drove as fast as she could to the hospital.

I was at the embassy when I received a call from Judith. She was in shock, crying, and could hardly speak, other than to say 'It's Adam. I am at the hospital. He is not breathing. I had a driver take me to the hospital immediately.'

I ran into the hospital, and down a corridor looking for the reception desk or Judith, and as I passed by a side alcove with a curtain half-drawn, I noticed a little bob of a baby's red hair showing from under a sheet on a gurney. It was rare to see a redhead in Chile. There was not a soul in sight. I stopped and hesitantly lifted the sheet.

I admit to a howl of grief, and the wave of anguish that followed was so overpowering that I could hardly stand. I felt as though every last breath of air in my body had been sucked out of me. I do not remember much about the next few minutes, but I believe I had taken Adam from the gurney and was found sitting on the floor with my back up against a wall crying, and in shock.

One of the emergency doctors must have been told of my finding Adam and came running. They tried for some time to settle me down and finally took Adam from me. I could not believe that he had passed away. He was supposed to have had a cold.

I was told later that I had sworn at the staff and had demanded to know what they had done to him. I think, upon reflection, that my initial finding of Adam alone on a gurney impacted me more with a feeling that he had been deserted and forgotten by the hospital staff. To this day, fifty-plus years later, I cannot avoid extreme sadness, and shortness of breath when I recall finding Adam like that. Writing about losing our son has been especially difficult. Parents are not supposed to outlive their children.

I was taken to the doctor's office and found Judith in worse shape than I was. She had been given a sedative, and thankfully, at least for the staff, I had quietened down and was more receptive in listening to what the hospital's paediatrician had to say. He advised that he had spoken to the GP who had been treating Adam and was told that Adam had developed a bronchial condition after his lengthy exposure outside on the street without adequate clothing during the evening of the earthquake. This had been compounded by the lack of any effective medication available in Santiago, and eventually led to his developing bronchial pneumonia.

The paediatrician was extremely upset and apologised profusely for not being able to do more to save Adam. His body was placed in my arms just prior to leaving the hospital by the paediatrician who apologised profusely again. He added that in his opinion Adam's death may not have occurred had we been living in Australia, North America, Europe, or anywhere else that had the necessary medication and appropriate hospital equipment and facilities to treat him.

The paediatrician's comments and Judith's two miscarriages while on posting to Moscow have added to a sense of guilt that I have continued to bear in having continually exposed my family, in this case our son, to such extremes that would not normally have been experienced had they been at home in Australia.

I did not realise it at the time or during the next six or seven years, but the sense of failing Adam and the family was silently eating away at me until finally, I was unable to efficiently carry out my duties. I would eventually have to seek help.

A group of our fellow embassy officers and their wives, plus Allen and Joan from the US Embassy had gathered when we arrived back at our home and were wonderful in comforting Judith while our First Secretary's wife Megan and I washed and dressed Adam to prepare him for the Funeral Director who would be involved in his transition home to Australia for burial.

Joan and Megan helped both Judith and I through a very emotional and difficult time, and we will always be most grateful to both of them.

Much of what happened that day and the days that followed are a hazy void, and I have had to rely on friends and family to provide and confirm details of that time.

This heartbreaking loss of our son occurred six months after Salvador Allende had been sworn in as the President of Chile and subjected the country to his Marxist brand of socialism. The introduction of Allende's radical ideology, with the considerable assistance of the Cubans, Russians, and others, resulted in chaos in government, riots, and unfortunately for all residing in Chile at that time, the forceful imposition of this doctrine reached the point that food was in short supply, meat of any kind was almost non-existent, supermarket and pharmacy shelves were mostly empty, and any medicine that could have helped Adam was no longer available in the country.

Figure 11. Author and son Adam, Santiago, 1971

I did not ask for permission from the department to take Adam home. I simply informed Ambassador Noel Deschamps that I would draw on my annual leave credits, pay for our own fares, and meet any other costs because we were going to take our son home to Australia. He did not attempt to dissuade me. This was apparently a first-case scenario for our people back in the department. They advised that they allocated funds for our fares, but I may have to later meet all the costs myself because the Public Service regulations known as DROS (Directions Relating to Overseas Service) did not cater for such an event. Prior to departing Santiago for Australia, I was provided with the capsules and syringes required to keep Judith sedated during the long flight home. We were met upon arrival in Sydney by the director of the Sydney office. He also took care of the arrangements for receiving Adam's body and the relevant paperwork when the casket arrived in Sydney a few days later. The department sent flowers and was represented at the funeral in Wollongong by the director. While with us he advised that I should report to the department in Canberra the following week.

During the interview in Canberra, I was asked to give an account of events leading up to, and after, the passing of Adam. I was also advised that the Public Service Board (PSB) had not as yet met to review whether there was to be any assistance provided to us in bringing Adam home to Australia and that I should not expect approval because that would necessitate a change being made to the PSB regulations. Unfortunately,

I lost control listening to the droning indifference and lack of understanding. I told the senior interviewing officer what he, the department, and the PSB could do with their review. I found the impersonal inferences of that discussion very difficult to overcome for some time.

Many years later I read the record of the conversation that we had that day, and on the side panel of the front page in handwriting was the comment, "Knox was a bit Bolshie!" To be fair, further comment in that document also recommended that the department should do everything in its power to ensure that we received every assistance possible.

The department's energetic efforts on our behalf were eventually successful after several meetings, and much discussion and argument with other home-based departments represented at the PSB hearing who were expressing concern about setting a precedent for future cases.

We may serve Australia as its representatives in foreign countries, but in the opinion of some members of the PSB at that time we may not bring our family members home for burial!

During this same meeting, I was asked if I would return to Chile and complete my three-year posting. I agreed, and we flew back to Santiago after a few days of quiet time with in-laws and close friends.

Our Thursday poker night in Santiago was usually held at the same location each week, but one day I received a call to advise of the change in arrangements. The game had been brought forward and rescheduled for that evening. We were all to meet at the home of an American businessperson in Chile. I was unaware of the reason for the change in location and day of the week until I arrived at his home.

I had met our host a few times at previous American Embassy functions, and at poker nights. The other players were there when I arrived. I was taken aside by Allen who explained that our host for the evening had been declared persona non grata. He had been identified, either correctly or incorrectly, by the Chilean government or their foreign cohorts as a CIA operative and had been ordered to leave the country.

The role of my poker-playing friends for the evening had been to ensure that the surveillance team who were parked close to the front of his house would not apprehend or otherwise harass the businessperson. US Embassy personnel and businessmen became targets of surveillance as the Russian presence increased and included the composition of the poker night participants.

I was given the choice of returning home after the normal close for the evening around midnight or remaining for the rest of the game which would continue until dawn. I elected to stay because one of the players in the group suggested that if I left the house alone at midnight, I might receive greater attention from the waiting "goon" squad parked outside, even with the diplomatic plates on my car which would identify me as an Australian diplomat.

The game over the course of the evening was serious enough, but it also had a little fun and distraction thrown into the mix to ensure we all stayed calm, and that adrenaline levels remained within relatively normal limits.

There was no alcohol consumed that evening or into the early morning. We played several hands of poker for most of our host's possessions that he could not take with him. The value of the pots became more expensive as the evening was drawing to a close.

I won a box of golf balls early in the evening, and later I won his golf bag and clubs. Then it was time for the last hand to be played. It was for our host's membership at the exclusive Prince of Wales Country Club, to which even our ambassador did not have a membership. The club membership was usually reserved for Chilean politicians, senior military officers, and CEOs of leading banks, mining and other foreign businesses. I won the club membership too.

I often invited the ambassador for a game of tennis at the club! I doubt whether the Australian Government would ever approve the cost of his membership! I handed the membership over to the embassy for the use of our officers when I was medically evacuated back to Australia the following year.

Dawn was approaching, and it was time to organise ourselves, pack up and leave, but as we were about to exit the front door, I spotted a pair of brown and white golf shoes that had been placed near the door. I asked what size they were, and once again my luck held. The only one who heard or paid attention to my question was the fellow on his way back to the US. The shoes were mine, no charge! No time for anything else other than concentrating on getting out the front door, and to our cars without any problems.

I had elected not to join the escort group. It would not be appropriate for an Australian Consular officer to participate in the farewelling of an American citizen being expelled under persona non grata conditions.

No-one took any notice of me when I walked away from the American party, exited the house and headed for my own car carrying the golf bag, golf shoes, and other items.

The plan was successful. The poker group stayed with the PNG fellow until they saw him board his aircraft and he was on his way home soon after.

We were now at a stage of the Allende regime in which curfews, riots, assassinations, kidnappings, and arrests were no longer a rare event. The Soviet and Cuban advisers had arrived in Santiago in such numbers that the Soviet advisers took over a high school to use as their dormitories. This activity gave cause for the Americans to also increase their numbers on the ground.

We heard that Cuba's president, Fidel Castro, was arriving in Santiago and that there would be a greeting party consisting of the president, ambassadors from several South American and East European countries, military chiefs, politicians, religious leaders, and a long list of other VIPs at the airport to meet and greet him. No-one from the

Australian, British, or American Embassies was invited to this event. My colleague mentioned that this was an event we should be at and suggested that we invite ourselves as members of the media.

I was initially hesitant about joining another of our embassy officers in this escapade, but the bravado of youth finally won.

As we approached the stairs leading up to the media gathering on the first-floor open terrace area, we noted the security officer was a local. We pocketed our Australian Embassy IDs and I produced my Soviet-issued *katoshka*, a red diplomatic identity card from Moscow which had the hammer and sickle emblazoned on the front cover and my photo and every other detail in Russian. I also pointed to a badge that I had affixed to my lapel, and then pointed to the badge on my companion's lapel which also had the same badge with the unsmiling face of Vladimir Ilyich Ulyanov, better known by the alias "Lenin". I spoke to the security man in Russian, and with appropriate gestures, I indicated that we were in a hurry. Fortunately, the man did not understand a word I had spoken and ushered us up the stairs.

The Russians and Cubans were normally heavily involved in all aspects of the president's security, but most of them appeared to be forming up on the lower lever, and with the waiting motorcade.

The media, mostly TV cameras and photographers, were already in position when we arrived and were focused on the aircraft taxiing to the arrival area directly in front of us, and what was unfolding on the tarmac. I did a lot of shooting that day, with a camera, of Castro and the reception party on the tarmac. It was interesting to see who was invited!

Figure 12. Author and Judith at embassy function, Santiago, 1970

Violent events directed at the diplomatic corps in Santiago were becoming more frequent and dangerous. For instance, we had no idea who was responsible for my counterpart at the British Embassy (Harry) receiving a parcel bomb. He had walked down his driveway to check his mail and found a parcel in the middle of the driveway. He picked it up to discover who the sender was. There was none. The lack of any inscription on it made him feel uncomfortable, so he placed it carefully back on the ground and moved quickly away. He only made it a few metres up the driveway when the parcel exploded. Fragments of metal and concrete shrapnel hit him in the back of his legs and backside. Fortunately, he only suffered minor injuries.

We did not spare Harry from several days of jokes and little sympathy in having to stand or lay on his stomach. If it had gone off when it was in his hands it would have been a completely different story.

A curfew was imposed soon after the parcel bomb and an escalation of other events of violence. Everyone had to be off the streets by 1 am, or they would be shot. Abundant stupidity was at the fore with our poker players, including my idiot self, as we waited until the last minute to leave the game for our homes.

Once Harry had recuperated from his wounds, he called to invite Judith and me to join him and his wife in driving over the Andes into Argentina for a couple of days in Mendoza.

The drive over the Andes was trouble-free on the corrugated dirt and rock-strewn roads. The only problem we had was with the Mustang's engine pinging briefly when we were up very high, but it never quit on us.

Relations were strained at that time between the Chileans and the Argentinians, but we were still surprised to find military machine-gun posts greeting us on the Argentinian side. I received a handshake from the ranking officer, once he had spotted our diplomatic plates and inspected our identification papers to establish that we were Australians and Brits.

We enjoyed the break in Mendoza. It was an attractive city, but the people we met appeared distant and cautious until they realised that we were not Chileans. The steaks and the red wine lived up to our expectations. Some of the best in the world.

The Marxist-socialist Chilean government had promised the farmhands of the foreign-owned or managed farms that they could seize the property as their own and follow the Soviet Union's example by operating them as collectives. Unfortunately, the workers had very little to no managerial skills, and the farms rapidly slipped into such decline that they could not be revived.

Animals normally farmed for markets and export were either sold off or slaughtered and eaten by the workers who thought that they no longer had to work the farms, or more likely, had little to no managerial farming skills. Crops were not sown. The wine industry was in better shape than most, but the entire country gradually became a low-echelon third-world economy with inflation soaring. The balance of trade was sorely affected with little to export, everything to import, but with little hard currency or credit to do so.

An American Embassy friend started flying over the Andes to Buenos Aires in Argentina every couple of weeks on business and returned with meat supplies for a couple of his embassy friends. In a rather gracious moment, possibly after watching me salivate over the steaks that appeared at one of his dinners, he offered to fill occasional orders for me also.

Luncheon invitations were a regular feature, but one was certainly more notable. I was invited to a midweek business luncheon by one of the American Embassy's regular poker crew, who I shall refer to as Ben.

Ben had been imbibing heavily of some of the best of Chilean wines that were on offer that particular day, and by the end of the lunch he was becoming quite animated. I had elected to be the designated driver because Judith and I had another function, hosted by our Ambassador Noel Deschamps, to attend that evening.

I suggested to Ben that we should stop at my place and have coffee once the others, mostly Chilean military officers and businesspeople had departed for their siesta break or had returned to their workplaces. He agreed, but after we had arrived at my home, he requested something much stronger to drink.

During the conversation that followed, Ben started to talk about his job as though I had been fully aware of who he and other members of the poker game were employed by. He mentioned that he had a law degree but was doing the work of an accountant. Without any enticement from me, he went on to provide some employment history on our fellow poker players, and others who were not.

Given Ben's state of inebriation I was not surprised at his mentioning his own duties at his embassy, but to name other

American Embassy officers, and their extremely sensitive duties would have been betraying one of the most serious protocols of his government.

I discretely passed details of the gross security breach that disclosed these sensitive details on to people within our own government in the belief that this information would assist our own people to identify and communicate quickly with their people should the need ever arise.

There has been no infringement of Australian security protocols in my mentioning any of the above matter relating to Ben because our prime minister at the time had confirmed in the House of Representatives during question time that Australian intelligence officers were in Santiago. That announcement by the prime minister made headlines in most, if not all Australian major newspapers.

Brisbane's *Courier Mail* of Saturday 4 June 1983 also had an article from Bruce Wilson reporting from Washington, DC on Seymour M. Hersh's book *The Price of Power* and the newspaper's headline read, "Australian spies helped CIA in Chile."

I fell ill soon after Ben's disclosure, and the action I had taken in passing this information to our government. I was subjected to several medical tests while bed-ridden at home in Santiago, and later at the University of Santiago Hospital. As time went by, I just got weaker and weaker with no confirmation on the cause of my ailment.

There was very little medication of any description

available in Chile during that period, and what was prescribed did not make the slightest impact on my condition. The treating doctor and his colleagues were at a loss to decide how to proceed following their exhaustive tests.

I ended up in a private hospital on intravenous drips. I never asked what was in those plastic bags slowly dripping their contents into my body to keep me alive.

Additional medication arrived from our embassy in Mexico City, but the treating doctors suggested that it would be best if I was medically evacuated to Australia for treatment as soon as I had shown sufficient signs of improvement that would allow for the long flight.

Judith had to pack up our personal belongings, sell our vehicles, and take care of all the other matters that had to be completed to get us on our way home quickly. Thankfully, Judith had the help of friends and our embassy staff, because I was completely incapacitated and still connected to a couple of tubes. This time Judith cared for me during my return to Australia. This was not the way I had planned on leaving Chile.

Despite suffering terribly with the loss of our son during this posting, and my own illness, the Chileans, our embassy personnel, and other foreign diplomatic representatives that we had contact with during those three years in Santiago were the most hospitable, sincere, professional, and interesting people you could ever hope to meet in a lifetime. We still remain in contact with several of our former colleagues and friends of other nationalities and embassies from that posting.

Chile was such a beautiful country when we first arrived, but it had turned so quickly into an economic and political basket case. It is no exaggeration to suggest that Marxist socialism was an absolute catastrophe for Chile.

Just before noon on 11 September 1973, Hawker Hunter jets from the Chilean Air Force flew in low across downtown Santiago and fired rockets into the Presidential palace. Gunfire from Chilean Army troops erupted throughout the city, and in the early afternoon, the troops, supported by tanks, stormed the Presidential palace. Soon after, Chilean military officers reported that President Salvador Allende had committed suicide. He was sixty-five years old.

The military junta that replaced Dr Salvador Allende in 1973 was led by General Augusto Pinochet Ugarte who remained in power as President from 1974 to 1990. The Chilean people continued to suffer under the new regime for years. From one violent extreme to the other for the Chilean people!

In closing this chapter on Chile, I will relate to you a story as told to me more recently by an American friend who remained in Santiago after we had left:

> The KGB personnel had angered the CIA team in Santiago for some obscure reason I was not privy to, and the exasperated Agency personnel decided that payback was well and truly overdue. They came up with a masterful plan. They circulated flyers and ensured that they were distributed to most if not

all, the environs of Santiago by every means possible. The flyers were offering a considerable sum of money to anyone who would donate a cat or dog to the Soviet Embassy. No telephone numbers were given on the flyers, only the location of the Embassy of the USSR in Santiago!

On the first day, several hundred cats and dogs were delivered by hand to the Soviet Embassy with requests for payment. It was chaos. The second and third days were even worse, as was the noise bellowing from the ever-increasing crowds and their animals massing outside the Soviet Embassy demanding that the Soviets honour their offer of payment for each cat or dog.

The operation was considered a major victory, and more than compensated for some of the mischief the KGB had engineered over the previous weeks.

15

Return to Australia & The Department of Foreign Affairs

1972–1973

Upon arrival in Sydney, I was taken directly to the School of Public Health and Tropical Medicine for more tests. The next stop was the Woden Valley Hospital in Canberra for ten days. There was still no definitive diagnosis, so I asked to go home. After another three or four weeks of various tests and medication, I thought I was well enough to get back to work at the department.

Two weeks after my return to work I was told to report to the Head of Staffing. I was asked whether I would like to work for the Secretary of the department, Sir Keith Waller, as his personal assistant, and also provide support to the two Deputy Secretaries, Lew Border and Mick Shann. I did not hesitate to accept, even though it was suggested that I should perhaps take a day or two to think it over.

I was also the liaison officer between the Secretary's office, the foreign minister's office, and the prime minister's office with trips to Parliament House around 10 am and 3 pm each day. Gough Whitlam was prime minister and for a while, he was also the Minister for Foreign Affairs.

I enjoyed this position and respected and admired the dedication and professional management of the department by the Secretary and his two deputies.

Our highest priority after I had settled in at work at the Secretary's office was for us to get out of a rental home and find a home that we could call our own. A friend advised that we could apply for a new home through the Canberra Housing Authority. We submitted our application and had a brand new three-bedroom brick home shortly after. It was in the new suburb of Holder. It cost A$24 500 and, as was the case in the Australian capital, all deeds on properties were in fact leases for a period of ninety-nine years.

I was preoccupied with my new duties in the department from Monday to Friday, and for an hour or two on most Saturdays and Sundays reading all inward cables for the Secretary to ensure there was nothing that could not wait until Monday morning or be handled by either of the Deputy Secretaries or a Head of Division.

The weekend hours that were free from work-related duties were engaged in tree and garden plantings, concrete laying, painting, etc., for the new home.

Judith was in a very pregnant condition at this stage and was busy unpacking after our personal effects finally arrived from Chile. I was on alert day and night with frequent requests from Judith for "Polly Waffles". The same old story. I had already been trained for this during the pregnancy with Adrian, and I was ready.

Judith's mother and father visited from Wollongong to assist as time grew close to Judith giving birth. At about 8 pm on 19 August 1972, just after the evening meal, Judith let us know, with a sense of urgency, that it was time to go to the Royal Canberra Hospital.

We had been advised that we were expecting a girl and were hoping that the baby would delay her arrival until after midnight so that she would share the same birthday as Judith's mother. It was not to be. She was in a hurry to make an entry into the world.

Samantha Alma was named and baptised in Wollongong, with her grandparents and a few close friends in attendance. She was a gorgeous, little, brown-eyed redhead like her two male siblings. A man could never hope for a more loving and beautiful daughter, and she still is.

Towards the end of 1973 I was told that Prime Minister Gough Whitlam had decided to bring Allan Renouf, then our ambassador in Paris, back to Australia to appoint him as the new departmental Secretary. Sir Keith Waller was due to retire.

A matter that could have had a considerable impact on the image of Australia's foreign service occurred during the final days of my appointment as PA to the Secretary. The incoming Secretary had let it be known prior to his departure from Paris that he was considering introducing what had been many years in the past a Mao-jacketed diplomatic uniform with its gold leaf adornments for officers accredited overseas. This early disclosure may well have been deliberate to gauge the reaction to his "idea". Fortunately, the majority of officers at the time were not impressed with the idea of the "Renouf Rig", as it was referred to, and it never did gain traction within the department.

My replacement as personal assistant was Dennis Richardson. He went on to become Director-General of ASIO; Australian Ambassador to the United States; Secretary of the Department of Foreign Affairs and Trade; and finally, Secretary of the Department of Defence. An impressive and well-deserved list of career achievements from a brilliant and personable officer.

I was offered and accepted the position of consul in Chicago, Illinois, reporting to Sir Patrick Shaw, our ambassador in Washington, DC.

When the Secretary of the Department goes, so does his personal assistant!

16

The Consulate-General Chicago USA

1973–1975

The pre-posting routines for the three-year posting to Chicago were completed, our packed personal effects were on their way, and so were we. We had rented out our home to an officer at the American Embassy, stored our furniture and other effects, sold our car, and made our farewells to family and friends. The usual routine!

The only stop on the way was Hawaii, then nonstop to O'Hare International Airport, Chicago. We arrived in late December 1973 and were welcomed by the bitter cold of Chicago's winter.

Upon arrival, we settled into a hotel that had been booked for us by the officer we were replacing. Judith got to work soon after to find us a home for the next three or four years. The home Judith had finally chosen was at 1211 Greenleaf Street, at Evanston, a leafy suburb on the north side of Chicago. It belonged to a Northwestern University Professor of Russian Studies who had accepted an exchange teaching role in Leningrad, USSR, for three years and that suited us perfectly.

The handover routine with the officer I was replacing was completed in two days. The third day was set aside for a welcoming cocktail party for us, and a farewell to the officer returning home. A crowd of government and business people with whom I may be in contact during the course of my duties was invited and introduced. I doubt if we ever saw most of them again during our stay in the "Windy City". You always end up making your own contacts and friends on overseas postings.

Chicago was an enjoyable and interesting posting for the family when compared to the repressive Soviet Union, and Chile which was beautiful one day, and politically turbulent the next.

Our Washington, DC experience with the Office of the Air Attaché and the Australian embassy from 1963 to 1966 helped a lot with the process of settling into the ways, means, and lifestyle of the American people.

The Consul-General was a trade commissioner and the post's priorities were centred around the business and commercial communities, which were considerable in Chicago.

My own consular reporting responsibilities on several areas of interest were restricted to the eight states of the Midwest. I was also expected to assist the Department of Trade officers with any useful information gathered while developing relationships with political and commercial contacts within those eight states.

An Australian Tourism Office opened in a building nearby,

but we rarely had cause for contact other than my initial call on them to introduce myself and meet their staff occasionally at official events.

Our son, Adrian, was just turning seven years of age when we enrolled him at the St Nicholas Primary School in Evanston, North Chicago. He was not happy at the school, but we thought it would be simply a matter of time for him to settle in and get to know a few of his fellow classmates. I could see that he was stressing about going to school one day and asked him what the problem was. He finally told me that he was being bullied by boys a lot older than he was, because he was a foreigner. I told him that I would talk to the headmaster if there was any more trouble.

I thought all was going well for Adrian until one day as I was returning home early and had driven into a street a couple of blocks from our house. I found a group of boys about three to four years older than Adrian on the side of the road kicking and hitting him while another boy was attempting to destroy his bike by stomping on the spokes. I pulled over nearby and ran towards them. They started to scatter, but two of them were too slow to get on their bikes. They both ran off rather than meet the wrath of the screaming madman (me) running across the street. I checked Adrian over. He was in a distressed state, and I was angry. I grabbed both the bikes and threw them over a fence surrounding a nearby park.

That evening the father of one of the boys knocked on our door. I was prepared for the worst. I invited him inside to avoid entertaining the neighbours. After introducing Judith and myself, I provided him with an outline on what had happened, including my disposing of the two bicycles. I was extremely apprehensive about how he was going to receive this explanation, but to my surprise he expressed his thanks on the way I had handled the situation and followed up with a handshake! He also added that he would speak to the other parents and the headmaster. Adrian had no more problems with the bullies.

Our daughter Samantha was only sixteen months old when we arrived in Chicago. She was a very quiet child and adored her protective big brother. The highlight of my day was to see both their smiling and excited faces looking out of the lounge room window as I arrived home.

The major focus for students of Adrian's age in Chicago appeared to be baseball, and therefore, the Chicago Cubs. Adrian went to the wrong person for advice on how to hold the bat, and hit the ball, me! I knew, like most Australians, how to hold and wield a cricket bat, and I thought a baseball bat could not be all that different.

That same evening Adrian and I were filling in time in the backyard waiting for Judith to call us for dinner. I asked him to throw, toss, or whatever they call the action with a baseball, and when he did, I must have had an unusual bit of luck because I hit it perfectly and sent it sailing over his head and through the window of my next-door neighbour. Basic inbuilt instincts had us both running for cover to hide out and trying to restrain our laughter.

We waited for the expected wrath of the neighbour. There was no sound at all to follow the loud smashing of the brittle glass of the double-glazed window. We waited a minute or two longer before I asked Judith to put a hold on dinner while I went to apologise to our neighbour.

There was no-one at home, so I left a note of apology and a promise to pay for any repairs. I did not feel this was sufficient restitution, so I left a case of Australian wine outside his side door. All ended well, and the neighbour later acknowledged it was an excellent idea of mine when I mentioned on the note that I had left him, that I would never pick up a baseball bat again, at least while I was his neighbour.

There was a small business community of ex-pat Australians living in Chicago. The sales manager of the Hilton Hotel, Ray Simpson, was from Sydney and was extremely friendly and generous to us. He often invited Judith and me to join him for drinks at the hotel's Tiki Bar, followed by dinner in the main dining room, or he would invite me to business lunches and introduce me to those people he thought would be of interest to me, and subsequently to Australia

Judith's mother and father, George and Alma, arrived for a stay of several weeks, and I casually mentioned to Ray during a conversation that I was planning on a seven-day road trip to Pittsburgh, Washington, DC, and Williamsburg with my in-laws. He immediately booked the in-laws and me into Hilton hotels in those cities for the duration of the week's road trip and ensured that we were really looked after at each location.

Our friendship was such that Ray invited me to give an official address as Australian Consul to several hundred people of his west Chicago suburb of Oak Park who had gathered for Thanksgiving Day's Annual Picnic in the Park.

Judith's most memorable evening during her entire stay in Chicago, or possibly ever, occurred when Ray invited us to dinner in the Hilton's ballroom where Tom Jones was to perform that evening. Our table had pride of place close to the stage. Late in the performance, Tom unexpectedly walked down from the stage, and approached our table while singing *Hey, Jude*. He then kneeled down on one knee next to Judith, continuing with the song while holding her hand. A great night, set up by Ray especially for Judith.

I presented Ray Simpson and his wife with an antique Russian samovar, with the royal seal and the year, sometime in the early 1800s, stamped into it. He had often admired and commented on it when visiting our home. I discovered it in a Moscow market. I treasured this item, but it was our way of saying 'Thank you' for all he had done to make us so welcome in Chicago.

I received a cheque from Canberra for A$1.3 million in the diplomatic bag soon after our arrival in Chicago, with instructions for it to be presented to the agents for Jackson Pollock's painting *Blue Poles* once the director of the National Gallery of Australia completed his scrutiny of the painting and took delivery.

The director and I were invited to attend at a city building that housed the painting in a vault and met the people involved in the transaction. A reception and "meet and greet" for invited guests had been arranged, and the painting was taken from a large walk-in safe early in the proceedings and brought up the stairs to where we were all standing.

The official side of the transaction, prior to and including the instructions on the handing over of the cheque, had been approved by Prime Minister Gough Whitlam.

Considerable debate in the political and public domain had occurred in Australia when the acquisition of the painting was first made public. The purchase price of A$1.3 million was a world record for an American contemporary painting at that time and had caused considerable controversy back in Australia.

In 2019, the painting's estimated worth was A$350 million!

An unusual consular case while in Chicago was played out at the Cook County Jail, which was reputed to be one of the worst prisons in which to be incarcerated in the United States. A prisoner was being held on an interstate drug-related crime and had declared to prison authorities that he was an Australian. An FBI agent, who became a good friend during this posting, had contacted me about the matter and asked me if I would accompany him to the prison to assist in establishing the prisoner's true bona fides.

I nearly gagged when we left the reception area of the

prison and were escorted to an interview room. The smell was quite overpowering with the main ingredient possibly being a chemical cleaning agent.

The prisoner was ushered in and was, at least visually, in a shocking state. He had fresh scars, with some stitches still in place on his face, his shaved head, neck and arms. He explained that he had cut himself to make himself look unattractive to other prisoners! He said he was raped the first day at the prison and added that his cries for help were ignored by prison officers on duty nearby.

It did not take long to establish that this particular Cook County inmate was not an Australian. There was no documentation such as a birth certificate or passport. There was also no indication or mention of a dual nationality made. His knowledge of Australia was negligible. We were on our way within minutes. The FBI agent was not impressed with the inmate's pitiful performance and berated him for wasting our time. Even so, I felt sorry for the man, and what lay ahead for him in that oppressive and dangerous environment.

That was nowhere near the worst of my visits to prisons while involved with consular duties, and it was not the worst prison I had visited either. Moscow's Lefortovo Prison, run by KGB staff, would have to rate as the worst of all the consular visits that I had made during my years of service.

An incident that required negotiation skills, diplomacy, and the capable assistance of the Chicago police occurred soon after Prime Minister Gough Whitlam had without warning or debate within his own Cabinet or Labor caucus, announced in Parliament the *de jure* recognition of the Soviet Union's annexation of the Baltic states of Latvia, Lithuania, and Estonia.

Gough Whitlam's provocative announcement had received considerable coverage in the Chicago press, primarily because of the huge population of Baltic émigrés that had settled in the Chicago area over many years, and it did not take long before we had a very angry crowd massing outside the Australian Consulate-General on East Wacker Drive.

The Consul-General was away at the time, and as deputy I received a Chicago police captain and two of his subordinates in my office. I was asked if I could suggest a strategy that would quickly assist in dispersing the crowd because traffic had been brought to a halt. I suggested that the easiest and quickest way to defuse the situation would be for one of his officers to go down and request one delegate from each of the parties participating in the demonstration outside to represent the rest and escort them up to my office.

The captain started the meeting as soon as the selected delegation arrived by emphasising the urgency in dispersing the crowd and getting the traffic moving. I listened to the delegates' case and explained the government's position to them. I then advised that I would send a report detailing their sentiments and arguments to the Australian Government the same day. The delegation reluctantly agreed to the action I had suggested much sooner than I expected, and one of the three representatives confirmed to the police who had remained at the meeting that he would immediately speak to the people in the street, and hopefully there would be no further problems. The police had been dealing with irate drivers in an increasing line of vehicles that had been in a holding pattern blocking several streets within the centre of Chicago since the demonstration had started.

Two Chicago police officers arrived at my office the next day to present me with a large bottle of Canadian Club whisky. I was told the bottle reflected the chief's appreciation of my assistance in dealing with the crowd the previous day, and also for my praise in the media a week before on the way Chicago police officers handled the capture of a kangaroo that had escaped from the Chicago Zoo! The bottle went missing sometime later. I think the trade people within the Consulate-General may have confiscated the bottle for their own use.

I experienced two incidents in Chicago that could have been life-threatening during this short posting. The first occurred at my home soon after Gough's announcement about the Baltic States.

My normal routine when I arrived home from work, and after I had reacquainted with the family, was to have a few minutes of quiet time to relax in the lounge room with a pre-dinner drink, before joining Judith and the children.

The back of my head was exposed to the street by a window when seated in a lounge chair. Judith had called out to me on this particular evening to request assistance in bathing the children. I had just moved my upper body to the left while still in the lounge chair to place my glass on a side table and prepare to rise when there was an almighty crash, and a granite-like rock between half and one kilogram in weight flew by and ended up in the lounge room along with the shattered remains of the double-glazed window.

The local Evanston police were called and a plainclothes officer asked several questions relating to why someone would act in such a way against me or other occupants of the house. They became more attentive when I mentioned that I was the Australian Consul and provided them with a briefing on the Baltic states issue, and the demonstration just days previously outside the Consulate-General.

The police officer advised that had I been sitting in a normal position in the lounge chair at the time I would have been extremely lucky to have survived. He added that a car would be placed out the front of our house for a few days. I asked for it to be removed the next day. I did not think the neighbours in this relatively quiet neighbourhood would have been very impressed at all.

Another incident that was considered life-threatening by some of the locals occurred at a cocktail party given by our Consul-General. Judith had risen to the occasion when she overheard our inebriated American locally engaged trade officer making extremely derogatory remarks about the Department of Trade and Australia generally. Judith had continued to hold herself in check until the American's abusive outbursts reached such a point that she felt obliged to quietly asked him to cease such inappropriate behaviour. The trade officer reacted by directing a venomous tirade of abuse at Judith and accompanied it by throwing the contents of his glass in her face. Judith did not hesitate to react and slapped his face as hard as she could.

Several guests, including a good friend that I had invited from the FBI, had been seated nearby, and witnessed this abusive discourse by the trade officer. The agent, with the assistance of a couple of other people at the function, removed him from the building, as he continued to scream abuse. Judith was applauded by those guests who had witnessed the occurrence.

I had been completely unaware of what had happened until I heard the applause and saw the trade officer being frog-marched out of the apartment. I had been engaged in conversation with several people, including the Consul-General, in another room. I was immediately briefed on what had happened. Judith was still shaking when I found her. A couple of women had taken her to another room for safety, and to provide time for her to settle down.

The FBI agent advised later in the evening that the inebriated trade officer had cried out, "I am going to blow your f... husband's head off" as he was being hustled out of the apartment.

The agent also advised that such threats were taken seriously in his country and asked whether I wished to take any action against the trade officer. I replied that I did not and suggested that we could manage any disciplinary action that had to be taken in-house.

I suggested to the Consul-General that we should meet in his office the next morning to discuss what action should be taken with this member of his trade staff.

The Consul-General advised that he had been fully briefed on the previous night's performance and related to me that the man had been a guest of the Department of Trade in Australia a few months previously and had behaved in a similar fashion there when he had consumed too much alcohol. His comments about the Australian Government, and more specifically the Department of Trade, had been unacceptable to all who had attended that function. He had received a disciplinary warning on that occasion.

I suggested that the removal of the trade officer as soon as was practicable would be in the best interests of the office. He was fired the next day, and the Consul-General returned to Australia soon after, not because of this incident, but because his posting had come to an end. As Deputy, I acted as Consul-General for a few weeks until the new Consul-General, a foreign affairs Officer, flew in directly from Athens sometime later. The new appointee had been ambassador to Greece.

This is simply an example of how spouses too have to face situations as they arise, and follow the required protocols, as I believe Judith reluctantly did on that occasion. Some may say that she should not have reacted the way she did — I say 'Rubbish' and applaud the way she handled herself. The message — don't mess with Australian women!

A myriad of choices for breaks away from Chicago were available for the family, and we often loaded up our VW Camper and took off every chance we had. A favourite destination when Judith's parents had been visiting was at Indian Head Lake, which was about 150 miles (241 km) to the north of Chicago in upper Michigan. We rented a log cabin and a small boat with an outboard motor for cruising on the lake for northern pike. This was a better fighting fish than it was for eating.

It was my turn to start preparations for the evening meal while the family group drove into the nearby village to pick up some supplies. I had decided to start cooking the potato chips for the fish dinner. However, there was a slight snag. I had tried to start the gas stove several times, and while kneeling with my head half inside the oven trying to find out why it would not fire up, it did and left me with superficial singeing of my arm and face. Hair would eventually have a rebirth on my arm, forehead, moustache, and eyebrows. The pain from the blast was extreme. The family arrived home to find a not-very-happy scene. The smell of singed hair and flesh was not at all appetising. No sympathy was given. That was my last attempt as the family cook, at least at Indian Head Lake!

I flew to Washington, DC on 8 August 1974 on a regular reporting trip, and as my cab passed the White House, I asked the driver what on earth was going on. There were so few people out and about, and the city's vehicle traffic was unusually light. "Nixon is about to resign" was the reply.

The Watergate scandal had not given Nixon any wriggle room. It was either impeachment, which had been initiated in February 1974 with the House of Representatives giving its Judiciary Committee the go-ahead to investigate whether enough evidence existed to impeach the president, or whether he should submit his resignation from the Office of President. Nixon did resign as anticipated, and Gerald Ford was the next president sworn in.

Allen, my American friend from the Santiago posting, was at this time back in Washington, and he had called me in Chicago to suggest we should meet for lunch and a catch-up the next time I was in Washington. I arranged to meet him for lunch once I had completed my call at our embassy, and before I caught my flight back to Chicago.

The conversation at lunch turned quickly to our experiences in Chile. I casually asked what had become of Ben and was told that he had been under investigation for some time before his indiscretion about fellow colleagues and had been sentenced to several years in a federal penitentiary for embezzling funds while employed by the US government.

One of the more interesting offers made to me while in Chicago was a Playboy Club gold card membership, including access to their executive dining room, which I used on a few occasions for official working lunches.

Overseas posts are always prepared for the endless parade

of official visitors who have to be briefed, entertained, and introduced to appropriate local contacts. I will only describe the one occasion, and I will not mention the visitor's name or the delegation that accompanied him.

I received advice from Canberra that a senior Australian Government official and party would be visiting. I was the designated contact officer for the official and his entourage, and for the first day of the visit I was requested to organise a luncheon that was to include city officials, appropriate media representation, and business leaders who could be of interest to the visitors.

I had been briefed that this official enjoyed good food, and good company. With this in mind, I visited the Playboy's Executive Club days prior to the lunch to discuss seating arrangements and the menu with the head bunny. I provided her with a glowing reference on the official, and the importance of his visit to Chicago to ensure that the best seating overlooking the city, and the best possible attention from the staff was achieved.

The group of visitors arrived on time, but the look on the face of the head bunny waiting with me to receive the official and his entourage at the entrance to the Club was an "OMG!" She turned her stunned look of disbelief on me. I did not know whether to laugh or cry. I am sure she thought I was playing a practical joke on her and her colleagues.

All went well for a while after the initial shock of the extremely colourful code of dress of the official, and the party had been seated in the executive room. The discussions and the meal were received favourably by all our visitors, and I thought we had passed muster on this day, that is until coffee was being served by an extremely attractive African-American bunny.

Figure 13. Author at an official function, Playboy Club, Chicago, 1974

A member of the delegation, not the official, did what no-one should ever do in the Playboy Club. This person grabbed the bunny's cotton-tail, that little white powder puff-like fixture attached to the rear end of her costume, with one hand and tried to grab her arm with the other. She danced away to avoid any further touching. I thought she handled the situation very well, but I could tell by the head bunny's attitude and facial expressions that she was not amused.

The party finally left with one of our trade officers who escorted them for the remainder of the day. I stayed behind to apologise and pay the bill. I am sure the tip that I had added to the bill that day was commensurate with the infringement and assisted in my membership not being cancelled.

We had only been in Chicago for a year of what should have been at least a three-year posting when I received a cable to advise that I would be returning to Moscow within six months as consul and First Secretary (Admin). I was also advised that funds were on the way to start me on Russian language training again.

I started my language training with the Berlitz School of Languages for two months, and then received instruction from a private tutor at Northwestern University for another three months.

Several days prior to leaving Chicago the Deputy Commissioner of Police Walter Vallee, who had been a regular invitee to our official functions, had a police car pick up Judith and Adrian for a surprise outing.

They were driven to the Marine Police Operations base on Lake Michigan by a Chicago police sergeant, given a tour of the base, and transferred to a police launch. They were then taken out on Lake Michigan for a spectacular view of Chicago from the water and a light lunch onboard.

Walter Vallee signed and enlarged the photographs taken that day for Adrian and me and had them delivered to the Consulate-General.

On return to the Marine Police base there was a car waiting to drive them to a park on South Shore Drive. The Mounted Police were quartered in this area. The police rode out from their barracks with Walter Vallee at their head and surrounded Judith and Adrian. A short speech was made by Walter who then led the police officers in a loud "Three cheers", which I believe they thought was the normal routine for such an occasion.

A police car then drove Judith and Adrian back home. They were still excited when I arrived home a few hours later and could not wait to tell me about their day out with the Chicago police.

Another hotelier who we became close friends with was the General Manager of the Intercontinental Hotel, the best of the hotels in Chicago at that time for entertainment and dining. Peter was a Canadian, and his wife Rosemary was an Australian.

Peter and Rosemary arranged our last, but most memorable, farewell dinner for us in August 1975. We were invited for pre-dinner drinks beforehand in the library. The library was a beautifully presented room with panelled redwood walls, red carpet, crystal chandeliers, and large leather lounge chairs.

We all left the library after a cocktail or two and were escorted by Peter and Rosemary up to the roof-top restaurant overlooking the city and Lake Michigan. As we entered the dining area the members of the group 'the Twelve Violins' commenced playing *Waltzing Matilda,* and between two and three hundred people in the restaurant clapped as we walked to our table. I am sure that most of those diners applauding would have had no idea who we were, what the occasion was, or what on earth that tune was the violinists were so enthusiastically playing as they moved between the tables until they had completely encircled our table as we sat down. During JFK's years as President of the United States the hotel's "Twelve Violins" were often summoned by JFK and flown to the White House in Washington for special occasions.

It was truly a night to remember.

Rosemary died a year later, a victim of a heart attack. A beautiful woman with whom Judith had formed a close friendship. Peter went on to open and establish the Intercontinental Hotel in Manila.

I received a phone call from the embassy in Washington during this final phase of departure from Chicago advising me that the ambassador, Sir Patrick Shaw, wanted to speak to me personally, and that I should plan to fly to Washington the next day. I initially thought that the Moscow posting had been cancelled, and that I could be off to another destination, or perhaps I was going to have my pre-Moscow briefings in Washington, but none of that made sense, because the ambassador would not normally be involved in such matters. I became very apprehensive about the reason for this summons to Washington. When I was shown into the ambassador's office, I became even more alarmed, because his secretary was sitting across from him in the lounge area with a note pad at the ready. My mind had been racing at this stage, and I was settling on someone close to us having passed away with the bad news about to be delivered.

Sir Patrick wasted no time in getting to the point and advised that he wanted to talk about the "honey trap" incident that occurred in Moscow in 1969 in the last days of that posting. He added that the incident had obviously continued to be the cause of some concern to others.

I was encouraged to recall as much detail as possible and at the conclusion of the interview the ambassador advised that Judith and I were to fly to the Canadian capital, Ottawa, the following week for a pre-posting security briefing with the Canadian foreign service, and that would entail an overnight stay. I was to report to the Australian High Commissioner in Ottawa after I had completed my briefings.

We arrived in Ottawa late on a Monday. The following morning, we arrived at the Canadian Department of Foreign Affairs, and after an hour in the waiting area we received an apology from the Canadians and were advised that the briefing had been cancelled. There was no-one available to provide the briefing! Our previous briefings in London, the discussion with Sir Patrick Shaw in Washington, and "on the ground" experiences in Moscow and Santiago must have sufficed.

A car returned us to our hotel and waited while we checked out. We were then taken to the Australian High Commission. A light lunch was provided by the High Commissioner, and our discussions were such that none of us had noticed the late hour. We had a plane to catch, and little time to make it to the airport.

The High Commissioner's driver told us on the way to the airport that we would not be able to make it so he pulled into a garage and called the High Commission. 'No problem' was all we heard from the front seat when he returned to the car.

On arrival at the airport, the driver drove past the main entrance, along the outer perimeter fence, and on to a manned security gate. He spoke to the guard who was aware of our arrival and gave directions on how to drive directly to the aircraft that was scheduled for departure to Chicago. We drove right up to the aircraft. The stairs were still in place and the engines were idling. The stairs were removed the moment we stepped onto the aircraft. We were shown into business class on boarding, and the curtain was closed. There must be better ways to get an upgrade. It took a while to settle down after that frantic ride through what may have been a very interesting city to visit, if ever we had the time.

I sent a cable to the fellow I was replacing in Moscow to ask what the current routine was in bringing vehicles to Moscow. I mentioned that I had two vehicles because we had expected to be in Chicago for at least three years and sought confirmation that my bringing both vehicles with us would not present a problem. I was told there would definitely be no problem.

In hindsight, which is a wonderful thing, we should have sent the VW Camper back to Australia and had the in-laws store it until we had completed the posting in Moscow. That would have eliminated a lot of problems that followed at the embassy in Moscow and back in Canberra with selling the two vehicles after only one year in Moscow when I had been declared persona non grata by the Soviet Ministry of Foreign Affairs. The rules were that we could only sell one vehicle after a year in Moscow. Apparently, the imposing of a persona non grata order, being no longer welcome in the USSR, was not taken into consideration. Rules are rules.

We survived the last of the farewells, and our personal effects were packed up and sent back to Australia. The house was handed back to the real estate agency people, and it was time to go.

We drove the vehicles onto the New York docks and handed them over to an agent for forwarding to Helsinki, Finland.

We booked ourselves into a motel not far from the airport for an overnight stay before catching a Trans World Airlines (TWA) flight from New York to Madrid for a two-week holiday in Majorca, before proceeding on a direct flight to Moscow.

17

Back in the USSR

1975–1976

We had been in contact with Colin and Mary-Lou Heseltine who had been posted to the Australian embassy in Madrid and had previously been colleagues in Santiago de Chile. Colin sent a car to pick us up at the airport, and as soon as we arrived at their apartment, they insisted we stay with them for a few days. We had a hard time convincing them that our schedule only included one night in Madrid.

Our hosts took us out to a restaurant after we had rested, and Colin ordered a beer and the house specialty for me at the bar while our wives and children were getting settled at a nearby table. I was not made aware of this specialty of the house until I had washed the last mouthful of the bull's balls down with a beer. Judith had obviously been briefed by Mary-Lou on what was happening, and they were both in hysterics. Nothing really special about the bull's jingly bits, other than possibly a little too much garlic, and they were a little rubbery!

We picked up the rental car that we had booked prior to

leaving Chicago, and headed southwest towards Malaga on the Costa del Sol.

Malaga was about a four to five-hour drive from the Portuguese border. We had also planned on spending three or four days in Lisbon and its surrounds, but unfortunately the border was closed. Spain and Portugal were having a dispute which I believe was over the supply of fresh water from Spain to Portugal. We were advised to turn around and head back to Malaga, and there we stayed until it was time to drive up the east coast to Madrid's airport to catch our direct flight to Helsinki.

I called our embassy in Moscow soon after we landed in Helsinki and requested confirmation that we had accommodation booked at the only hotel we were allowed to stay at in Novgorod. The booking was confirmed by one of the Russian clerks at the embassy, which was a relief because our previous experience six years earlier had not been a good one.

The first task after arrival was to pick up the vehicles from Customs at the port. I was not surprised to find that the vehicles had been stripped of all our maps, spare parts, manuals, transmission and motor oil, plates, cutlery, and other items that I had placed in the VW Camper cupboards in Chicago prior to dropping it off in New York. "Expect the worst, and hope for the best", as the saying goes.

Replacement of the lost items during the shipment from New York to Helsinki and general items for servicing of the vehicles along with food supplies, clothing for the children, and the other necessary supplies for the next several months were purchased at Stockmann's department store in central Helsinki. We were old hands and knew the drill.

It was August 1975, and with the previous experience in 1968 still implanted in our minds, I had also cabled the embassy before we left Chicago and requested advice from the officer I was replacing if another call could be made to the hotel to ensure that there would be no problem in Novgorod. I was told emphatically that there would be no problem as the booking had been confirmed twice. I was assured that we would all have a bed and a meal awaiting us on our arrival at the hotel.

The next day we drove on to Porvoo for an overnight stay. We knew from previous experience that it was the last place that we could get accommodation and a decent meal before we crossed the Finnish-Soviet border at Vyborg the next morning.

We were up early to bid farewell to Finland and crossed into no-man's-land. There was very little vegetation between the Finnish border station and the Soviet border guards' inspection building.

It was after 10 am by the time we left the border inspection area, and we had at least another six or seven hours drive to Novgorod. With stops along the way and diverting into Leningrad (now St Petersburg) for fuel. It was after 7 pm when we arrived in Novgorod and found the hotel.

Judith and Samantha stayed in the car while Adrian helped

me carry our luggage from the camper into the hotel reception foyer. The receptionist was the only person in the reception and foyer area, and she did not look up or acknowledge our presence. We had amassed a pile of luggage in the foyer once we had emptied both vehicles. We knew from experience that we could not leave anything of value in the vehicles overnight in an open yard.

The receptionist continued to chat on the phone for another few minutes, while completely ignoring Adrian and me. When she did finally decide to hang up, she said, 'passports'. That's all. She then looked at what I understood to be the booking register, and without any hesitation handed me back the passports and said, 'No room'. I went to great lengths to explain the confirmations of the booking from Chicago, Moscow, and Helsinki, that we were exhausted and hungry, and that my wife and daughter were waiting outside in the car. All to no avail. She just stared at me and repeated, 'No room.' Deja vu!

We did not think this could possibly happen to us again after the number of confirmations that we had been booked in on this occasion, and the letter of complaint that our embassy sent to the Ministry of Foreign Affairs in Moscow describing the treatment we received previously in 1968 from the same hotel in Novgorod.

I knew I would get nowhere with this person; the instruction had been given. We had to conform. I decided to play for time and see if someone else turned up behind the desk. I asked her if we could at least have something to eat. She did not seem happy with that request either but pointed towards the empty dining area.

Our meal order was taken, and sometime later the potatoes and meatballs arrived. We were told that was the only meal available. We could smell the meatballs before the plates were set down on the table. They were foul. A lot of garlic had been added to the mix of whatever meat it was. Judith had a taste and gasped. We bundled the meatballs up in several tissues and placed the packages in an empty shopping bag. We ate as much of the black bread and potatoes as we could and left. Both children were almost asleep and thankfully were not interested in food.

I returned to reception, but there had been no shift change. I asked the cantankerous woman for help in recommending somewhere we could sleep. She had mellowed a little since I last approached her for assistance and suggested a camping ground near a village several kilometres south of Novgorod, which was at least in the right direction to continue on to Moscow in the morning. We had no other option because we were not permitted to park on the side of the main road to Moscow, and I had no wish to drive down any side roads after our previous experience in 1968 when we found ourselves in similar circumstances with nowhere to stay late at night.

We retrieved our luggage, and on my final exit out the front entrance of the hotel, I emptied the rancid meatballs into a tall pottery vase in the foyer. Not much of a "thank you very much" parting gift, but it helped with our morale.

We found the camping ground easily enough and were shown to a room on the ground floor of a two-floor block. There were only two single beds and one lamp on a bedside table. The children joined us in the beds, one at each end. We did not dare to change out of our clothes. It was not possible to get into a sleeping position, because if there had been any springs, they had given up long ago.

We tried to get some sleep before we faced the hours of driving to Moscow that lay ahead of us the next day. There was no other alternative because the "camp commandant" said we could not stay in our camper van. Rules are rules and must be obeyed!

Judith and the children were either asleep or almost there, and I was just getting to sleep when I heard a strange noise coming from where I understood the door of the room to be. I turned on the only bedside lamp and opened the door. The mangiest cat I have ever seen was sitting just outside the entrance to our room, and it was chewing and crunching on a sizeable but very dead rat. That was it. Game over. Everyone was awake at this stage, and we were all spellbound just watching the cat, which was completely ignoring us. We packed what little we had taken out of our bags, carefully stepped over where the rat and cat had been and crept out of the place.

We piled into the camper, which was within the grounds,

and tried to get as much sleep or rest as we could before dawn, and before we were spotted. Bugger the rules!

We drove into the embassy grounds in Moscow at dusk, and as we parked the cars, I saw the fellow I was replacing talking to a Russian driver only a few metres away. He completely ignored us and kept on with his discussion. Not the warmest of welcomes from a fellow colleague! Was it the two vehicles?

In contrast, one of the Soviet drivers I had known from six years earlier came rushing over to greet us. The first thing he said after the pleasantries was 'We were all so sorry to hear of the death of your son in Chile'. I was stunned because I was reasonably sure that not even the Australian staff members would have known. Absence does not necessarily make the heart grow fonder. I felt as though I had never left the place.

The total of Australian officers had increased from five to fifteen during our absence of six years. It now had a trade section, increases in the political section, and a scientific affairs officer, and Poland was no longer our responsibility! However, we had no increase in our consular and administrative section. The long hours would continue.

I was very disappointed to see that the Down Under Club had closed. It had been replaced by a kindergarten following an influx of additional staff, some with children. Other friendly embassies also enrolled their children in our kindergarten.

When we were in Moscow previously, we had a tiny one-bedroom apartment on the top floor. The privilege of rank as First Secretary and Consul had us provided with three bedrooms, and the apartment was on the ground floor. This was the same apartment that had been occupied by my former boss in Moscow six years previously.

We were given a nanny by the Directorate of services to the Diplomatic Corps (UPDK) soon after arrival. As already mentioned, there were occasional lapses with the degree of caution by some UPDK staff. It was obvious nothing had changed in that area either. Our nanny was the daughter of a Russian admiral, and soon after starting to work for us, and while outside the building helping us carry in supplies, she apologised in a whisper that she could be a little late on Thursdays. She added that she had to be at UPDK's head office each Thursday morning from 7 am to 8 am to report.

The nanny often made other revealing remarks to Judith while outside the apartment, in particular about how difficult life was, with emphasis on the difficulty of finding anything in the stores. She must have known every word she uttered was being recorded, or perhaps she was fed up with the Soviet system. She was not with us very long! We were not told what had happened to her. An older woman turned up soon after and introduced herself as the new nanny.

Soon after arriving in Moscow, we were invited to attend a function at the American ambassador's residence, Spasso House. I had just parked our car when I saw Yuri Mishin leaning against a car in the driveway. I can only guess what other guests who were arriving and walking past this reunion must have thought with me being given a joyous bear hug from a Soviet driver. Yuri was the driver who accompanied me in 1968 to a bus accident involving several Australians near the Polish border. He was now the Irish ambassador's driver.

In addition to my normal duties, I was also responsible, as consul, for the Operation Reunion effort, that we conducted out of our embassy during 1975 and 1976. It's function was to assist Russian Jews in obtaining visas to emigrate. A Brit and a Canadian, both wives of diplomats, were employed in clerical roles to assist on this program. This was not a role we would hand over to Soviet clerical staff. I had several calls from as far away as Armenia requesting assistance.

The Special Jewish Department was established within the KGB in 1971 in an endeavour to intimidate Soviet Jewry and discourage emigration attempts.

Although the Jewish population were officially classed as a "nationality", they were not allowed to communicate in Yiddish or Hebrew, while Ukrainians, Armenians, and most other minorities could use their own languages. The Soviet State's official support of the Arab states against Israel further complicated the situation.

The Soviet Union's Jewish population in 1975–1976 numbered roughly three and a half million, and had more limitations placed upon them than Christians or Moslems.

Entertainment choices had not changed so we decided to go off the beaten track, be more adventurous than we were on our previous posting in Moscow and discover what those citizens of Moscow who had no special privileges were doing to entertain themselves.

We visited small stand-up soup kitchen-style cafes and watched plays in Moscow's parks. There was one theatrical performance, *My Fair Lady*, spoken in Russian, that we attended together with the children, after being recommended by our nanny. It was playing in a suburban theatre rarely visited by foreigners, certainly not diplomats, and had actors that could have passed as those playing the major roles in the film of the same name, Rex Harrison and Audrey Hepburn. We thought it was brilliant. The performance would have been applauded on Broadway if it had been in English.

Adrian and I loved to cross-country ski. Samantha had just turned four years of age and had her own set of skis. I often took her out to the southern outskirts of the Moscow city precincts, away from the crowds, to ski slight inclines and slopes. She loved it, even with a padded snowsuit, and other heavy winter gear on. Her big brother Adrian did not have the patience to guide her.

Adrian at eight years of age played ice hockey with the Russian boys from the buildings opposite the one we lived in. They used the outdoor frozen surface of a basketball court in front of our building. They all got along very well. Kids will be kids.

Judith accompanied Adrian and me a couple of times when we cross-country skied through the birch forests outside Moscow, but she would not venture onto the frozen river with us. She quite sensibly reasoned that she, as the sole survivor, would have to explain to family members how we disappeared while foolishly skiing down whatever river we were on at the time.

A friendly embassy couple invited us to join them at their dacha for the weekend. The dacha provided country living relief away from the suits, traffic, and Disney-like Stalinist buildings of Moscow.

I had promised Adrian that we would find time to do some cross-country skiing the next day. He woke me the next morning. He was fully dressed in his ski clothes and indicated that I may have forgotten that I had promised to take him on a cross-country trek down the nearby river. As any parent would know, an eight-year-old does not forget promises made so recently by his father, nor is he ready to accept lame-duck excuses that may be offered in an attempt to avoid the inevitable.

It must have been approaching late morning by the time we had eaten and organised ourselves for the trek. I informed Judith where we intended to go and headed off for the track that would lead to the frozen river. Judith had not been happy about us going.

There had been a light snowfall during the night, leaving a crisp powder covering the narrow track. Adrian led the way with considerable enthusiasm. Our movement through the white birch forest line to the river's edge was a magical experience. It felt like time had stood still. Not a sound was heard — not a bird chirping. No other human, animal, or insect betrayed its own presence.

We had only been into our smooth, measured strides for a few minutes on the frozen river when a strengthening breeze whipped up the covering of powdered snow and froze its minuscule particles to our cheeks. It had also become necessary to lower our muskrat shapkas, fur hats with fold-down ear flaps, and raise our woollen scarves just enough to leave a very narrow line of sight exposed to the elements.

With heads down, we almost skied into what appeared to be a small tent in front of us. A light flickered within the enclosure. Curious, we approached the entrance and called out a greeting to the occupant. The greeting was returned, and a face long ago savaged by smallpox and adorned with the most remarkable moustache appeared. With a grin and a toss of his head, he beckoned us to join him inside after we removed our skis.

The man tossed his catch of several grey and half-frozen fish out through the narrow entrance flap to make room for us both to sit opposite him. He returned to his position on a wooden crate covered with a heap of what we would call wheat bags and sat in front of a hole in the ice. We settled our backsides onto the pads of hessian, canvas, and straw that he had placed on the ice for us.

He may not have bathed since before the 1917 revolution, and his breath was so foul that you instinctively ducked whenever he opened his mouth to speak. Spittle flew in every direction and at such close quarters it was impossible to avoid. But that laugh — his eyes would disappear into the folds of weathered skin. Adrian was held spellbound by the jerking movement of the enormous ice-encrusted moustache from which hung shards of yellowish ice shielding the entrance to his cavernous mouth.

Our host introduced himself as Vladimir and apologised for his poor English. I did the same and apologised for my Russian. Adrian cheekily said he would help me by translating. Our language limitations were aided by gestures and general theatrics.

Vladimir mentioned that once the Volga warmed, he again became a boatman First Class. He reached into his multilayers of clothing, and emerged with a bottle of Hunters vodka, which contained a large red chilli. He advised it was for additional warmth. He had been drinking tea or coffee and threw the remaining contents of the mug into the hole in the ice before pouring a generous serving of vodka and handing it to me. I took one mouthful, and my lungs seemed to have had the air sucked out of them, and a fire progressed slowly as a flaming torch down through my body until thankfully it slowed to a mellowing warmth. Speech was again possible. Once again that laugh, moustache, dancing tonsils, and Adrian leaning forward in awe.

While I was recovering from the initial impact of the vodka, Vlad set about preparing a feast, and with a flourish large chunks of sour black bread appeared from a sack at his side. The bread was placed in our hands, and we were told to hold the pieces in front of us while he added thick slices of sausage, chunks of cheese, and a large pickle. This wonderful spread was washed down with his fiercely hot vodka.

Pausing briefly during the meal Vlad told us of his love for the Volga, and of how it was his one and only mistress. She was his life! He was still relatively articulate at this stage. When it was obvious that I was having trouble understanding he would talk slower and provide greater theatrics with his hands.

Vlad put the vodka bottle aside and released a fart that would surely have had the dead fish outside come back to life and flee across the ice. We could not open the flap to ventilate the small space as the breeze outside remained bitterly cold, and I would have offended our host if I had shown or indicated any measure of disgust. Adrian on the other hand thought this was the greatest experience ever and was laughing louder than the old man. The racket in that small space could have surely alerted the militia back in Moscow!

Vlad's multiple layers of clothing did save us from a nasty end as the stench that followed slowly filtered its way through whatever escape route was available.

I had to reluctantly make our apologies, because it was getting late, and I had noticed the air outside had become still. We had to get back to the dacha before it became dark. The farewells were made with much hugging and brushing of his beard on our faces as we all leant over the hole in the ice. I felt as though I had known the old man for years.

When we arrived back at the dacha, Adrian could not wait to tell anyone within listening distance about his day with Vlad and Dad.

Of all the restaurants I have visited around the world since that day I have never remembered a meal so clearly as the one provided by Vladimir, the boatman First Class, squatting on a straw and hessian mat on the surface of a frozen river in the middle of a Russian winter with my son Adrian by my side. Adrian also retains pleasant memories of that experience.

A major interest for Samantha during winter, in addition to her skiing, had been sledding. That is, until one evening when I took her up to the Lenin Hills near a Moscow university, called Patrice Lumumba University at the time, which overlooks the city. We were the only non-Soviets there.

I had started Samantha out on the more moderate slopes, but she insisted on sledding down a steeper one, because several other children her age and younger were on it. There did not appear to be all that much of a difference in the angle of decent, so I gave in to her. During her first decent she hit a small bump, and her left leg dropped off the sled altering her direction. She crashed head-first into a tree.

I think my heart stopped that night. It seemed to take forever for me to scramble and slide down the incline. A small group of children who had been on sleds themselves had gathered by the time I got to Samantha and were trying to console her. She was in considerable distress, and I thoroughly checked her out to ensure there were no serious injuries before moving her. I put her back on the sled, and the Russian children helped me by pushing and dragging the sled back up the steep incline to the road.

I expected and received a severe dressing down from Judith when I arrived back at our apartment carrying a sobbing Samantha.

The next morning Samantha looked a mess with both eyes swollen and a lot of bruising. The British doctor was not due back from London for several days, so we bathed her wounds, and applied whatever ointment we had at the time. The application of iodine made the injuries look even worse. I was concerned she may have had a concussion, but after reading my medical handbook I conducted some rudimentary tests and decided to let her out of bed the next day.

We eventually decided it was safe to take Samantha out for a break in a nearby park, but soon after exiting our building complex a trio of babushkas, elderly grandmothers, stopped in front of me on the street. They berated me and accused me of mistreating my daughter. I tried to explain what really had happened, but they refused to listen, and walked away. Judith adjusted a pair of her sunglasses to fit Samantha. They looked ridiculously large for her, but at least our venturing outdoors was a lot easier to deal with.

It was almost Christmas 1975, and I had been visiting an

Australian woman who had slipped on the ice on a Moscow street and had a skull injury. The male patient in the bed next to her also had a bandaged head. I commented, with some amazement, that the bandages were moving! The Australian patient advised that she had witnessed the hospital staff regularly using leeches to cleanse open wounds of the patients in her ward. I mentioned how I had also used leeches on my sores and cuts when I was a child, and that it was an effective treatment!

Christmas eve had arrived, and our thoughts focused on this woman isolated in a Soviet hospital. We had to do something. Judith prepared a plate of food as soon as our family had finished a late lunch with friends on Christmas Day. I also included a bottle of red wine and a couple of books in our hamper for the patient. Judith and the children came with me, and we stayed at the hospital for some time. We left after a toast with the wine was made for as speedy a recovery as was possible under her circumstances.

When I called the hospital the following afternoon, I was told the patient had been discharged, and was able to travel out of the Soviet Union with the assistance of a friend who had arrived from France.

We now had our own broomball team drawn from the additional staff members, which included our embassy security members — the Australian Federal Police officers. I thought this new line-up of teams in the diplomatic broomball competition were a lot of wusses. They were now using helmets, elbow and knee pads, heavily insulated clothing, and deep treaded heavy footwear with which to gain greater traction on the ice. Gone were the days of simply sliding, out of control over the ice, and beating the daylights out of each other when you collided with no helmets, padding, or other aids. Perhaps this was the start of the workplace health and safety era! There were no more offers of beer in the Finnish sauna after a game either! I lost interest.

One of the Irish embassy officers willingly assisted us by joining the team I put together to travel to Stuttgart to pick up three new vehicles for our embassy, and then drive them back to Moscow via Germany and Poland. Unfortunately, the local Soviet drivers could not be utilised because of restrictions on travel outside the Soviet Union. I gave our vice-consul, Terry Fahey, the responsibility of being our group task leader. He got everyone, and the new vehicles, back to Moscow without a mishap, and within the time frame given, which was an excellent achievement. Wherever you are Terry, I wish you good health and happiness.

The staff at the British Embassy in Moscow continued to be distant with anyone outside their own walls. This was further emphasised when the Malaysians and New Zealanders were advised by the British Embassy to approach me during this posting to assist them with advice on opening their respective embassies.

Easter 1976 was only a month away, so I planned a trip to Kyiv with a fellow Australian Embassy officer and our wives to cover the Easter service and compare it to the failed attempt in 1968. Unfortunately, the Easter service ended with a similar result with a bussed in rent-a-crowd forming a wall of protest, and the inability of the clergy, and others involved in the proposed service, to even open the doors of the church.

I had briefed my companions on what to expect, and sensed some obstruction was in the works from the crew who had been surveilling us since departing our hotel for the church. I suggested we observe the ritual of disturbance by the organised rent-a-crowd from a safe distance. The rest of that visit to Kyiv fell into the "business as usual" basket.

I was surprised and delighted to find Yuri Knox had been promoted and was commanding the full complement of shifts of the border guard detachments at Sheremetyevo Airport. He was just as affable and helpful as ever, particularly in continuing to assist me with prompt access to Australians who had been arrested or detained, usually for reasons such as arriving with incorrect entry visa details.

When visa holders arrived in Moscow earlier or later than shown on their visas, they would be incarcerated by the border guards in a holding annex at the side of the airport. They were then put on the first available flight out of the country. This happened to a couple of our DFA officers who had been conducting several embassy audits in eastern Europe and had arrived in Moscow from Warsaw.

I met the auditors as soon as they left the aircraft. I had to leave them at the arrivals area of the border guards' passport control booth and went on to the arrivals lounge to wait for them to be processed.

When they did not reappear sometime later, and there were no more passengers being processed, I asked a border guard officer seated in a booth nearby if I could speak to his commander. Unfortunately, Yuri was not on duty. The officer with whom I was placed in contact advised that the auditors had arrived three days earlier than was indicated on their visas, and they were being held in the quarantine area at the airport. They further advised that they would not be released until advice was received from the Ministry of Foreign Affairs.

I sent an application to the ministry requesting their release as soon as I returned to the embassy and provided an outline of the reason for their visit to Moscow. However, our visitors were travelling with official passports — not diplomatic passports, and consequently, my approach to the ministry was not successful. They were placed on the first available flight the next day. The only notification from the ministry was to advise that the two Australians had left.

In more serious consular cases confronted at Sheremetyevo Airport, those detained were removed to the more formal detention location at the KGB's Lefortovo Prison on the outskirts of Moscow.

I never looked forward to my visits to the infamous Lefortovo Prison. My rare visits to this uninviting and oppressive fortress were made to ensure that any of our citizens held there were being treated in accord with the

Geneva Convention, and to pass on letters from family and friends.

We were extremely restricted in what we could do to assist Australians in custody or convicted of crimes within the Soviet Union during those years. We could apply in writing to visit those being held and enquire how they were being treated to ensure they were not being treated any worse than other prisoners. We could also request to be advised of any court appearances and insist on being present for such hearings.

Legal representation and appeal were non-events in the Soviet Union. In most other countries we could also provide the Australian prisoner with a list of lawyers to select from. That does sound very lame, but the reality was that that was all we, or other countries bound by the Geneva Convention, could do.

The prison visits were almost always a disturbing encounter, but the simple action of bringing mail or word from home and providing a few minutes with a fellow Australian appeared to give them hope that they were not forgotten. Prior to this happening, however, any mail would have to be handed to the prison's escorting official, who would then pass it on to their superiors for screening prior to it being received by the inmate.

When I was allowed to speak to an inmate at Lefortovo it would have to be in the presence of the officer in charge, usually a KGB colonel. Five minutes were all I was allowed with the prisoner, who had to stand with his back against a wall, and look straight ahead, not at me. I would be seated to the side of the prisoner, on the other side of the room. When I asked the prisoner how he was being treated there would be one word offered — 'fine' or 'good'. Once the few minutes were up, and I had passed on any information I had received from Australia I then asked for any words he wanted to pass on to family members. He would then be marched out to heaven only knows what standard of incarceration he was being subjected to.

The standard period of sentence for those caught with drugs in the Soviet Union was eight years, with no parole, appeal, or another possibility of a shortening of the sentence.

The consul in Moscow in 1969, my boss, was a former British Army Major. He had been posted to Warsaw about the same time that I arrived back in Moscow. He sent me a cable via our network inviting Judith and I to visit him and his wife.

We received approval from the ambassador to travel to Poland over a long weekend and arranged with one of the embassy wives to look after Samantha while we were away. Adrian had been encouraged by his teacher at the American Embassy's Anglo-American School to write an essay on his visit to Warsaw. This should have been a simple trip. All arrangements had been processed in the required manner, including a letter to UPDK. The approval to travel should have taken between seven and fourteen days maximum but ended up taking between four and five weeks.

We were not off to a good start with having the Soviets reschedule our timetable at least twice and to finally advise that we could not fly to Warsaw. We could only book the train and only one way. UPDK also suggested that we would have to book the journey back to Moscow while we were in Warsaw. I cabled our embassy in Warsaw, and they confirmed that the return trip would not be a problem because of the choice and frequency of train or plane.

We were late being picked up by our embassy driver on the departure day to Warsaw, and we became very anxious about whether we were going to make the train on time. When we thought we had arrived at the train station and had started to relax the driver apologised and said he had made an error in taking us to the Leningrad Station which was some distance from our true destination, the Warsaw Station. This was not acceptable, and I let him know in no uncertain terms.

We arrived at the Warsaw Station as the train started to move. The only people on the platform were railway staff. Running was out of the question with our bags and heavy clothing. Adrian and I were well in front of Judith. I threw our luggage up onto the landing of the last carriage and hoisted Adrian up onto the steps of the carriage while on the trot and leapt up onto the bottom step to help Judith up. Another few seconds, and we would have been too late. All I could think of was — *what next?* It did not take long to find out what was next!

We had to walk through several carriages before we finally found our compartment. There was yet another problem. A Russian glanced up at us from his position stretched out full length on one of the bench seats as we entered and went back to reading his paper. We had booked this compartment for ourselves and had to pay a premium in foreign currency for the privilege. I asked the fellow to check the details on his ticket, because he was in the wrong compartment, but he simply ignored me.

I left Judith and Adrian with the luggage in the corridor and found a conductor moving along our carriage checking tickets. I explained the situation to him, showed him my diplomatic identity card, passport, and tickets, and motioned for him to follow me. It took a few minutes, but we finally had the fellow ejected. It all seemed to be an act playing itself out. I had the feeling nobody expected us to have made it to the train.

We had hardly left for Warsaw, and I was already growing concerned about our return to Moscow.

Our hosts, the Major and his wife were most gracious in their welcome to Warsaw, and in providing accommodation and an excellent dinner as soon as we arrived. We toured the city the next day and spent time in the Old Warsaw district with a light lunch in the picturesque town square. The following day, sensing a disruptive force at work, I decided it best to check on our travel arrangements for the return to Moscow.

The embassy staff in Warsaw offered to assist us with train bookings, but they were told that all seats were booked for several days. The Major decided that we should go to the main train station for a face-to-face with the booking people. We were sent from one desk to another, with each appearing to give a signal to the next one that we were approaching.

We finally and reluctantly gave up and decided to forget the train and fly back. We were becoming extremely concerned with the obvious and determined obstructions to our travel arrangements that had been in progress even before we had left Moscow.

The Warsaw Embassy staff told us that the flight back to Moscow had been booked, but we would have to front up at the airport ourselves with our passports and diplomatic identity cards before the tickets would be handed over because that was the required procedure for persons other than those diplomats who were accredited to Poland. Our parish no longer included Poland, and therefore I had no accreditation other than being a foreign diplomatic passport holder.

Fortunately, the Major insisted on accompanying us to the airport. The "game" started as soon as we arrived at the check-in desk. No-one would acknowledge the booking had been received. We were told to stand in a long queue while the matter was sorted out. This was yet another delaying tactic to either test our resolve or ensure we did not get on a flight.

Judith and I were both starting to resign ourselves to another day of this obstruction, and frustration. However, the Major lost his long-held British reserve and told us to take a seat nearby. A few minutes later, apparently after ignoring the *apparatchik* desk-dwellers, he demanded and received assistance from the Polish Border Control Commander. We were told we would not be travelling to Moscow that day, but we were given our tickets for an Aeroflot flight for early the next morning. There were no further problems in our return to Moscow. I will make a few personal observations in the next chapter on the people of the USSR, the "Elitists" who destroy the illusion of a classless society, and the Catholic Church, under the yoke of communism.

18

The People, the Elite & the Church in the USSR

1967–1976

"Socialism is a philosophy of failure, the creed of ignorance, and the gospel of envy."

Winston Churchill

The People of the USSR (Soviet Union)

It would be remiss of me if I did not make mention of the Soviet public persona that existed during the years my family and I lived in the Soviet Union, so that you, the reader, will better understand the system that was imposed on the Soviet citizenry who lived, endured, and interacted, or not, with us, while those of the "elite" classes enjoyed privileges that the average citizen could only dream of.

The challenge for most of us who had been posted to Moscow during this period was to get to know and understand the Soviet people. Unfortunately, during the 1960s and 1970s, this was an incredibly difficult, if not almost impossible task. You could live among the people of the Soviet Union, mix with them during the normal routines of the work day at the embassy when out and about, or when travelling, but still not truly understand how they felt about the existence they had inherited, and been subjected to.

The mechanics of segregated living did not make it absolutely impossible for a curious and purposeful Russian-speaking foreigner to meet and get to know the average Soviet citizen. What the restrictions did ensure, however, was that by and large, those with whom foreigners tended to mix were "official" people only, and this obviously affected and coloured an outsider's view of the Soviet Union.

An exception to the rule of keeping the general Soviet citizenry away from foreigners must not have been applied to elderly Russian women who were generally considered the backbone of the Soviet family and were fiercely protective of young children. I have already mentioned the dressing down I received on the street from a group of *babushkas*, or grandmothers, when they spotted our daughter's sledding injury. I have another example for further amplification. One mild summer's day Judith and I were walking in a park, and I had Adrian, who was probably between one year and eighteen months old perched on my shoulders. The two *babuskhas* stopped me in my tracks and began to loudly berate me in front of a small crowd. They were quickly joined by others, and I became quite concerned thinking it was because I was a foreigner. We eventually understood what was upsetting them. The action of a *babushka's* finger prodding at my chest, and tugging at Adrian's trouser legs, was enough to get their message. He had been showing some bare skin. Not allowed, even on a warm day!

The further one travelled from Moscow, the less inhibited and less strictly indoctrinated the people appeared to be. I recall an evening at dinner in a restaurant in Tallinn, Estonia, on the Baltic coast, when the lid fell off the teapot while the waiter was serving our table of four travelling companions. The waiter, without missing a beat, leant over our table, picked up the lid, and with a straight face whispered, 'made in the USSR'. A small comment that meant a lot coming from an Estonian.

All Soviet citizens wishing to move to Moscow had to apply to live in the capital and had to carry their internal passport (ID) to prove that they were indeed approved residents. The internal passport had to be kept on their person for checking purposes by police and other government officials at any time.

If too much celebrating had taken place by a Soviet citizen he or she could voluntarily or involuntarily sober up in the "special stations" where showers, a bed and a hot drink were provided with no criminal charges made. This was to ensure that people do not freeze to death on the streets during the winter months. On questioning my driver about this facility, he mentioned that they only charge between ten and fifteen roubles a night (US$8). The driver added that the stations always filled up during and after New Year's Day. The detail he provided in telling this story indicated to me that he may have experienced a stay in one of the stations himself.

There was the occasional exasperated or derogatory outburst about the Soviet system from a Soviet staff member, more often than not from an embassy driver, maid or nanny, but such outbursts would almost immediately be withdrawn or amended in fear of a reprimand or worse if overheard or reported on. Controls were so tight that the system almost shut you out.

An example of how a low-echelon member of State Security really thought at times became evident when my driver injected the following comment into a conversation we were having while taking me to an appointment one day: 'The USSR was like a rotting fish, it always starts to rot at the head!'

I also recall another driver's sudden outburst while driving me back to the embassy on one occasion. We had just passed a family from Ghana in colourful African garments and headwear walking to their embassy nearby. The driver grunted in a derogatory way and commented, 'You can tell the state of a man's soul by the colour of his skin!'

The Soviet Class System and the Elite

An entire false veneer of the people, running into the thousands, had been created by the Soviet system for dealing with foreigners. These people were referred to as "official Russians". Practically every Soviet institution from the Red Army to the Writers' Union or the Russian Orthodox Church had its Foreign Department set up for contacting foreigners. These "official Russians" also had the task of projecting *Pravda's* Russia, the Russia of scientific success, Soviet workers' democracy, and the modern welfare state. Nearly everyone was involved in some way or other in hiding the fact that Soviet life did not measure up to the Party's propaganda, such as the artless fiction that Soviet writers were not censored, or the laughable claim that the more than one hundred Soviet nationalities lived in harmony. One reason why the life of a Soviet citizen was so deceptive was that they were, through necessity, masters at the art of lying low, and of adopting a protective colouration of conformity in order to simply get by. Important elements of Russian culture and the very existence of intellectual life survived that way.

Official and other prominent or privileged Muscovites could pass through the entries to our diplomatic residential compound checkpoints if attending diplomatic receptions and other special occasions only by showing written invitations that had the approval of the appropriate Soviet ministry. Those not in the elite category, or not in possession of the required paperwork, were challenged and questioned.

Many visiting diplomats, businessmen, politicians and journalists arriving in Moscow were completely unaware that within the Soviet Union's so-called classless society there was a highly privileged class whose members were secure, so long as they conformed. If they lost favour, they lost the privileges that belonged only to those of the elite.

The nerve centre of the system guaranteed both power

and privilege and was referred to as the *Nomenklatura*. It was like an exclusive club with membership offered to party leaders or those in the most sensitive positions within the Communist Party power structure known as the apparat or the *apparatchiki*. It is this hierarchy that was rewarded with access to special stores and other facilities.

There was another way to join this exclusive club, and that was reserved for those who could contribute as outstanding performers in science, the arts, sport, or in the military. However, while they may receive the status of the elite class, they had no power.

A monthly allotment of gold roubles was also provided to the upper echelon of the Soviet elite which permitted them to buy foreign goods in the *Gastronomes* and *Beriozkas*, or as they were known locally, the *Valuta* shops which were generally restricted to tourists, diplomats, and other holders of hard currency.

In addition to the *Gastronomes* and *Beriozkas*, there were special stores that were never advertised with a shopfront and were impossible to locate or identify unless you were one of the privileged few, or like some of us, curious foreigners who discovered what to look for. The usual tell-tale sign was the black Soviet-made Volga sedans illegally parked in groups on the footpath. Their licence plate letters were also a dead give-away.

The drivers of these vehicles would gather in groups and most of them would focus their attention on the entrance doors of a particular building waiting for the privileged class to exit. If we wanted to observe further to confirm our discovery, we would wait to see if they were carrying "booty". It was never possible to see what they were carrying because their purchases were always hidden in plain wrappings or boxes, and the drivers would move their cars as close as possible to the entrance to ensure the exit and loading procedures were conducted as quickly as possible. These stores existed in every major city in the Soviet Union to service the elite.

The majority of the Soviet people who had no elite status or access to special stores at that time had to form lines outside any shop that had food, shoes, or clothing items for sale. Every woman carried a "perhaps" string bag, and men carried briefcases for the same purpose — perhaps they may find shoes, perhaps toilet paper, or perhaps meat, potatoes, etc., may be in a store.

It did not matter that items were not required at the time. Shoes or clothing items did not have to fit, they were simply items that had arrived in that store and could be traded with other people for something they did need. If there was a line outside a store people quickly joined it in the hope that perhaps they would be able to buy something to use, eat, wear, or trade.

Salaries of top officials in the Soviet Union in the 1960s and 1970s were supposed to be top secret. It may, therefore, be surprising to learn that the wage of Leonid Brezhnev, General Secretary of the Central Committee, and leader of some 250 million people from 1964 until his death on 10 November 1982 was the equivalent of approximately A$900 a month. There were, however, extensive fringe benefits other than money that were accorded to the Soviet leader, and some 255 000 other Communist Party elite, as the prerogatives of power.

The upper levels of the elite were also entitled to their own apartments in the city; country dachas or country houses; superior medical care; and State-supplied vehicles and drivers, depending on status and rank. Some also had that most prized of privileges, the opportunity to travel abroad and mingle with foreigners without fear of arrest.

Some of the other additional comforts and benefits available to this privileged hierarchy were in access to other special establishments that were also tucked away from prying eyes. They consisted of special kitchens for prepared food; special tailor shops; special clubs; and special dry cleaners! There was even a special hospital, called the Kremlin Hospital, although it was not in the Kremlin complex where the highest level of the elite could be treated by the country's best doctors using the latest imported western medical equipment. This was a fine example of socialism hard at work for the masses, or not!

The country's best doctors were apparently not good enough to treat Leonid Brezhnev, General Secretary of the Communist Party of the Soviet Union and Chairman of the Presidium of the Supreme Soviet. A Swiss businessperson friend of mine who represented a European company based in Moscow told me that Brezhnev had been experiencing heart problems since the early 1960s. The businessperson mentioned during 1969, while we were having a beer after a game of broomball, that Brezhnev had suffered another heart attack, and had a Geneva-based heart specialist looking after him on a regular fly-in/fly-out regime. It was widely suspected that Brezhnev was being pumped full of drugs to get him through conferences and major events.

This same contact also told me that Brezhnev had one of the best collections of European and American vehicles, and both Brezhnev's apartment and dacha were fully equipped with expensive European appliances and furniture.

However, there was one thing that no Soviet citizen could own, no matter how exalted his or her position, and that was land. The land belonged to the State, not a person, and therefore could not be bequeathed to any heir.

The elite watched TV on the latest foreign-made colour sets instead of the antiquated black and white sets produced by Soviet manufacturers, and they had priority access to the waiting list to purchase a car. The waiting time for the citizen without elite status for a Soviet-made Moskvich or Volga was seven years during the 1960s. The wait had dropped to four or five years by the mid-1970s.

Diplomats wishing to buy a Soviet-made vehicle did not have to wait longer than a couple of weeks. The Soviets wanted the hard currency, and that had precedence over supply to its own citizens. I bought a Russian-made car, called a Moskvich, in the early days of my first posting. It caused me nothing but grief.

I was recently reminded of the occasion we had gone to the Bolshoi Theatre, and upon leaving we discovered that it had been snowing heavily. We found the Moskvich and cleared enough snow to get into the vehicle so that I could start and warm it up. I turned the ignition key, and after a lot of noise, cutting out, and restarting for a second or two, it burst into flames. We exited the vehicle as quickly as possible as smoke was pouring into the interior of the vehicle. Bystanders were frantically calling out and pointing to the engine area. Russian theatre-goers came from all directions and started to scoop up and throw snow onto the burning vehicle. I motioned to everyone to step back, and just let it burn. No-one took any notice of me; perhaps their pride was at stake. It eventually burned down to its metal shell.

I also recall an incident a day prior to the car burning that may have contributed to or had been the cause of the fire. One of the fuses had failed three months after I bought it, and the car became inoperable. One of our drivers came to the rescue and mentioned this was a common failure in the vehicle and that it was no problem to fix. The word "improvise" in the Russian language is exactly the same as in English and was used by the driver as he reached into his coat pocket and came out with a pack of cigarettes. He tore off a piece of the silver paper that surrounded the cigarette packet interior, pulled the fuse out, wrapped a piece of the silver paper around each end, and inserted the fuse back into the fuse-holders. The ignition key was turned and the vehicle started. I thought his improvisation was brilliant. Perhaps the silver paper only lasted a couple of ignition starts before it set the car alight!

On a lighter note, Muscovites often joked about their leaders, when with very close friends. One story that has been told and retold over many years may still be new to some. It goes something like this: Brezhnev was very close to his mother, who lived in Ukraine, and he really wanted to impress her with the trappings that went with being the leader of over 250 million citizens. So, he invited her to Moscow, and showed her around his huge apartment which consisted of one whole floor of a nine-floor building at 26 Kutuzovsky Prospect, and all she could say was 'okay'. So, he took her out to his dacha in his ZIL (aka Russian Cadillac) limousine with motorcycle escorts, and several cars of minders. The dacha's previous tenants included Stalin and Khrushchev. He took her on a tour of the multiple rooms and the landscaped grounds, and all she could do was move her head from side to side, and not a single word was uttered. Frustrated, Brezhnev called for his helicopter and flew her to a hunting lodge with huge entertaining rooms, an impressive array of animal heads mounted on every wall, and racks of guns of multiple calibres. There was continued silence, and he could no longer restrain himself. He hesitantly asked, 'Mama, what do you think?', 'Well,' she muttered, 'It's nice, but what will you do if the Communists come back?'

The other Soviet elite that set itself apart from the rest, was the Committee for State Security, the *Komitet*

Gosudarstvennoy Bezopasnosti, or as more commonly known, the KGB. The top echelon of senior officers of this organisation were up there with the elitists. In addition to all the perks mentioned for the elite Soviets already referred to, the KGB, like a parallel universe, had their own special dachas, stores, etc., that they had access to without the scrutiny of the *apparatchiks* of the Kremlin.

Those not included in the senior ranks of this organisation and therefore not considered elitists, clawed, connived, and climbed over whoever stood in their way to partake of the rewards that awaited those who had the privileges. The junior ranks did have middle-level stores with fewer luxury items, and they had to pay more for their purchases than their bosses!

The Church

The founder of the Soviet State, Vladimir Ilyich Ulyanov (Lenin), once said, 'Any notion of a Lord God, even any trifling with a Lord God is an unspeakable abomination.'

Millions of Soviet citizens paid at least some observance to religious faith during this period up to the late 1970s, and I believe the approximate religious composition in the Soviet Union at that time was as follows: Russian Orthodoxy, 30 million; Roman Catholics, 10 million, mostly in Lithuania; Protestant numbers were mainly confined to the 700 000 Lutherans of Latvia and Estonia; and the Russian Baptists numbered more than 500 000. There were also several million Muslims in central Asia and some Buddhists.

Russian Orthodoxy was caught unprepared when faced with the rise of the communist revolution of 1917. The Soviet leaders, Lenin and Stalin, between them wiped out over 50 000 priests, monks, and nuns, and demolished all but 6 400 of the 48 000 Orthodox churches in the pre-communist era. Religion was clandestinely controlled in the Soviet Union. Soviet State Security controlled the Church hierarchy and recruited bona fide clergymen as agents. This organisation had many means at its disposal to suppress young believers by alienating them from their peer groups, blocking career possibilities, and ensuring that seats at universities and other places of higher learning were not available to them.

The State also allowed only those with government licences to preach. A deal was finally struck between the Soviet State and the Church with the result that priests no longer filled labour camps. In return for a relatively quiet existence, the Church refrained from criticising Soviet policies. A win-win for all.

The Ukrainian Orthodox Easter service in Kyiv suffered even greater scrutiny and harassment, and many in the West considered that one could gauge the state of the Church within the Soviet Union, or more specifically, Ukraine, because Ukrainian Orthodoxy had been brutally persecuted and controlled by the Soviet authorities.

Although we had intended to ignore the presence of those who tried to disrupt or deny entry to the Russian Orthodox Church in Moscow, we found it quite disruptive, and not worth the attention and stress. We only went to the Russian Orthodox service twice, and that was out of curiosity more than religious fervour.

When we Christian diplomats wanted to attend a Catholic Mass or other Christian service we would have to wait for a priest or pastor to arrive from Helsinki or London twice a month or later to conduct a service in the small chapel at the British Embassy. The American Embassy also had periodic visits from a Catholic priest.

Parish records were not kept in the USSR, but in an interview with leading Russian Orthodox priests by a group of American journalists in the mid-1970s, it was disclosed that the believers go to divine services lasting three to four hours, and they stay to the end! One cleric mentioned, 'If you came to our churches, you would find faith and worship, not coffee-drinking, dancing, or clubs'. He added, 'There may be fewer churchgoers than in Czarist times, but there is no comparison in the quality. People go to our churches today out of conviction and to obtain inspiration rather than out of habit or tradition'. He finished by suggesting, 'This is our strength'.

The Church within the Soviet Union appeared to be increasing its influence in the early 1980s. People were generally becoming more cynical towards their government. Western music which had been almost completely expunged from the Soviet Union was slowly but surely making its presence known. The youth of major Soviet cities were organising themselves in setting up underground concerts and promoting their local musicians.

By the mid-1980s the outright persecution of the Church was no longer a priority preoccupation of the State. Perhaps there was an appreciation that religion is like a nail that gets more deeply embedded the harder it is hammered.

There was also a well-oiled underground flow of bibles and other religious materials reaching eager hands throughout the Soviet Union. Religious organisations under the guise of tourists were a steady source of supply.

Before I leave the subject of the people and their Church in Soviet Russia, I believe it worthwhile mentioning a cultural and religious experience that we attended outside the environs of Moscow. I had been on an excursion with Judith and a group of Canadian and Australian embassy staff visiting the Zagorsk Theological Academy and Seminary which was located approximately 100 km from Moscow and had been a major tourist attraction for some time.

The atmosphere and structure of the service we attended at the Church of the Assumption were nothing we had witnessed before in the Soviet Union. The church was very dark inside with the only light provided by the hundreds of candles on and around the altar held by the aged parishioners who had arrived on the grounds earlier by horse and cart, or by foot. I discovered later that this was the only form of transport used by that generation of "Old Believers", as they were referred to. They firmly believed that all forms of motorised transport were the vehicles of the devil.

There was no seating in the chapel. The parishioners stood facing the alter which was manned by bearded priests dressed in gilded vestments. Parishioners and visitors were separated from the priests who stood on a slightly elevated platform. All in the congregation were chanting in what we agreed was possibly some form of ancient Russian that we could not understand. The services went on for several hours. It felt like a pagan ritual of the past was being re-enacted. Very eerie, but unforgettable with the lighted candles further enhancing their ghost-like figures. We foreigners did not stay for the full service!

I have already mentioned my involvement in the Jewish "Operation Reunion" program we operated from the embassy. My only other face-to-face association with any of the Jewish community in Moscow was during a very brief private meeting organised by a US Embassy Military Attaché. This meeting occurred towards the end of my first posting to Moscow in 1969. I joined two US Military Attaché Officers in an American Embassy vehicle to do a "drop and go" visit to an underground art gallery run by a group of Jewish dissident artists, for no other reason than to buy some paintings, and provide the artists with some hard currency.

Buying or otherwise transporting works of Soviet artists out of the Soviet Union was forbidden unless full disclosure of the art pieces and the artist were made known to UPDK in writing, and approval was given to remove them from the

Soviet Union. As far as I know, no-one was ever successful in following this routine.

There was also the problem of meeting and mixing with unapproved Soviet citizens, especially dissident Jewish artists. To acknowledge we had mixed with and purchased art pieces from these dissident artists would more than likely have caused considerable problems for them, and possibly us.

The need for secrecy on this art purchasing run was emphasised. We were assisted on this occasion by a Marine gunnery sergeant who was our van driver. He dropped us off outside our destination and drove off immediately with instructions to come back in fifteen minutes. If we were not out front, he was to return ten minutes later. We missed the first run and had to be ready for the next one because the diplomatic plates would draw too much attention to the building and its occupants in this part of Moscow.

There was no time for a session of art appreciation. We had to make a hurried selection, and after paying for three paintings each in foreign currency we waited just inside the building's front street door until we saw the 'Gunny' return.

The Marine had us back within the US Embassy grounds in a matter of minutes. The Soviet guards at the front gates of the US Embassy were not happy as we sped through. Another fun day in Moscow.

The three paintings I bought were transferred to my car within the compound of the US Embassy, packed with our personal items when we left Moscow, and still hang in our home today.

19

Persona non grata & Farewell to Moscow

1976

Many unwelcome events had been directed at my family and me in Moscow during our first posting from 1967 to 1969 and had increased from 1975 to 1976 with regular overt entries into our apartment made while we were out. Our secure area in the apartment had a lockable cage for storing items such as canned and packaged food, cigarettes, liquor, and personal items required for other seasons, such as clothing, skis, etc.

Our efforts at trying to keep the caged area secure were futile. The intruders made no effort to conceal their activity, even leaving the front door unlocked when they left. Locks to secure cupboards were left on tables to show they could do what they liked; they signed off on their presence in the apartment by leaving their unmistakable Russian cigarette *Papyrosi* stubbed out on the floor, on a plate, or even left in the kitchen sink; they turned back clocks; they turned lights on; and they would often ring our phone several times a night, every night for several days. I had to answer every time because it could have been an emergency consular case. As far as I could tell the intruders never took anything. I believe the tactics employed were simply to harass and wear us down.

A disturbing and unacceptable event took place that signalled the opposition team were getting serious when they initiated what appeared to be a mock kidnapping attempt of Judith and our children outside a *Beryoska* store in central Moscow.

I was sitting in our car several car lengths from the front entrance of the building waiting for Judith and the children to come out when two Soviet-made Volga cars pulled up near the entrance. Although I was initially interested in the cars and their occupants, and the dramatic way in which they pulled up, I soon lost interest thinking they were probably an escort party waiting for an elite *apparatchik* to emerge from the building.

Judith and the children finally came out and stopped in front of the entrance to look for me. I had started to get out of my car when the occupants of the two vehicles exited and encircled Judith and the children and tried to usher them towards the curb and the waiting cars. Judith was unsure what was happening. She stood still and held the hands of both the children and was looking back to where I was parked. One in the group stood apart from the others, near an open car door, and turned around to look back at me. The group was in no hurry as they broke away, strode back to their cars, and drove off. It all happened so fast that by the time my mind had computed what was happening they were on their way while I was still running towards them. The whole incident would not have taken more than a few seconds, but at the time it seemed a lot longer. The only witnesses to this escapade other than ourselves were two Russian drivers waiting for their masters only metres away. They just went on chatting when I raised my hands face up in the universal hand language of, "Did you see that, what the hell just happened?"

The continuous, repressive, and blatantly overt surveillance was humorous at first, then it became extremely trying and annoying, and finally, when my family were included in the escapades it was "enough is enough". Such behaviour from people with such an adversarial interest in us must seem so mundane today to anyone who has not experienced that time and place, during the height of the Cold War.

I was only halfway through my two-year posting in early 1976 when John Rowland, the ambassador to the Soviet Union during my earlier posting, flew in on an official visit to the embassy. We had a long chat in the embassy's Secure room, and I briefed him on some of the smothering and restrictive occurrences that had been taking place since I arrived back in Moscow. He mentioned that he was aware of much of what had been happening from reports from the ambassador, Sir James Plimsoll.

Not long after John Rowland's visit, I received advice from the department that my posting had been cut short.

Arrangements commenced almost immediately for our

return to Australia. Sir James Plimsoll held a farewell lunch for me, and once everyone had left, he invited me to join him for coffee in the *Bolshoi Zal*. This was a huge room used for the annual National Day function, and other events that required room for large numbers of guests. Once the niceties of the day had been dispensed with, Sir James informed me that, 'The Soviet Ministry of Foreign Affairs had instructed me that you are no longer welcome, and you are never to return to the Soviet Union or any of its associated States or Territories.'

I had been declared persona non grata. The official meaning given to this term is "unacceptable and unwelcome and must leave the country". No specific reason was provided or mentioned by Sir James, and I did not ask for any. I was, if anything, delighted to hear the news. I just wanted to take my family home. I had definitely had enough!

We had not been able to send our Mustang back to Australia from Santiago because of my being medically evacuated at that time, so we decided to bring the VW Camper home with us after we had left Moscow.

We had planned to take whatever outstanding leave I had left at the completion of the supposed two-year posting to tour Europe in the VW Camper, and then send it home from England at the end of our holidays. However, our sudden departure imposed by the Soviet Ministry of Foreign Affairs had caught us unawares and made all this impossible. It had to be sold, and quickly. We had already sold our other vehicle only weeks previously, and therein lay a problem that continued after we had left Moscow. I should have set the vehicle alight to make everyone happy. Only one vehicle a year could be sold by diplomats and other foreigners.

With only days to go before departure, I received a frantic phone call in the evening from the Australian Federal Police (AFP) officer on duty at the embassy requesting me to come as quickly as possible. The embassy was on fire, and there were firemen moving throughout the Chancery and the secure area.

I arrived at the narrow street that the embassy was situated in, and found it packed with several fire trucks spread around, with one partially inside the embassy grounds.

At a rough count made on the run into the embassy, there were ten or eleven fire trucks. Fire hoses were laid out all over the street and the pathway side-entrance leading into the ambassador's official residence on the ground floor, and up the stairs to the first floor where our secure offices were located. It was chaotic.

The official residence did not appear to be in immediate danger as I entered the building so I moved quickly up to the first floor where the stressed Australian Federal Police duty officer was unable to maintain even cursory surveillance of the firemen to ensure they were not carrying anything other than normal firefighting equipment as they went into, and out of the active fire area. At the same time, he was trying to brief me on what had happened, and where he thought the seat of the fire was. Not good news, it was definitely in our secure area.

John Burgess, the counsellor (second-in-charge), emerged from the dark smoke that was invading the entire area during the AFP's briefing. John was exhausted. I took his antiquated Russian mask and oxygen bottle and set out for the secure area to see what I could do.

Some of the flooring had been burned through. For safety's sake, I had to place one foot in front of the other on the main beam that had supported the hallway flooring so I could proceed into the secure area. It was a mess. The walls were so hot I could only briefly touch them with my hands to balance myself. I was competing for a footing with the firemen all the way. It was impossible to remain inside for long to try and monitor the activity within the Secure Room. There was little light to go by, and this was hindered further by the constant presence of thick smoke and the firemen.

It was a very long night. We managed to save a lot of files and other sensitive material and had to keep an eye on the firemen at the same time. We did not know the cause of the fire at that time.

Once the fire was under control, hours later, and most of the firemen had either left or were in the process of doing so, I went down to the official residence, and asked a couple of staff to assist me in taking all the paintings down, and carrying them to the trade commissioner's residence, which was across the other side of the parking area, and safely away from the main building. Water and ash had started pouring down into the main entertaining room from the first-floor fire area.

While engaged with the paintings I spotted a well-dressed middle-aged man in a European-style beige raincoat, and a dark Fedora hat wandering around and peering into rooms. I thought he may have been a journalist. I asked him at least twice to identify himself. When he did not reply I identified myself as an Australian embassy officer and told him in no uncertain terms to leave the premises. He continued to ignore me until I became a little more vocal and animated. I pointed to the side-entrance door and escorted him out of the embassy grounds. It had been an extremely stressful night.

The ambassador joined us once the fire had been extinguished, and just as the dawn was at last beginning to show itself. Sir James applauded our efforts and told us to go home and get some sleep. I was more interested in attempting to unclog the ash and residual smoke debris that I had accumulated in my eyes, nose, mouth and throat. I was also contemplating a long hot shower, a change of clothes, and breakfast.

John Burgess had already organised the first order of business for the morning before I arrived back at the embassy. He had arranged for us both to meet the appropriate officers at the Directorate for Services to the Diplomatic Corps (UPDK) to discuss the cause of the fire, and what temporary arrangements could be put in place as quickly as possible to ensure the embassy could continue to function.

John and I arrived on time and were escorted into the director's office. The most noticeable item in the room, as was the norm in most if not all Soviet government offices, was a large portrait of Lenin looking down on us all. Seated at an impressively ornate desk was the well-dressed man I had removed from the ambassador's residence the previous evening. It was the director! I felt very uneasy. All I could do was pretend I did not recognise him and hope he did not recognise me!

The usual pleasantries were exchanged, but only between the director and John. I was being completely ignored. He had recognised me all right! I decided it best to just sit back and shut up unless asked a question directly. John commenced by stating that we had no idea how the fire started. The director advised that his investigators had already established that it had started when a light switch on the ground floor had been turned on and had shorted out. The electrical short had run up the length of the wiring and started the fire in the upper floor. We were not qualified in fire safety or whatever other qualification was required to question the director's findings.

John mentioned later that he could not understand why the director completely ignored me during the discussions that morning. I told him of my meeting with the director the previous evening. I do not recall John laughing.

I have no idea what ensued later, and whether we or UPDK would be held responsible for the cost of repairs and renovations. John and my replacement would have to take care of the consultations with UPDK, and all that would follow in getting the embassy up and running again.

I only had a couple of days left before leaving Moscow and returning to Canberra. All departure procedures, documentation, and packing had been completed. We could not wait to get on our way home.

There were numerous other experiences with what American President Ronald Reagan described as the "evil empire", but I believe enough energy has been expended on this subject. Suffice to mention that life behind the Iron Curtain was never boring. It is time to finally bring that "curtain" down.

20

Return to the Department & Resignation

1976–1981

There were so many incidents that impacted heavily and adversely on my family and me during the years serving overseas that when I arrived back in Canberra in August 1976, I found that I could not focus on my work. I simply wanted to get away from everybody and sort myself out. I knew I had gone beyond just feeling tired, disoriented, depressed, and unable to concentrate on my work. I finally realised that I needed help.

I had only disclosed to my Section Head that I was exhausted and needed time off to rest and recover. I was convinced that my general condition would not be understood by friends, and departmental colleagues, and that I would possibly be seen as not being able to withstand the pressures of overseas service. I had continued to have bouts of sadness, depression, and guilt in losing our son, particularly when considering the comments made by the treating doctor in Chile that our son Adam would have survived if we had been at home in Australia or in another country where appropriate medical assistance and medication would have been available to treat him. I had interpreted this advice to mean that my choice of career was responsible for our son's death.

I realise that I had agreed to serve in Chile, and I could not possibly have foreseen the events that tore such a beautiful country to pieces. However, that has not diminished the pain within me that I continue to feel all these years later. A father is not supposed to outlive his children.

The final blow to my confidence in continuing with a career with the department culminated halfway through the second posting in 1976 when the Soviet Ministry of Foreign Affairs notified the ambassador that I was no longer welcome in the USSR. I thought this reaction from the Soviet Ministry of Foreign Affairs could severely limit my range of posting options for overseas service in the future and encourage continued and unwarranted attention from those who still held the cords of the Iron Curtain.

I was personally treated by the Head of the Social Psychiatry Research Unit at the Australian National University (ANU) for what was described as the worst case of "battle fatigue" that he had seen in peacetime. Today, this is referred to as post-traumatic stress disorder or PTSD. I paid for all the treatment regime myself and took my three months of accredited Long Service Leave (LSL) to get myself well again, and back to work. I had to take LSL because I had used up almost all my sick leave during my treatment and hospitalisation in Santiago, and at Woden Hospital in

Canberra upon arrival back in Australia in 1972. The treating ANU Head of Psychiatry, in his final summation wrote, in part:

> Along with Hippocrates, one may concede that the sorrow that hath no vent in tears may make other organs weep. His was in large part an unresolved grief reaction following his son's death.

I am certain that the early success in my recovery after I had requested to be taken off all medication, eventuated mostly with the assistance of my family, and to a lesser but valued degree by the silent companionship and aid of Lady, a beautiful four-year-old Labrador that a friend gave me prior to his proceeding on posting overseas. Lady was my constant companion, and we walked together for hours every day, and sometimes late at night. There were a lot of long one-way conversations with her. She was a good listener.

Upon completion of my treatment at ANU, and because of what had been described as the uniqueness of my case I agreed to be taped in an interview situation with the treating professor. His students listened in at an overhead glassed-in observation area.

The interview was conducted over a question and answer session covering all the areas that were understood to be triggers that had slowly but surely contributed to my slipping into that dark period. I was told the interview exercise would later be used as a teaching project at the university.

Following the completion of the treatment I had received

at ANU, I requested an appointment with a Australian Government doctor and was cleared to return to work once my three months of LSL had been used.

Once back in the department my first task was supervising the translators and interpreters, and the document preparation and distribution team assisting the representatives of the thirty-six countries at the 1977 Antarctic Treaty Consultative Conference in Canberra. After the conference, I was attached for a short period to the staffing section and travelled Australia-wide as a recruitment officer.

My next appointment was as state director in charge of the Department of Foreign Affairs office at Westfield Towers in Sydney during 1978-1979. The position also included oversight of one hundred and fifty of our passport personnel in a separate location near Sydney's Circular Quay. The Sydney assignment was for only one year to fill in for our High Commissioner in Cyprus who would take over the position once she had completed her posting.

This was not much of family life for us, because I had to fly from Canberra to Sydney on Monday mornings and return back to Canberra on Friday nights. The department had leased an apartment in Randwick for my accommodation.

I had one request for political asylum during my year in Sydney. I had to charter a light aircraft to fly me to Newcastle to interview an Ethiopian male who had been found stowing away on a ship and had been handed over to Customs officers (Border Force) upon arrival at the port of Newcastle.

The work in Sydney was interesting with a lot of interaction with other government departments and members of the consular corps.

My last position with the department after the Sydney assignment was as the senior foreign affairs representative to South Australia from 1979 to 1981. I was responsible for providing briefings, when requested, to the South Australian Premier, politicians on both sides of the House, and other government officials and departments as requested, as well as being available to business leaders, universities and the representatives of the consular corps in South Australia. There were many speaking engagement requests from various service groups.

Figure 14. Author and Judith at Government House, Adelaide 1980

The general administration of the Adelaide passport office was also part of my brief. My second-in-charge covered those tasks admirably, and without much involvement from me.

Consular assistance and advice to the general public was also demanding at times, particularly when parents had lost touch with their children travelling overseas or had fallen prey to various cults that flourished during those years.

Protocol duties were a regular occurrence in Adelaide, with many visits of VIPs and international visitors. These visitors had to be facilitated upon arrival and departure and were often accompanied by Department of Prime Minister & Cabinet or Department of Foreign Affairs escort officers. Either the protocol section of the prime minister's department or I prepared the programs of places to visit, and people for the visitors to be introduced to.

Once again, our posting was cut short after two-and-a-half years. Canberra advised that I was about to be replaced by Alexander Downer. Politics were at work in a supposedly apolitical workplace. Alex was about to enter federal politics via a seat in South Australia, and my office in Adelaide was the perfect launching pad.

Alex was a great choice, and I admired his ambition and hard work in achieving success with a seat in the House of Representatives, followed by his appointment as Minister for Foreign Affairs, Leader of the Liberal Party, and later as High Commissioner in London.

Arrangements for the selling of our home in South

Australia commenced immediately, but there was little else we could do, such as schooling for the children, and packing our furniture and personal effects, until we heard from the department where we would be going next.

There was also our home in Canberra that was still being leased by a counsellor at the US Embassy. That lease would have to be terminated if we were to return to Canberra for any considerable time. We did not have to wait long for such advice. I was asked to fly to Canberra for a meeting with the Head of Staffing soon after Alex's posting to South Australia had been officially announced.

I did not appreciate it at the time, but the department had provided time for me to get back in shape by posting me to State offices in Sydney and Adelaide before sending me off overseas again.

I met with the Head of Staffing in early July 1981 in Canberra and was asked whether I would be interested in opening the Consulate (later a Consulate-General) in Bali. I would also have to spend at least three months at our embassy in Jakarta before arriving in Bali.

Several of the Qantas representatives in Bali had been requesting their head office in Sydney for years to appeal to the Australian Government for permanent diplomatic representation in Bali to be seriously considered, and as soon as possible because the average death rate of Australians in Bali had reached one a week, mostly from tourists not wearing helmets while riding motorcycles.

This posting was an extremely tempting offer. However, at that time Bali had very little in the way of medical facilities, and no appropriate schooling for our children. When I brought this up with the Head of Staffing, I was told we could choose the boarding schools for our thirteen-year-old son and eight-year-old daughter, and that they would be flown to us in Bali twice a year during the school holidays.

The idea of having to leave our children, and only seeing them twice a year during their holiday periods was the proverbial last nail in the coffin. Resigning was not a long and difficult decision to reach. I felt it was long overdue for me to "pull the plug". My family had been through enough. I also had to consider Judith's parents who had missed their daughter for such long periods and had so little time with their grandchildren. It was time to put my family first.

I offered my resignation a day after returning to Adelaide and commenced preparations for the handover with Alexander Downer.

When I joined the department, I had no idea of the hardships, health issues, and dangers we would face in the years ahead while serving overseas. Despite all that, I shall never forget the great times, the valued friendships of many nationalities or the hard-working, selfless and dedicated people at the Department of Foreign Affairs with whom I had the honour and privilege of serving. I would like to make special mention of one man whom I hope has been truly appreciated for his exemplary contribution to the support and wellbeing of those under his charge, and those with whom he came in contact — David Rutter.

21

The Sunshine Coast & Into Business

1981–1986

Once the decision to resign was made we immediately set about selling our home in Canberra. It had been leased to the American Embassy since our move to Adelaide in 1979.

We enrolled Adrian, a thirteen-year-old, at St Joseph's College, Nudgee, in Brisbane, and put him on a plane a couple of weeks before we left Adelaide. The college arranged to pick him up at Brisbane airport and kept in touch with us on how he was settling in.

Judith, Samantha and I returned to Canberra on 31 July 1981 to finalise my resignation formalities with the department, and to make my farewells to the secretary and colleagues before departing for the Sunshine Coast of Queensland where we had a year earlier purchased and leased out the rundown 52-seat licensed Shearwater Seafood Restaurant and Bar at Kings Beach, Caloundra. It had been our intention for the restaurant to be plan B should we ever decide it was time to leave the department and seek a sea change. We must have felt the end was nigh even then.

21 The Sunshine Coast & Into Business

We really did jump in at the deep end when we left the department to go into business. Even with kitchen staff, front-of-house staff, and a chef on the payroll, we would not get to bed much before midnight. I would be at the Mooloolaba Seafood markets, 18 km away, to attend the daily auction which commenced at 6 am and would race home around 5 pm to shower and change after a day of preparing the seafood, stocking the bar, and the many other tasks that have to be taken care of, and be back at the restaurant by 6 pm. Judith and I met all our customers at the door and assisted them throughout their dining experience.

My father-in-law (GB) had a couple of world records as a big-game fisherman and was still active in his late 1970s. He missed the sea so much that soon after he and Alma moved up to the Sunshine Coast from Wollongong, New South Wales, he bought a forty-five-foot commercial fishing boat, studied, and obtained his Queensland Master Fisherman's licence. He was a reliable supplier of fresh crabs to our restaurant.

I occasionally accompanied GB on his crab runs to the northwest of Moreton Island on a Sunday during the slow season. Once the traps had been dropped overboard in a long line, we shut down the twin Volvo diesel, racked open the ice-cold beer, and dangled a rod and line over the side to fill in time, while the crabs marched into the traps. The cooking process of the crabs started as soon as we reached the shore. They were great days spent with a great guy.

State politicians, Brisbane TV hosts and crews, and so

many other "notables" were regular visitors to the restaurant. Tourist companies called to request that we cater for busloads of forty or fifty visiting interstate and international visitors. A special seafood lunch menu was adapted to meet their particular requests and tastes.

Figure 15. The restaurant at Kings Beach, Sunshine Coast, Queensland, 1981–1986

There was never a dull moment in the restaurant business, as any owner or operator in that industry will confirm. One problem that has often been recalled by family members occurred on New Year's Eve in 1983. We had never had air-conditioning in the restaurant as we were right at the seaside and relied on the sea breezes. During the previous summer, we had some very uncomfortable warm and humid evenings so we installed air-conditioning for the comfort of our diners during any future hot and humid summer evenings.

New Year's Eve arrived. We had double sittings. The first sitting was for families from 6 pm to 8 pm. There was no breeze, and it was getting uncomfortable in the restaurant so I turned on the air-conditioner. Rather than having a full house of happy diners, I found quite the opposite. People started to complain that it was getting hotter, not cooler. I thought they were an ungrateful lot. The perspiration on diners was the clincher. Something was wrong. I opened all the bay windows as wide as possible, but still no relief. Some diners asked if they could take their tables and chairs outside. I assisted them, and we set about solving the ever-increasing heat problem. I erected a step ladder and went up to check the air-conditioning unit. It was set on high heat! Most people laughed, but some did not! The free beer for the rest of the night certainly cooled everyone down.

We often received approaches from tourists to buy the restaurant. They were naturally enraptured with the beauty of the beaches of Caloundra, the people, the climate, and the restaurant's location facing the sea at Kings Beach. However, we were not ready and continued to build the business. We wanted to complete the considerable renovations and improvements that we had been working on for over five years.

We finally sold to a couple of Myer executives from Adelaide who visited Caloundra each year for their annual holidays and ate in our restaurant almost daily. We were exhausted. The long hours were getting too much for us, and we wanted a new challenge after almost six years.

During the final months in the restaurant, we had a phone call from my brother Bob in Western Australia. All his hard work and research over several years had finally come to fruition with his discovering, one by one, the whereabouts of our younger siblings, and contacting them. A reunion with our siblings after a separation of forty years was going to happen at last.

22

The Family Reunion after Forty Years

February 1985

Figure 16. The newspaper headline of the family reunion, 1985

B ob had been interviewed by the West Australian newspaper in early February 1985 when they heard what was unfolding from his extraordinary efforts in finding as many of our siblings that he did. The media had described the event as follows:

A bizarre reunion of brothers and sisters formerly unknown to each other has completed one man's thirty-year quest to find his family. It is indeed an incredible story of one man's application, commitment and dedication.

Judith and I flew to Perth for the reunion with my five brothers and sisters and their families. The five-hour flight provided time to ponder what I would say when I met them. I was, after all, the eldest and would be expected to lead and set an example on the day. I ended up saying very little at all — it was Bob's day, and I wanted all the attention to be focused on him. He did us all proud. I have always been absent, living thousands of kilometres away on the other side of the continent, or in another country.

The experience was and continues to be so difficult to define. Before our arrival at Bob's home for the reunion, I felt great sadness in all of us never having had the opportunity to grow up as a family unit, and experience our youth together, but that feeling was eclipsed when I saw those faces and their smiles. I felt the enormous love, joy and excitement that we were all experiencing as we embraced. There were a quite few tears shed that day.

As wards of the state, Bob, Muriel, and I had very different early life experiences, and had less choice in career paths or education than the three younger siblings, Kerry, Andrew and William, who had either been adopted or fostered out as infants and had become part of the families that had taken them in.

Bob and I had always been together through the years of Castledare, and Boys Town, that is, until at almost fourteen years old, when I was taken from Clontarf Boys Town and admitted to hospital, and never returned to Boys Town. Bob remained until he turned fifteen, and was then taken to the railway workshops, and signed on as an apprentice fitter and turner.

It would be many years before Bob discovered that his apprenticeship had been under the tutelage of the man who had adopted our youngest brother, William.

During this search for family by Bob, a young woman phoned him and introduced herself as his younger sister Kerry. They met and Kerry spurred Bob on to find the other family members.

Kerry, at between the age of one and two years, and Muriel, at four years of age, had been placed at St Joseph's Foundling Home. Kerry was at that institution for only a very brief period before being fostered out. Although the new and loving family were experiencing tough times, they ensured that Kerry did not want for anything.

Kerry won life's first prize when she met academic Andrew Hunwick. He had been teaching French Studies and Language as an Associate Professor at the University of Western Australia. In more recent years, Andrew was decorated by the French government for his contributions to French culture and language. Kerry is extremely proud of him, as we all are.

Bob continued to patiently and quietly continue his search to find the others by reading newspapers, listening to the radio, and generally remaining on alert for mention of the names of our remaining siblings to appear, and they did.

While at his National Service Army training in Northam, north-west of Perth, a friend mentioned to Bob that he had met a girl at the Saturday night Town Hall dance named Muriel and added that she bore a striking resemblance to him. That was enough to encourage Bob to go AWOL every Saturday night that he could to visit the Town Hall dance. Then, one night he spotted her. After having witnessed Kerry's family resemblance, he knew in his heart that this young woman was indeed his sister.

Not a word was mentioned to Muriel for months, during which time Bob turned up at the Town Hall, and danced with her every chance he could. On a couple of occasions, he even took her home! He decided that he had to wait for the right moment to mention the possible familial link to her.

Bob had to also consider if Muriel would want to learn of other family members or whether such news would be too upsetting for her. The right time eventually came for him. He told her of his search for his sister, named Muriel. She was stunned at first, and then started to open up to him about her past. Bob let her finish, and then told her she was his sister. She cried and hugged him, and they both sat and talked for ages. She was absolutely delighted with the news. She also told Bob that she had thought he was a bit strange, because he had never tried to kiss her or show any interest in her as a girlfriend during the past weeks of their growing "friendship". They have had a good many laughs over that.

What little I have learned of Muriel's life until she reached the age of twenty-one is truly heartbreaking. We were probably too occupied with our own situation to think of anything other than dealing with what came every day in our own confinement. We believed Muriel and the other children were still in the care of our mother.

Muriel was fostered out of St Joseph's at age seven. The foster family also took another two girls from the same institution. They were all "enslaved" in the environment of the foster family's boarding house that accommodated twenty-four boarders. I have not used the word "enslaved" lightly or irresponsibly. The girls rose each day at 5 am to prepare breakfast and lunches for the boarders. They attended school up to the seventh grade and would be beaten severely if they were not back at the boarding house by 3:30 pm each day to assist with preparing the evening meals. There was never time for homework.

When Muriel finally left the place at age twenty-one, she only had the clothes on her back, and a few extra pieces of personal items in a small bag.

While still at the boarding house, Muriel met and later married Kevin Kidd, a police constable in the Western

Australia Police Force. They raised three children, and were extremely active in community and sporting activities, no matter where they were sent on duty. Kevin retired from the police force in the late 1990s with the rank of inspector. Each year as winter approaches, he and Muriel don the cloak of the grey nomads, pack up their caravan, and spend six months travelling around Australia visiting family and friends. They have been very happy in retirement and continue to be as robust and appreciative of life as any couple I have ever met.

The next ten years were not so fruitful, until one day Bob read an article about a football umpire named Andrew Hocking who had a successful wager on the outcome of the Australia Football League's Sandover Medal, which is an award for the best and fairest football player in the state. A picture of Andrew appeared with the story and people in Bob's office were congratulating him on his big win. The likeness was so striking. The article also mentioned that Andrew trained harness racing horses.

Once again, Bob was reluctant to immediately locate and approach Andrew. He patiently plodded away at checking with friends in the racing industry to confirm Andrew was enjoying life and was reasonably happy.

Bob became a regular attendee at the trotting races on a Saturday night, and often spotted Andrew around the various facilities of the track. Finally, taking the bull by the horns, he approached Andrew and made his pitch. It was not the response he had expected, especially after his initial contact experiences with Muriel and Kerry. Andrew was so shocked and disbelieving of Bob's approach that he told him to 'get lost'.

Several weeks passed, during which Bob could not face up to going to the track and possibly running into Andrew again. He had almost given up trying to make any further contact with Andrew.

Bob eventually threw caution to the wind and returned to the Saturday night trots. Almost immediately after walking into the betting ring, he noticed Andrew. From that moment every time Bob glanced around, he found Andrew nearby. It was obvious that Andrew was following him, and like a cautious animal approaching its prey, he circled closer and closer until he suddenly stepped in front of Bob, held out his hand and said, 'Hi, brother'.

They embraced and started to laugh because people were milling around and watching them. One punter shouted, 'What did you back?' Another, 'How much did you win?' Bob shouted back, 'We both won. We have found each other. We are brothers!'

I only had two opportunities later to sit down and have a chat with Andrew after meeting him for the first time at the family reunion in 1985. His daytime job for several years was as a livestock inspector with the Western Australian Department of Agriculture.

Several years ago, I received word that he had remarried and experienced a severe heart attack during a holiday in New Zealand. He died in Dunedin, which was ironic, because the city's main thoroughfare, the university, and several other major sites and industries were named Knox, the name he initially inherited from his biological father.

The final link between our brothers and sisters was perhaps the most bizarre. Bob had finished his four-year apprenticeship as a fitter and turner at the Western Australian railways, and soon after decided that was not the work that he wanted to pursue as a career. He started working in a city shoe store and worked his way up to the position of manager of a city boutique shoe store, which was part of the largest chain of shoe stores in Australia.

During this period, Bob became close friends with a fellow employee named William (Bill) Choules. Bob had no idea that Bill Choules was, in fact, the adopted son of the supervisor who had supervised him at the railway workshops so many years earlier. The friendship with Bill had grown over a period of twenty years in the close proximity of their business relationship. They were in daily contact with general sales discussions, strategy meetings, and seasonal purchasing arrangements.

Bill had become the footwear chain's national handbag buyer, and Bob was by then Executive General Manager with responsibility for the selection and buying of women's fashion footwear for over 200 stores around Australia.

At one point during the search for siblings, Bob's wife Kay had invited her brother to dinner, and during the course of the evening, he mentioned that he had played cricket with a fellow who looked so similar to Bob that they could be brothers. His name was Bill Choules!

At the first opportunity when they were alone Bob asked Bill for his full family initials. He knew that the last remaining brother to be found had the first name initials WD but thought the surname had been Childs. When the initials had been confirmed Bob did some more checking and discovered that Bill's surname was Choules, William (Bill) D. Choules!

Bill had never been told he was adopted. The breaking of the discovery to him had to be considered long and hard over several months, particularly as the man who had adopted Bill was dying.

A few weeks after the funeral Bob took Bill to lunch during which he told him that in addition to being such good friends, they were also brothers. The news was not accepted, and Bob was told that the gesture although kind, was not believed.

Bill was confused by Bob's announcement. He wanted clarification quickly, so the next morning he put the question to his mother by adoption. Later the same day he telephoned Bob and emotionally accepted him as his brother. Although they had known each other for so many years in business, they at first did not know how they would react to each other as brothers. What would change in the relationship? They decided nothing would change, with the exception that they would now have a greater bond, not only as friends but also as brothers.

One final irony came to light at the reunion. Bill discovered that when he was in his teens and working at Northam, north-east of Perth, he had been a boarder with Muriel's foster family. Muriel had cooked him breakfast for over a year without him knowing she was his sister, and Muriel had no idea that she was cooking for her younger brother each day during that period!

We all continue to live our own separate lives, but with the confidence and assurance that we are all part of one enlarged family. We all keep in contact. We belong to each other, no matter what cards we have been dealt, and it is comforting to know that we will always be there for each other. Isn't that what families are all about?

23

The Last of Business & Return to Public Service

1986–2022

Following the sale of the restaurant, we had to look for a home once again. Adrian had completed Year 12 at St Joseph's College, Nudgee, in Brisbane and was back home again. Samantha had been enrolled at a college in Buderim on the Sunshine Coast.

We also sold our apartment in Caloundra, and Judith found a home close to her parents in Mooloolaba on the Sunshine Coast of Queensland.

We were still cautiously searching for a business opportunity when Bob mentioned that a friend of his had been appointed Managing Director of Filmpac, a new film distribution company. It had 35mm films for theatres, 16mm films for smaller theatres in clubs and pubs, and had just started buying into the video market in the USA.

Bob passed on details of our involvement in business and a brief outline on my Public Service history to his friend at Filmpac, and I was invited to fly to Sydney to meet with their executive team for an interview. I was taken on board immediately and thrust into the movie industry as the Queensland State Manager.

The company's opening presentation included all senior management including the state managers flying to Hawaii to join the Film and Video Industry's annual ten-day conference.

The experience with this company was good while it lasted. They had some excellent commercial products which included their opening film *Dirty Dancing* with Patrick Swayze and Jennifer Grey.

Two years later, I was on my way back from a sales trip in northern New South Wales when I received a call in my car directing me to instruct all employees to cease work, go home, and await further instructions.

The next day I received the instructions I was hoping would not come. The company had shut down without any warning. I had to tell everyone they were no longer employed. Staff were generally dumbfounded by this decision. They had all worked so hard and had turned in such great sales figures on some excellent film products that the company was considered a success in the industry.

The major stakeholder in the company had decided to go in another direction in business, and in doing so the remaining directors were asked to pay him out to the tune of several million dollars to retain the business. They could not afford to do so.

Tow trucks arrived the next day to take away our leased company vehicles, and other trucks turned up to take our complete archive of films, videos, and equipment. I was finally left with only a rubbish bin turned upside down to sit on before I turned out the lights.

The "bush telegraph" system worked well in the film and video industry, and within a week I was invited to join the Palace Entertainment Corporation as their State Manager in Queensland. Three years later I was appointed their National General Manager (Video) distributing their films to 4 100 stores throughout Australia. Several trips to Las Vegas for film and video conventions were a necessary and enjoyable part of the job.

The Palace Entertainment Corporation was a Melbourne-based family-run business and had a son working and learning theatre operations with his father. The son was promoted into my position a couple of years later, which left me out in the cold once again. This was a normal family business transition of appointments of their own family members into key positions, and I could see the sense in that. There were no hard feelings.

Soon after, Bob asked if we were interested in establishing an agency for Bollé's safety eyewear in Queensland. While on a business trip to Canada, he met a friend for lunch in Montreal. This friend brought along another fellow who was a director of the Bollé company, also on a business trip. During lunch the Bollé director had mentioned that he was looking for an agency to represent his company in Queensland, to work with his main office and warehouse in Melbourne. This well-known and well-established French company had a solid global reputation. I contacted the Melbourne office and following a lengthy interview in Melbourne we were taken on board as distributors of Bollé's products in Queensland.

We enjoyed working with this professional and enduring French company. We worked hard, and our territory grew to encompass not only Queensland, but also the Northern Rivers area of New South Wales and the Northern Territory, promoting and selling Bollé products, especially their safety eyewear range, to councils, police and hardware outlets.

The company's senior management in Melbourne invited us to join them for special events, and we were well looked after and appreciated by the company.

During 1996, while we were with Bollé we received an invitation from Allen and Joan, with whom we had been close friends in Santiago, to attend a ceremony celebrating the dedication of the George Bush Chair for Leadership at CIA Headquarters, Langley, Virginia. Allen had been appointed as its first Chair by the then US President George H.W. Bush and thought it would have been entertaining for us both later to have sat down with an intake of new recruits into his organisation and talk about our experiences in Santiago. I suggested that all I could talk about were our tennis games, golf, and poker nights, at which, as I had reminded him, I usually won. He did not agree with anything in the last statement, perhaps with some biased justification! We had to send our regrets because we were now seriously committed to business with Bollé and could not leave at that time. A year after Allen had completed his role as Chair at Langley, he was decorated with the agency's Distinguished Intelligence Medal. He and his wife Joan remain close and dear friends to this day and reside happily in retirement in Florida.

When we decided to retire, we sold the Bollé agency to an Australian of French birth who had made an approach sometime earlier after we had assisted him in visiting the Bollé factory in France.

Business activity had ceased, and the enjoyment of once again playing golf five days a week was starting to wane when a new chapter presented itself when I joined Volunteering Queensland.

My first appointment with Volunteering Queensland was as a team leader in charge of the swimming, diving, and cycling venues at the Brisbane-held 2001 Goodwill Games.

The Games were followed soon after by Brisbane's hosting of the Commonwealth Heads of Government Meeting (CHOGM) to be held on 6 October 2001. I was appointed as team leader, as was Doug Carroll, a former Victorian homicide detective. We were both tasked with the training and general indoctrination of a team for positioning at five major hotels in Brisbane where the Queen and major leaders of the Commonwealth countries would be staying.

CHOGM staff were selected over a period of weeks, their uniforms were issued, and phase one planning had been completed. An excellent team was ready to go. However, we were suddenly told to stand down. CHOGM was postponed because of the September 11 terrorist attacks on the New York Twin Towers in the United States.

A month or so after CHOGM, Doug and I were selected to join the Royal Queensland Show (Ekka) as team leaders to select and train 160 staff and appoint supervisors and coordinators.

Immediately following the Ekka, Doug Carroll, who was the Director of International Hotel Security, another former homicide detective from Victoria (Scotty), and I flew to Bangkok to spend a week at Sheraton's Royal Orchid Hotel to provide all aspects of hotel security training to twenty-five security managers from the SPG group of hotels, which included the Sheraton Hotels, the Westin, and Le Meridian Hotels in Thailand, Cambodia, and Vietnam.

Doug flew out to the Philippines on another assignment upon completion of the training exercise in Bangkok. Scotty and I flew to Phuket to conduct a three-day covert security audit of the Le Meridien Hotel at Karon Beach, not far from Patong on the Thailand Coast.

Judith and I were past the norm for retirement age and had progressed with reasonable success through the impositions and challenges of a demanding foreign service career, and the ebbs and flows of business. Along the way, we have managed to raise two children and assist and steer them through their early years to achieve the confidence to be their own masters.

Retirement was great for a while, but once again, the strong work ethic I was brought up on from an early age managed to put a stop to the idle times. I just had to get back to work.

I answered an advertisement for a position with the Federal Court's Administrative Appeals Tribunal (AAT) in Brisbane. I was successful and travelled to court houses all over Queensland for the next six years.

In 2011, while still with the AAT, I visited the Director of the Department of Foreign Affairs and Trade (DFAT) office in Brisbane to do some research on my personnel files, which I had requested to be sent from Canberra. While there I was asked by the DFAT State Director whether I would be interested in joining the Department of Prime Minister and Cabinet's (PM&C) Protocol & International Division as a protocol officer facilitating the visits to Brisbane of royalty, foreign presidents and prime ministers. I was definitely interested. I joined PM&C and soon after resigned from the AAT.

Several years later I received and accepted an offer to also join the DFAT as a protocol officer with similar duties to that of PM&C in facilitating the official visits to Brisbane of foreign ministers. Workloads from both these departments keep me very busy, and I have the privilege of working with a group of highly motivated and professional people.

I may have to give up trying to establish just what may have contributed to the last ten years (1971–1981) of my departmental personnel records not being available when requested for personal research from the department and from the National Archives. DFAT advised that they did not have them and suggested that I should try the National Archives. I did, and on 16 December 2015 I received a reply advising that:

> The Information exempted is of a nature such that its disclosure could lead to an unreasonable intrusion on the personal affairs of a person or persons, and there is no evidence in the record that suggests that when the information was gathered, the subject expected it to be made publicly known or that it has become known in the intervening years. Disclosure of the information would involve the unreasonable disclosure of personal information.

Six months later, in an email from the National Archives dated 11 May 2016, I was further advised, "The agency advised that they have recorded mega-data on file for yourself. Unfortunately, after an extensive search, they were unable to locate the file and have recorded it as missing."

I was sure I had been on the right path for some time in bringing the matter of my missing personnel file to the surface, but to continue to pursue the matter could have only caused difficulties for others, and possibly myself. I may have to resort to applying via the *Freedom of Information Act* — or not.

This memoir, which I started so many years ago had originally been intended for family members only. However, my immediate family in Queensland and siblings in Western Australia have insisted on having the story published. It took quite a while for me to work up the courage to do so. It has been an emotional and exhausting experience

When time allows, I also assist our son, Adrian, with his

TV program *Blokesworld* which has been running for over twenty years in Australia and New Zealand. Some may say that I am referred to, irreverently, on his program as camera 83! It's a much kinder description than a lot of alternative titles that could be given to an octogenarian.

In closing, I would like to add that I believe the meaning of life that we hear so much about may relate quite differently to each one of us, but to me, it simply means to love and to be loved by family. I have always tried to put my family first, but unfortunately, I have not always been as successful in that pursuit as I should have been.

Thank you so much for picking up this book and taking the time to read it. Now, why not sit down, apply "bum glue", as author Bryce Courtenay once suggested to me, and write your own story? Everyone has one.

Figure 17. Father and son — thank you.

www.ingramcontent.com/pod-product-compliance
Lightning Source LLC
Chambersburg PA
CBHW020135130526